Worship and Mission
After Christendom

The old ways in the church no longer ring true. These authors invite us to follow where the Spirit leads, even against our most treasured conventions.
—Walter Brueggemann, Professor Emeritus, Columbia Theological Seminary

Worship and Mission After Christendom is ground-breaking and boundary-crossing, with fresh biblical interpretation, insights from church history, a passionate plea for Christians to integrate mission and worship, and very practical resources to help us do this.
—Stuart Murray, founder of Urban Expression, author and church planting consultant

A wonderful history of Christian worship in relationship to the *missio Dei*. Making use of the best of liturgical, historical and theological scholarship, this book will be read with profit by all who struggle with the proper relationships between worship and evangelism in church and world today.
—Maxwell Johnson, Professor of Liturgical Studies, University of Notre Dame

The Kreiders insightfully describe a Spirit-filled church whose mission grows out of narrative-based, table-centered worship that will cause seekers to ask, "What kind of people are these?" "What do they know?" and, "Who is this God they worship?"
—David W. Boshart, Executive Minister, Central Plains Mennonite Conference

A Peaceable Kingdom, Edward Hicks (1780–1849)

Worship and Mission
After Christendom

ALAN KREIDER AND ELEANOR KREIDER

Herald Press
Scottdale, Pennsylvania
Waterloo, Ontario

Library of Congress Cataloging-in-Publication Data
Kreider, Alan, 1941-
 Worship and mission after Christendom / Alan and Eleanor Kreider.
   p. cm.—(After Christendom)
 "First published in 2009 by Paternoster Press ... Milton Keynes,
UK"—T.p. verso.
 Includes bibliographical references and index.
 ISBN 978-0-8361-9554-5 (pbk. : alk. paper)
 1. Public worship. 2. Evangelistic work. 3. Missions—Theory.
I. Kreider, Eleanor, 1935- II. Title.
 BV15.K72 2011
 264—dc22

                                             2010046606

WORSHIP AND MISSION AFTER CHRISTENDOM
Copyright © 2011 by Herald Press, Scottdale, PA 15683.
 Released simultaneously in Canada by Herald Press,
 Waterloo, Ont. N2L 6H7. All rights reserved.
Library of Congress Control Number: [to come]
International Standard Book Number: 978-0-8361-9554-5
Printed in United States of America
Cover by Merrill Miller

16 15 14 13 12 11   10 9 8 7 6 5 4 3 2 1

To order or request information please call 1-800-245-7894 or visit
www.heraldpress.com.

For Stuart and Sian

Contents

Foreword to the North American edition:
    John D. Witvliet 11
Series Preface: Stuart Murray 15
Acknowledgments. 17

Introduction 19
1. Worship After Christendom   **23**
    From Italy to Britain 23
    Worship: Actions and Emotions. 25
    New Testament Words for Worship Imply Mission. 26
    Worship: Ascribing Worth to God. 28
    Worship Is for All of Life 29
    Worship Services Must Be in Keeping with God's
        Character and Mission. 31
    Worship Services Reveal the Character and
        Purposes of God 33

2. Mission Under Christendom   **35**
    Characteristics of Classical Mission 36
    The Christendom Origins of Classical Mission 38
    Classical Mission in Late Christendom. 40

3. Mission after Christendom: The *Missio Dei*   **43**
    Missio Dei: The Bible's Grand Narrative. 45
    Wolves and Lambs 46
    A Feast for All People. 47
    The Means of God's Mission: Sending 48
    Characteristics of the *Missio Dei* 49
    Implications of *Missio Dei* Thinking. 53
    Criteria for Discernment. 55
    An Exemplar of the *Missio Dei*. 56

4. Post-Christendom Worship: The Recovery
   of Narrative   **59**
   The Power of Story 60
   The Stifling of Story in Christendom 61
   God's Story: A Five-Act Drama 63
   Worshipping God in the Present, Between Past
      and Future 64
   The Past: Acts of Worship in the Bible Tell
      the Story of God 65
   Narrative Worship that Tells an Odd Story 67
   Ways of Telling the Story. 70

5. Narrative Resources for Worship: Hoping the Past,
   Remembering the Future   **77**
   Hoping the Past 77
   Drawing on the "Gap Years" 79
   Drawing on the Immediate Past: "Reports from
      the Front" 81
   Remembering the Future 85
   The Loss of Hope 86
   Regaining Hope 87
   Anticipations Little and Big 88
   Long-Sighted Christians 89

6. Early Christian Worship: Multivoiced Meals   **91**
   Inculturating the Gospel 93
   Inculturating Worship in Corinth. 94
   1 Corinthians 11–14 Is All One Piece. 97
   1 Corinthians 11—The Meal. 97
   1 Corinthians 14—The After-Dinner Conversation 101
   Paul's Objections: Disorder and Incomprehensibility . . .102
   Outsiders Are Present 104
   Paul's Vision for Table and Word 106

7. After Christendom: Multivoiced Worship
   Returns   **111**
   The Disappearance of Multivoiced Table Worship 112
   1 Corinthians 11–14 in Christendom 115
   Multivoiced Worship: Bubbling to the Surface 117

Churches After Christendom 118
Paul's Vision of Meal and Word for Today 120
In Small Churches: Experimental 123
In Small Churches: Inherited 124
In Churches that Combine the Small with the Large 125
In Larger Churches 127
Testimony: Three Ways. 130
Symposium-like Worship as a "New" Sacrament 134
Inculturating Worship and Witness in the
    Post-Christendom West 134

8. Worship Forms Mission I: Glorifying God, Sanctifying Humans   137

Worship Edifies Attractive Christians 138
Glorifying God, Sanctifying Humans. 141
What Christians Do in Worship. 143

9. Worship Forms Mission II: Actions of Worship   147

We Gather 147
We Praise God 152
We Confess that Jesus Is Lord. 154
We Tell the Big Story .157
We Tell the "Little Stories". 159
We Perform Baptism, Eucharist, and Footwashing. 160
We Make Peace and We Pray. 167
We Sing. 170
Transformations 175

10. Worship Forms Mission III: Worshipping Christians in the World   179

Witness. 180
Being 180
Affections 181
Actions 183
Deviance: Individual and Corporate 187

11. Missional Worship in the Worldwide Church   189

We Worship the God of All the Nations 190
The Worldwide Vision of the New Testament 191

Pre-Christendom: A Worldwide Vision. 193
Christendom: The Vision Narrows 193
Christianity Becomes Worldwide Again 194
Post-Christendom: Worldwide Interdependence 195
Relationships 196
Gift Sharing: Structures .201
Changes in Worship and Mission 207
Gifts for Worship 209
Gifts for Mission 214
Worldwide Christianity: A Transcultural Community . . .216

12. Outsiders Come to Worship I:
   What the Outsiders Experience   **219**
Worship and Outsiders in Christian History 219
Why Outsiders Come. 221
What the Outsiders See: Paul's Concerns 224
Where the Outsiders Meet Christians: A Liminal Space . .225
The Outsiders in Christian Worship: Inculturation. . . .227
Five Models of Church: Domestic, Megachurch,
   Cathedral, Congregation, Outsider-Directed 230
What the Outsiders See: Actions of Christian Worship . .233
What the Outsiders Intuit: The Church's Ethos. 237
What the Outsiders Intuit: About God. 239

13. Outsiders Come to Worship II:
   Hospitality and Wholeness   **243**
Attending Church by Choice. 243
Hospitality: A Task for All Christians. 244
Hospitality in Worship .246
Outsiders and the Table: Three Approaches 248
Worship and Mission in a Body Made Whole 255
Breathing In, Breathing Out. 256

Appendix: Are Americans in Christendom? 259

Notes. 265
Bibliography. 309
Index. 315

Foreword

I n an age when books—even books about Christian ministry—are often lauded because they are punchy or pugnacious, celebrity-driven or attention grabbing, it is gratifying to encounter a book that represents a quiet protest against all of that. *Worship and Mission After Christendom* represents the patient learning and honest struggles of two wise and seasoned Christian disciples and leaders. As I have come to know the Kreiders and as I read their book, I find myself discovering again the beauty of the fruit of the Spirit. This is a book that, among its virtues, quietly exudes joy, peace, patience, and self-control.

For this reason this book is valuable not only for people interested in worship and mission, but also for anyone who struggles with the practice of faithful ministry today. It holds great promise for spurring reflection on four central and perennial questions related to Christian ministry.

How can we conduct ministry with a sense of passionate urgency, but without a sense of anxiety or despair?

All too often, Christian practice oscillates between lukewarm indifference and overheated zealousness, both of which ultimately derive from a lack of confidence in the sovereignty of God and an overconfidence in either settled or innovative ministry practices. This book clearly has no patience for tepid ministry practices. It is a book that arises out of a passionate desire for vital and faithful ministry. At the same time, this book avoids both an anxiety-prone search for quick-fix techniques and a triumphalistic announcement of some grand innovation that will usher the church into a new golden age. It commends time-tested practices: disciplined prayer, engagement with the entire narrative sweep of Scripture, testimony, deeply attentive participation in the Lord's Supper, and more. And it does so with a calm and buoyant confidence in the way that God's Spirit freely

11

chooses to work through these practices, resting in the conviction that the mission in which we participate is God's, not ours.

What is the best way to draw upon a rich body of ecumenical wisdom while remaining rooted in a particular tradition?

Worship and Mission After Christendom is a resonant contribution to Christian thinking from an Anabaptist voice in the ecumenical choir. But it is also deeply informed by voices from other traditions. It not only describes the value of the church's catholicity, but also models it, demonstrating what is possible after a generation of fruitful ecumenical exchanges. Thus, the book avoids two common extremes: a narrow and exclusive approach to one's own tradition on the one hand, and, on the other, a kind of grab-bag approach that creates an ultimately unstable post-modern pastiche of motifs that lack coherence and traction.

This ecumenical approach challenges readers to reciprocate. Those of us who are not Anabaptist would be shortsighted if we merely read the book as a window into one strand of current Anabaptist thinking. Rather, we should read it as a prophetic challenge to the coherence and faithfulness of our own thinking. For many of us, this book provides an opportunity to detoxify ourselves of the subtle but persistent yearnings for the trappings of Christendom that may quietly cling to our work.

How can ministry practices be deepened by the entire spectrum of theological disciplines?

Too often, books about ministry practices are disconnected from thoughtful engagement with recent work in biblical, historical, and theological studies. In contrast, this book is an attempt to synthesize energy and insight from significant recent work in biblical studies (especially 1 Corinthians 11–14), historical studies (especially the periods that featured the rise and fall of Christendom), and systematic theology (including insights from not only Anabaptist thinkers but also a number of Reformed and Catholic writers). While specialists in each of the fields may find details of this analysis to quibble with, they should also value the attempt to draw upon insights from each of these fields. In a world filled with an increasing deluge of information and the hyperspecialization of work within each of these complex fields, we need books like this that organize, relate, and calibrate all of these insights into a coherent vision. Some day the world of theological education may offer a broader discussion about the proper uses of biblical, historical, and theological study in the shaping of contemporary ministry (as opposed to engagement within each of those fields as an end in itself). Until then, it is wise to pay attention to volumes like this that simply do this integrating work.

What is the best way to calibrate approaches to Christian worship and mission?

Finally, this volume is also a helpful and challenging reflection on the practice of mission and worship. It challenges a zero-sum approach to worship and mission, in which strength in one area entails weakness in the other. Too often, emphasis on mission ends up diminishing worship, treating it as a pragmatic, instrumental event to attract people. This approach ends up unwittingly baptizing the very cultural elements that the gospel would otherwise subvert. At the very same time, in other places, worship ends up diminishing mission, exhausting resources of time, energy, and money in pursuit of liturgical excellence at the expense of mission. In contrast, *Worship and Mission After Christendom* describes the fundamental importance of robust, participatory, narratively-conceived, theologically rich worship services as a non-instrumental but indispensable cornerstone of a missional vision for church life.

In response to all four of these questions, then, this book points a way forward that avoids pitfalls on both sides of the road. It is urgent, without being anxious; ecumenical, without being relativistic; multidisciplinary, without being scattered; missional, without being utilitarian. For this reason, "poise" comes to mind as an apt description of the Kreiders' approach. May God's Spirit use our study of this book to build up the body of Christ and to elicit ministries of uncommon fruitfulness—all to the honor and praise of the triune God.

—*John D. Witvliet, Director*
Calvin Institute of Christian Worship
Calvin College and Calvin Theological Seminary
Grand Rapids, Michigan

Series Preface: After Christendom

Christendom was a historical era, a geographical region, a political arrangement, a sacral culture, and an ideology.

For many centuries Europeans have lived in a society that is nominally Christian. Church and state have been the pillars of a remarkable civilization that can be traced back to the decision of Emperor Constantine I early in the fourth century to replace paganism with Christianity as the imperial religion. Christendom, a brilliant but often brutal culture, flourished in the Middle Ages, fragmented in the Reformation of the sixteenth century, but persisted despite the onslaught of modernity. While exporting its values and practices to other parts of the world, however, it has been slowly declining during the past three centuries. In the twenty-first century Christendom is unraveling. What will emerge from the demise of Christendom is not yet clear, but we can now describe Western culture as "post-Christendom."

> Post-Christendom is the culture that emerges as the Christian faith loses coherence within a society that has been definitively shaped by the Christian story and as the institutions that have been developed to express Christian convictions decline in influence.

This definition, proposed and unpacked in *Post-Christendom*, the first book in the After Christendom series,[1] has gained widespread acceptance. *Post-Christendom* investigated the Christendom legacy and raised numerous issues that are explored in the rest of the series. The authors of this series, who write from within the Anabaptist tradition, see the current challenges facing the church not as the loss of a golden age but as opportunities to recover a more biblical and more

Christian way of being God's people in God's world. The series address-es a wide range of issues, including social and political engagement, how we read Scripture, youth work, mission, worship, and the shape and ethos of the church after Christendom.

These books are not intended to be the last word on the subjects they address, but are an invitation to discussion and further explora-tion. One way to engage in this discussion is via the accompanying website: www.postchristendom.com. Additional material can also be found at www.anabaptistnetwork.com/AfterChristendom.

—*Stuart Murray*

Acknowledgments

To write is to incur debts. Ours are many. We grew up in the United States in Mennonite missionary families that were excited by the recovery of "the Anabaptist Vision." We are grateful to our parents and the Mennonite congregations that formed us and taught us to love and follow Jesus.

We have been shaped by Christians of many traditions, and especially by worshipping with them and becoming their friends: in Anglican parishes in St Albans and York, England, in which for two and a half years we were regular worshippers; in Baptist churches in Manchester and Oxford, in which for nine years we were members; in London prayer groups of peace activists, many of whom were Roman Catholic; in a table church in Oxford, whimsically called "Group," with which for five years we met every Thursday; in charismatic churches in many parts of the United Kingdom, which we visited frequently. During our seventeen years in London with the London Mennonite Centre and the Wood Green Mennonite Church, we learned much, formed by community and solid, lasting relationships. As the Anabaptist Network developed in the 1990s, its members became our friends who taught us by word and faithful life. We are grateful.

Since our return to the United States in 2000, we have found a home and nurture in the Prairie Street Mennonite Church in Elkhart, Indiana, where we are committed members. This has also been a time of travel for us; we have worshipped with Christians of many traditions in many countries. A particular influence on us has been monastic communities both Protestant and Catholic where we have spent extended periods of time—La Communauté de Grandchamp near Neuchâtel, Switzerland, which lives by the Taizé rule, where we lived for two months in 1984; and Saint Benedict's Monastery, St. Joseph, Minnesota, among whose sisters Alan twice spent months as a Studium scholar. To all these, who have taught us by inviting us to worship with them and share in their lives, we are grateful.

Our work has also been shaped by the people we have taught in churches, colleges, and conferences in many countries. We are especially grateful to Whitley College, University of Melbourne, Australia, where in 2005 we gave early versions of these chapters in their annual School for Pastors; also to two 2007 meetings of the Anabaptist Network in the United Kingdom—the annual conference and the theological circle—in which our ideas were further refined. Our students at the Associated Mennonite Biblical Seminary's "Worship and Mission" course have inspired and instructed us, especially the effervescent 2007 class, whose members responded to early drafts of many of these chapters. We are also grateful to the seminary itself, which granted Alan a sabbatical leave that enabled us to complete the book.

Our friends and colleagues have taught us much. We never studied with John Howard Yoder, but he was a friend, and he influenced us in more ways than we realize. We often sense that he is looking over our shoulders, "watching" us! We think of John Rempel, whose passionate commitment to the Lord's Supper has stirred us; also of biblical scholars Lloyd Pietersen and Willard Swartley, who read our chapters on 1 Corinthians with both affirmation and correction. For help in assessing the practicality of our writing for congregational life, we turned to David Boshart, a gifted missional Mennonite pastor from Iowa, who has critiqued the entire book. Our friendship with Trisha Dale began many years ago when she transcribed a speech on "social holiness"; it has been a particular joy to collaborate with her as she has expertly copyedited this book. For the North American edition, we are grateful to Byron Rempel-Burkholder and Amy Spencer for editorial assistance, and especially to John D. Witvliet for writing the foreword.

To our friends Stuart and Sian Murray Williams we owe a particular debt. Their lives and thinking have challenged us and given us hope, and we have spent many delightful hours in their kitchen, conversing and eating together. From the outset of this project, Stuart, the editor of the After Christendom series, has been a generous companion, reading and responding to the chapters as we have written them.

We have not always agreed with our readers and friends; what we have written is not always what they would have written. But we know that they stand with us and value our contribution. The responsibility for the book is our own.

Introduction

Worship and Mission is a challenging title. Worship and mission—each is a specialized discipline, with its own scholars and practitioners. We have learned much from the writings and friendship of many of them. We ask ourselves, is it arrogant for us to try to interweave the two disciplines? Adding *After Christendom* to the title magnifies the challenge. This brings a third discipline—the history of Christianity in its broad sweep.

And what, after all, is Christendom? Our own experience of European Christendom began in the 1960s when we, young Americans, went to England as students. We were astonished to read about bishops in the House of Lords; we were delighted by public Christmas music that was explicitly Christian (where was "Rudolf the Red-Nosed Reindeer"?); we were dazzled by the architecture and music of the English cathedrals. As we stayed in England to follow our vocation as missionary teachers, we observed complex realities of Christendom. Our son at school every morning attended the act of worship that was required by act of Parliament, and he took obligatory courses in religious education. We met attractive Christians in vital congregations. But we also observed that our neighbors, who saw themselves as "good Christians," went to church only for funerals and weddings. Television comedians and sitcoms portrayed vicars as fuzzy-minded dunces.

What was Christendom? Whatever it was, during our years in England we observed it slipping: Christmas became "winterval"; church attendance plummeted; and some church buildings became carpet warehouses, dance studios, or exclusive housing. When we left England in 2000, the twenty-six bishops were still in the House of Lords, but the United Kingdom had become self-consciously multicultural, and its tone had become secular. It had entered a new world, the world of post-Christendom. To be a Christian was to belong to a religious minority, still relatively numerous, that engaged in the peculiar form of recreational activity called worship. As we reflected about all this with friends, we came to see that Christendom, for all its beauties that we enjoyed so much, had been problematic for the welfare of Christian faith in the United Kingdom. Or, as we increasingly were coming to understand it, Christendom had been an impediment to the mission of God. But there was hope: new ways of Christian living were springing up that, along with revivified old ways, were creative and had the potential for broad impact for God's kingdom in the United Kingdom and beyond. What we say about worship and mission first of all grows out of our experience in a country we love, one we have watched becoming a post-Christendom society.

Since 2000 we have lived in our native country, the United States, which we also love. Our years in the United Kingdom have shaped us, and so we have attempted to see whether the United States—whose written Constitution separates church and state—is nevertheless a society with Christendom characteristics. As amateur missionary anthropologists, we observe parts of the country that are as secular as any part of the United Kingdom, but we also know a town whose citizens do not think that it is incongruous to have a cross on the top of their municipal water tower. We listen to sociologist Robert Bellah, who finds it "difficult to see where church leaves off and world begins" in the United States.[1] We nevertheless find that, in the country as a whole, figures for religious adherence are inflated and the general trajectory of this very materialistic society is toward post-Christendom (see appendix). And so we hope that what we say in this book will be as relevant to the United States as to the United Kingdom and the Western world in Europe, Canada, and Australasia.

We write as Mennonite Christians in the Anabaptist tradition. In recent decades we have seen Anabaptism emerge as a voice in the Christian choir, a potential resource to all Christians. Both of us have also found that studying the worship and witness of the Christians of the early centuries has stimulated, stirred, and changed us. As we state in our acknowledgments, we have been taught and transformed by Christians of many traditions. We have studied under these Christians and alongside them; we have worshipped and engaged in missional action with them; they have become our friends. We take the many traditions seriously, because we believe that God has given charisms to them—including the young traditions that seek emerging, "fresh" ways of being Christian. We believe that traditions are truest to themselves when they listen well to others. We want our book to contribute insights that are Anabaptist, evangelical, and ecumenical to the post-Christendom churches. May we all—in the diaspora existence that we now share—worship freely and passionately the God whose mission is reconciliation.

As we write, we have gratefully drawn on the writings of others. These appear in our endnotes and bibliography. We mention one short book in particular, *Worship and Mission*, which J. G. Davies of the University of Birmingham in England wrote almost fifty years ago (SCM Press, 1966). We single this out both because it is an insightful study that attempts the daunting task of marrying missiology and the study of worship and because there has not been anything like it since. Now, with the advent of worldwide Christianity and the crisis of Christendom in the West, the task that Davies began—thinking about worship in light of the mission of God, thinking about mission as a means of ascribing worth to God—can gain momentum. Charles Farhadian's recent *Christian Worship Worldwide* (Eerdmans, 2007) shows how Christians from many parts of the world can inspire us to discover missional ways of worshipping God. We want our book to contribute to this task, shaping a Christlike people who joyfully worship God and participate in God's work in the world.

Finally, a brief word about writing a book together. Our book grows out of a shared delight in worship and mission, fed by books we have read aloud to each other, vigorous conversations, and innumerable teaching sessions in churches and conferences of Christians of many traditions in many parts of the world. Through writing and speaking we have pulled the threads of our learnings together and tested the strength of the fibers. Writing this book has been a weaving of the cloth. Reading, conversing, drafting, redrafting, editing, reediting—this is the work of writing any book, but for us the productivity and the pleasure were multiplied by more than two.

—*Alan Kreider and Eleanor Kreider*
Elkhart, Indiana, United States
Epiphany 2009

ONE

Worship After Christendom

During the Christendom centuries, the phrase "worship and mission" occurred rarely, if ever. Worship was what the church in Christendom existed to do; worship was its central activity. Mission, on the other hand, was peripheral and rarely discussed. Mission took place "out there," in "regions beyond," in "mission lands"—beyond Christendom. In the last centuries of Christendom, a small number of enthusiasts promoted mission, and an even smaller number of specialists traveled abroad to carry it out.[1] But worship services were nearby, in one's immediate neighborhood, not out there but "here," in every town and every parish. The main task of the clergy—the large corps of religious professionals—was to preside over these services.

From Italy to Britain

Across Western Europe, worship services provided cohesion for Christendom societies and articulated their values. Consider two examples, one glorious and one homely.

> In the sixth century, a great artist created the mosaics in the dazzling church of San Vitale in Ravenna, on Italy's Adriatic coast. On both sides of the chancel the artist depicted processions heading toward the altar—on the north wall the Emperor Justinian carries the Eucharistic bread, surrounded by clergy, civil servants, soldiers and a donor; on the south wall the Empress Theodora bears the Chalice, in the company of attendants and civil servants. Over the altar the artist depicted Christ, King of kings, of whose rule Justinian's reign was to be an image.[2]

In Christendom, in which the reign of Christ was actualized, human potentates played a prominent role in the central act of the civilization, the worship service, the Mass. And the Mass, with its regal setting, gave legitimation to the emperor's rule. In 529 this emperor, Justinian, had issued an edict requiring all inhabitants of the empire to be baptized and to attend services of worship.[3] In a Christendom society, worship was unavoidable; thanks to government compulsion, mission was unnecessary.

In contrast to the splendor of San Vitale, a parish church deep in England's Norfolk countryside is unimpressive.

> The parish church of Tivetshall St Margaret is conventional in design, with a modest-sized nave separated from the chancel by a filigreed carved gothic screen through which the laity can observe the eucharistic action. Originally, a rood (crucifix) stood high and central on this screen flanked on each side by statues of the Blessed Virgin Mary and St. John the Evangelist. In the 1560s, however, the local power-holders, the gentry, decided that the statues were idolatrous—graven images—and they removed them. We may assume that some people were unhappy with this. And in 1587 the gentry replaced the discarded images with a wooden panel that filled the chancel arch up to the roof. On the panel an artist expressed Christendom values which, as in Ravenna, involved the "powers that be": the coat of arms of Queen Elizabeth I was central; under this in neatly calligraphed letters were the Ten Commandments, the words of Paul in Romans 13—"Let every soule subiect hymselfe vnto the auctorite of the hyer powers"—and a prayer: "O God save our Quene Elizabeth." And to each side of this central ensemble were the names of the churchwardens (possibly local gentry) who may have paid for the improvement. Royal arms, Bible text and local gentry—a formidable visual evocation of Christendom.[4] In this space, week after week, the local agricultural workers and their betters were supposed to gather, by royal command, for services of worship.

Worship in that culture was essential; mission—through which God changes minds and subverts inevitabilities—was in nobody's mind.

So, for centuries in places like glorious Ravenna and rustic Tivetshall, ordinary Christians—the laity—were expected to attend the services of worship led by the clergy. Gradually European church and civil law established regulations for attendance at worship services. The Fourth Lateran Council of 1215 required Roman Catholics to take Communion once per year; laws in Elizabethan England required people to attend a Church of England service every week in their local parish church; in England the 1944 Education Act required all children, of whatever religious conviction, to attend a daily act of worship in their schools. In Christendom, worship was the responsibility of the religious professionals. Nonprofessional Christians were expected to attend. The professionals spent a lot of their time organizing these acts of worship; liturgical theologians thought about what happened in the services of worship; and the laity—who, the clergy complained, often skipped the services put on in their behalf—spent most of their time engaged in secular activities.

Today, after Christendom, we're in a different world. The clergy still organize services of worship, and some lay people attend them. But, in Europe and in many places in North America, Christianity has come to be "a minority cult in a cross-cultural situation."[5] For most people in the West, worship services are strange; they take place in an unfamiliar environment, using archaic vocabulary and an incomprehensible ritual language. And so, mission has emerged as a major concern for Christians who think about worship. But post-Christendom, in which Christians at last think about worship and mission, has not only caused some Christians to think about mission in new ways; it has also caused them to reexamine what they mean by worship.

Worship: Actions and Emotions

In Christendom, in which Christians could assume that most people would attend church, one way of talking about worship predominated. Worship denoted religious actions, which scholars call cultic actions. (Here, cult is descriptive, not pejorative.) Worship was what Christians did when they gathered in church. "Worship consists of our words and action, the outward expressions of our homage and adoration, when we are assembled in the presence of God." So wrote the Scottish theologian W. D. Maxwell in the 1930s,[6] and it expresses one dimension of worship that continues to be important—the cultic actions of humans in response to the presence and action of God.

But in the 1970s or so, as people in many places increasingly absented themselves from the churches and as Western cultures became more emotionally expressive, a second way of talking about worship became common. Worship—or "true" worship, as it was often called—now came to be associated with experiences and feelings. These emotions occur through an encounter with God that is *real* and *personal*. We "really" worship God when we sing or when we praise God or when "our hearts worship the Lord."[7] Worship, according to Sally Morgenthaler, occurs when humans "meet God," when they have "a heartfelt response to a loving God." The task of the worship leader is to enable this personal, affective encounter to take place; the leader must "allow the supernatural God of Scripture to show up and to interact with people in the pews."[8]

In a culture in which legal compulsions to attend church have disappeared and social compulsions are withering, in which there are many attractive ways to spend leisure time, and in which consumer values have become pervasive, people attend worship services because they want to receive something. This emphasis on heartfelt encounter is important. Like Maxwell's emphasis on cultic action, it is an essential part of the picture. And we may realistically note that, in a post-Christendom world in which religious participation is uncoerced, if people find that worship services don't make them feel better, they will simply not come back.

New Testament Words for Worship Imply Mission

But worship is more than cultic actions and potent experiences. The New Testament writers used three words that deepen our understanding.[9] One of these words, precious to the liturgical traditions, is *leitourgia*. Etymologically this means "the work of the people," and in the ancient world it often had to do with a service that someone performed voluntarily for the state or the wider community. This is the word that the book of Acts uses to describe the worship of the Christian community in Antioch: "While they were worshipping (*leitourgounton*) the Lord and fasting, the Holy Spirit said, 'Set apart for me Barnabas and Saul'" (13:2). Was this worship "liturgical" in its order of actions and use of psalms and other set prayers? The worship was clearly flexible enough to allow for the spontaneous breaking in of the divine word. And this worship led to action. It led to the missionary journeys of Paul, and eventually to his role as a public servant; *leitourgos* is what Paul called himself as he brought a redistributive financial gift from the Gentile churches to the impoverished Christians in Jerusalem (Rom 15:26; 2 Cor 9:12). It is thus not only Christians in the "liturgical" traditions that are drawn to *leitourgia*; so also are Christian social radicals who remind us that authentic worship expresses itself in mission—in action that makes justice.[10]

Many Pentecostal and free-church Christians, on the other hand, ignore *leitourgia* altogether but discuss a second word—*proskynēsis*—as if it were "the Greek New Testament word for worship."[11] Ancient writers used *proskynēsis* to designate the custom of prostration before persons, reverencing them and kissing their feet or the hem of their garment. New Testament writers such as Matthew used *proskynēsis* and its derivatives to connote affective, whole-bodied reverence (Matt 2:2; 4:9; 28:9); in his Apocalypse, John depicts scenes in heaven in which worshippers prostrate themselves before God and the Lamb (Rev 5:14; 7:11; 19:4; 22:8). The term *proskynēsis* is almost completely missing from the Epistles. The exception is significant—1 Corinthians 14:25, in which outsiders, experiencing the presence of God in the multivoiced Corinthian Christian assembly, "bow down before God and *worship* him, declaring, 'God is really among you.'" *Proskynēsis*—worship that engages the affections and mobilizes the body—gives Pentecostal and charismatic Christians New Testament warrant for their emotionally and physically expressive worship. And there is a strategy of mission here. Pentecostals contend that today, as well as in first-century Corinth, worship of the *proskynēsis* sort attracts, touches, and converts people.

A third New Testament worship word, *latreia*, connoted formal religious acts, especially sacrifice. According to the evangelist Luke, the aged Anna engaged in *latreia* day and night in the temple, praying and fasting (Luke 2:37). For Paul *latreia* had come to refer not to ceaseless temple worship but to worship that permeates all of life. In a famous passage, he urged the Christians in Rome—in light of God's amazing work of incorporating Gentiles along with Jews in God's peoplehood—to offer their bodies as "a living holocaust," which is their *latreia* "that makes sense" (Rom 12:1-2).[12] As a result of their worship—sacrificial, life-encompassing, and ceaseless—the Roman Christians would be distinctive, not conformed to patterns of the Roman world but transfigured within the Roman world into the image of Christ. *Latreia*—worship that involves total personal holocaust, that affects one's body and all areas of

letting worship go for given

life—is radical. As missiologist Jonathan Bonk has written, "True worship involves sacrificing that which is most dear to us."[13]

Although contemporary writers on worship tend not to give much attention to it, *latreia* has historically often dominated the awareness of theologians; in fact, the Seventh Ecumenical Council of 787 explicitly subordinated *proskynēsis* to *latreia*, which it asserted is the "true worship of faith which alone pertains to the divine nature."[14]

Worship: Ascribing Worth to God

But Greek words may seem beside the point; after all, most readers of this book think in English. What English word can we use that encompasses what we have seen so far—worship that involves words and actions, that is emotionally heartfelt, that is the work of the people, that is full-bodied and emotionally expressive, that is radically sacrificial? If we probe the inner meaning of the English word worship, we find that it is surprisingly able to convey the large, all-encompassing meaning of the biblical words.

Of course, every language has its worship words. German has *Gottesdienst* (the service of God); Spanish has *adoración*; Indonesian has *kebaktian*, which combines meanings of adoration, loyalty, and obedience—"adore–obey." Each of these words holds out special possibilities. Each of them also has limitations that are inevitable, given the size of the reality that we are asking this word to denote.

As a single, shorthand, all-embracing word, the English language has *worship*. This is a strong word. *Worship* is an Old English compound, made up of *weorth* and *scipe*—worth/worthiness and create/ascribe. Ascribing worth: in the most basic sense, this is what we do when we direct our lives toward God. When we ascribe worth we reveal what preoccupies us, what we ultimately value, what is most important in our lives. As the Hebrew prophets pointed out, we worship what we trust for our security. We are like the merchant in Jesus' parable who found treasure in a field: we worship what we will sell everything to get (Matt 13:44). We worship what we organize our lives around and what we are willing to die or kill for. Philip Kenneson has put it well: "Every human life is an embodied argument about what things are worth doing. . . . All human life is doxological"—of God or of something else.[15]

In light of this understanding of worship, every worshipper must ask whether our lives and our priorities ascribe worth to the God who has been revealed in Jesus Christ. Our words may ascribe worth to God but our life choices may indicate that our deepest concerns are estranged from God's concerns. The Old Testament prophets saw this estrangement and labeled it idolatry. They inveighed against it. The prophetic critique assumed that the covenantal relationship between God and Israel had two parts: God's saving acts and God's "call to ethical obedience."[16] Israel ceremonially repeated this foundational covenant at times of revival. The recitation of God's acts and the people's response in word and ceremony were "the essence of worship."[17]

The Old Testament prophets were particularly alert to the constantly lurking temptation to trust in human sources of security. They were convinced that we worship what we trust; we ascribe worth to the sources that we rely on for our comfort and security—wealth, oppression, and military strength (Isa 30:12; 31:1; Hos 10:13). Jesus, too, taught in this tradition: "No one can serve two masters. . . . You cannot serve God and wealth [*mammon*]" (Matt 6:24). So idolatry's essence is not genuflecting to graven images; it is using words and cultic actions to ascribe worth to God and then undercutting this by choices and commitments that ascribe worth to other sources of security. As Paul put it, idolatry is worshipping "the creature rather than the Creator" (Rom 1:25).

Worship Is for All of Life

The vision of the biblical writers is deeply holistic. The biblical writers invite us to worship God—to ascribe worth to God—in all of life. For them there is no sacred-secular divide that confines worship to religious places or cultic acts. The *latreia* that Paul describes in Romans 12:1-2 involves the transformation of all aspects of the believers' lives so that they will be conformed to Christ. And in the Hebrew Scriptures the prophets' most terrifying warnings come to people who place their trust in conventional sources of security. In the temple or assembly, with word and rite they proclaim that God is Lord; then, in their everyday activities, they ignore God's law, defy God's priorities, and trust in their wealth and weaponry. Such people want God's blessing without committing themselves to live in response to God's saving acts. They think that by participating in the cult they can short-circuit the route to blessing. They do not need to behave according to God's law. But, in the words of Nicholas

Wolterstorff, "The authenticity of the liturgy is conditioned by the quality of the ethical life of those who participate."[18]

God, according to Isaiah, could not "endure solemn assembles" of people whose lives were unjust and whose hands, lifted in prayer, were "full of blood"; when the worshippers refused to advocate for the oppressed, orphans, and widows, God hid his eyes and would not listen (Isa 1:13-17). Similarly, in Jeremiah's day the Israelites assumed that if they stood before God in the temple and engaged in cultic actions, their nation would be secure—even if in their everyday life they oppressed immigrants and orphans and widows, shed innocent blood, and worshipped other gods. Not so, said Jeremiah. When the worshippers do not live compassionately and justly, the temple is a "den of robbers" and God repudiates their cultic acts (Jer 7:1-11). As Isaiah and Jeremiah realized, the worshippers' words in worship that ascribe worth to God must be congruent with the worshippers' lives which are conformed to the character, purpose, and mission of the One whose worth they proclaim. Wolterstorff's pithy phrase catches the prophetic vision: "*not* authentic liturgy *unless* justice."[19]

Jesus of Nazareth, a "prophet mighty in deed and word" (Luke 24:19), stood in this tradition. The distillation of his teaching, the Sermon on the Mount, ends with his reflections on worship and life. Jesus was concerned that people would worship him but ignore what he said. They would call him "Lord, Lord" and not do "the will of my Father in heaven." They would hear his words and not act on them. Their responses would be disastrous for them: in judgment Jesus would not recognize them, and their whole worlds would collapse (Matt 7:21-27). Jesus' vision parallels that of the prophets: *not* authentic liturgy *unless* discipleship.

Wherever the congruence between word and life is missing, there is idolatry, false worship that God judges. Christian leaders across the centuries have often restated this theme. In mid-third-century Carthage, for example, Bishop Cyprian stated as one of 120 precepts to be memorized by catechumens (people being prepared for baptism): "That it is of small account to be baptized and to receive the Eucharist, unless one profits by it in both deeds and works."[20] In sixteenth-century Holland, the Anabaptist leader Menno Simons, on the run from the civil and religious authorities, berated the Protestant clerics:

O preachers, dear preachers, where is the power of the Gospel you preach? . . . Shame on you for the easygoing gospel and barren bread-breaking, you who have in so many years been unable to effect enough with your gospel and sacraments so as to remove your needy and distressed members from the streets, even though the Scripture plainly teaches . . . [that] there shall be no beggars among you.[21]

There was, however, another way—the way of repentance, which would make the words and behavior of the worshippers congruent with the character of God. According to Isaiah, God invited the people to "cease to do evil, learn to do good; seek justice, rescue the oppressed, defend the orphan, plead for the widow" (Isa 1:16-17). According to Jeremiah, God promises the people, "*If* you truly act justly . . . *if* you do not oppress the alien, the orphan and the widow . . . *then* I will dwell with you in this place" (Jer 7:5-7, our italics). According to John the revelator, God will reward his servants, both small and great, when they reverence God's name and refrain from participating in the destruction of the earth (see Rev 11:18). God's people can repent by repudiating worship services that offer God brilliant music and solemn sacrifices without challenging their unjust living: "Let justice roll down like waters, and righteousness like an ever-flowing stream" (Amos 5:24). Then the people will ascribe worth to God consistently, with integrity, in "lives offered up to the agenda of God."[22]

Worship Services Must Be in Keeping with God's Character and Mission

In worship, all of life is the point. All of life must be lived in keeping with God's character and agenda. But although the ritual events are secondary, they are still important.[23] Lives that ascribe worth to God must have times of concentrated attention to God. We call these "worship services," or, in short, "worship." These are not the sum total of worship, but they are an essential part of worship, both weekly and daily. They are essential because if we do not give God specific, dedicated times in which we verbally and ritually ascribe worth to God, we will soon not ascribe worth to God at all. As Eugene Peterson has written, "Worship is the time and place that we assign for deliberate attentiveness to God—not because he's confined to time and place, but because our self-importance is so insidiously relentless that if we don't deliberately interrupt ourselves regularly, we have no chance of attending to him at all at other times and in other places."[24] So in this book, we insist that all of life is worship. But we also assume that dedicated cultic acts—these markers of life that we call worship services—are indispensable.

Why indispensable? Because worship services enable us by God's grace to encounter the God of life. This encounter is God's gift. In fact, worship is not simply a human activity; it is "primarily something that God does."[25] The Holy Spirit is at work, taking the initiative, beckoning us to gather in God's name.[26] God's voice speaks; Jesus is present in our midst; the Holy Spirit bestows gifts to heal our wounds, restore broken relationships, and empower us to participate in God's mission. Worship is "the self-communication of the Triune God."[27]

When we worship God, we enter an environment of praise. We read the Scripture and proclaim the good news; we pray and sing and bring testimony; we share in the Eucharist. And, even in our brokenness and sin, God graciously encounters us. Through these means, God enables us to tell and retell the story of God and God's people; God reorients us by the story; and God reforms our habits and re-reflexes our instinctive behavior. In short, as we worship God, God nourishes in us the character of worshippers—humility, trust, obedience.

As we worship God, we experience what Gerhard Lohfink calls "de-idolizing."[28] With new alertness we see the tools and instruments, the forces and institutions that cast God in our own image and "whose exacting demands elude scrutiny and technique"—and whose unwitting instruments we would be if it were not for worship.[29] When we say "Jesus is Lord" and bow at his feet, we radically restrict the worth we ascribe to Caesar. And as people who are freed from the thrall of false gods, we respond by giving thanks to God, by praising God, and by committing ourselves to live in light of God's mission so that we flow with it and not impede it.

Speaking specifically of the Eucharist, J. G. Davies asserted that "one of the fruits of communion, i.e. growth in the likeness of Christ by the reception of his humanity, is identical with one of the goals of mission." He continued, "To partake of Christ's person in the Eucharist is to be engaged in" the task of Christ's mission.[30] When we as worshippers recall or enact certain historical events, we become participants in the significance of those events. Since "the context of the divine acts was mission, . . . [so] our present evocation and participation in them includes us in the mission" of God.[31]

Of course, the worship services themselves can be unjust. As the biblical writers warn us, they can be instruments of irrelevance and oppression that reflect the rebellious daily lives of the people. In his first letter to his Corinthian friends, Paul said that the humiliating way that they organized their common meal kept it from being "the Lord's supper" (1 Cor 11:20-22); in its injustice it stood in the way of God's mission. Without justice there was no worship. Jesus' response to the Jerusalem temple was similar. In it he found a worship system that was functioning efficiently but actually was blocking God's mission. Its cultic enterprise zone in the court of the Gentiles excluded the outsiders and oppressed the poor. So Jesus quoted Jeremiah and Isaiah: "My house shall be called a house of prayer for all the nations. . . . But you have made it a den of robbers" (Mark 11:17).[32] Angrily Jesus upset the tables of the temple *bureaux de change* and drove out the sellers of animals. Dramatically and offensively, Jesus indicated that, even in this holy place, without justice there could be no worship. The worship of God must be an expression of the entire lives of the worshippers; their acts of worship must be in harmony with the mission of God. That mission is just and peaceable.

Worship Services Reveal the Character and Purposes of God

This, indeed, is the point: in worship we encounter our God, Creator and Redeemer, and in this encounter God's character and purposes shape us. As we shall see in chapter 3, the God whom we worship is passionately committed to moving history in a particular direction, toward cosmic, creation-encompassing, unimaginable reconciliation. In Christendom, in which both rulers and peasants were Christian, Christians assumed that Christ's rule had already been realized and that the established order had been divinely ordained. After Christendom we are aware that the world—the world of Christendom and the world of post-Christendom that is succeeding it—is deeply flawed and marked by rebellion and idolatry.

But when we are formed by worship and by the story of God that we tell and enact in worship, we confess that God is committed to a different kind of world whose future will be realized by alternative means. Through Christ, according to a lyrical passage in the letter to the Colossians, God will reconcile to himself "all things, whether on earth or in heaven, making peace by the blood of his cross" (Col 1:20). By suffering, by servanthood, God has worked and is working to bring about reconciliation of people with God, of people with their enemies, of people with the created order. This is God's mission—to bring right relationships in every area of life, to make multidimensional shalom. We cannot participate in God's mission without worship. We're not strong enough or clever enough. But when we respond to the Holy Spirit and assemble for worship, the Spirit meets us in our weakness and equips us to live toward God's vision. This is why "the very act of assembly is part of the mission of God."[33] As we attune ourselves to God's mission and align ourselves with God's purposes we ascribe worth to God. We discover, in all of life, that worship and mission belong together.[34]

So how do we evaluate the worship services of our churches? Not by the expertise and flair with which they are led; not by the emotions they elicit or the way they move our hearts; not by the way they break through the "culture barrier" by employing "the language, music, style, architecture, and art forms of the target population";[35] not by their pizzazz, which certain English evangelicals call the "wow factor."[36] Rather, we ask, Does the worship of our churches ascribe worth to the missional God? Does our worship give space to the Holy Spirit, who equips God's people, to take part in God's mission? And we ask, with Stephen Holmes, whether is it possible that a God who "is properly described as 'missionary' . . . can only be worshipped by a missionary church."[37]

TWO

Mission Under Christendom

What is mission? When many people today think about mission, they have "missionaries" in mind. According to the conventional stereotype, missionaries are Westerners—often British or American Westerners—who leave their homes in the prosperous North to take the Christian message to people in the global South. There are fewer of these people today than there were fifty years ago, but there are still hundreds of thousands of missionaries.[1] The media in the post-Christendom West often portray these missionaries as "colonizers at prayer," bearers of stifling prohibitions and cultural restrictions to people who were happier in their pre-Christian innocence.[2] At times there has been truth in this stereotype. But a substantial minority of people in the West are not dissuaded by the stereotype and support churches that engage in sending missionaries to many countries.

We have vivid personal recollections of the missionary movement. We grew up in missionary families: Eleanor was born in India of missionary parents, and Alan grew up in Japan at a time when there were many North American missionaries there. For much of our adult lives, we ourselves were missionaries, sent by Mennonite Christians in North America to work with other Christians in England. Throughout our lives, our families intermingled with missionaries, rallied support for them, and advocated for them. While there have been some missionaries whose behavior we thought dishonored the cause of Christ, we ourselves know many missionaries whom we respect deeply.

Don and Dorothy McCammon were wonderful examples of this kind of missionary. In 1947 the Mennonite Church sent them from Indiana in the United States to Chendu in western China. They were close friends of our families and were important to us personally. So, when we stood at the train station and sang "God Be with You Till We Meet Again," it was with commitment and passion that we were sending them off. We had no idea what they would face. After language study, they settled in their city, met with the local Christians, and collaborated with them as they shared their faith in Christ. Within a year they were engulfed by the Chinese Revolution. "Red-star soldiers," initially friendly, turned hostile. Rumors were spread about the unsavory actions of the "imperialist Christians." Don was arrested, brought to the center of Chendu, accused before a Peoples' Court of anti-revolutionary acts, and sentenced to death, while members of the crowd shouted, "Shoot him." He was deported, not shot. Later, after months of negotiation, suitable loss of face, and a perilous voyage down the Yangtze with newly born Julia, Dorothy was deported too and eventually reunited with Don in California. Don and Dorothy had tried to stay in China, but the revolution had defeated them. As missionaries, they had failed.[3]

Or had they? Decades later, word came from their Chinese friends, courageous Christians, who had been imprisoned for many years during the Cultural Revolution, and who now wanted to be in touch again.[4] By the 1980s the Christian church in China—Catholic, Protestant, house church—which Communist might had apparently crushed, was growing rapidly. Indeed, it was growing far more rapidly than it had before the revolution—and, we may add, more rapidly than the church in prosperous Middle America from which Don and Dorothy had been sent as missionaries. Today, according to historian of worldwide Christianity Lamin Sanneh, China may be "well endowed to assume a leadership role in the scheme of post-Western Christian developments."[5] The Chinese church is simply one aspect of a worldwide Christian reality of which Don and Dorothy were a tiny part. Christianity in the twenty-first century is not a Western phenomenon but a world phenomenon.

Characteristics of Classical Mission
Don and Dorothy were participants in "classical mission," which is still present but was a typical phenomenon of late Christendom. What were the characteristics of classical mission?

- *Sender*: The sender is the church. A Western missionary society called Don and Dorothy to go to China; a church—in fact, an entire denomination—ratified the call and provided financial support for them, laid hands on them, and sent them with its blessing. Other classical missionaries, who often raised their own support, were commissioned by parachurch agencies.
- *Territory*: The destination of the missionaries who were "sent" was the "mission field." Mission took place "out there," often separated by cultural, linguistic, or political barriers from the place that the missionaries came from. The missionaries could be sent to the inner city of a Western metropolis, but more frequently they were sent to some "non-Christian" country—some country beyond Christendom. Missionary activity primarily took place in heathendom, which Western missionary societies carved up and cantonized to prevent undue competition between missionary organizations. Don and Dorothy, after consulting with other expatriate Christians, went to a carefully specified part of western China.
- *Agents*: Don and Dorothy were missionaries. They were specialists, who had received training that prepared them for their work. They were parallel to other specialists—parish priests, pastors, deacons, counselors—who did full-time work for the church. In Roman Catholic missions, the missionaries were typically members of religious orders. All these specialists were "serious" Christians, distinctive and different. Ordinary Christians, in contrast, worked at their jobs at home, worshipped God on Sundays, and supported the specialist priests and missionaries with their prayers and donations.
- *The goal of mission*: To bring salvation to individuals and to build the church. Don and Dorothy shared their faith in Christ with individual Chinese people whom they loved with sacrificial abandon. They tried to nurture a congregation that met near their home. This task was a daunting one, which in the end they could not carry out. Missionaries elsewhere were more successful. In Rwanda, in central Africa, for example, efforts by missionaries both Catholic and Protestant made it "one of Africa's most evangelized nations."[6] The vast majority of its people were baptized. Of course, at times the evangelization was somewhat superficial. Given the number of people who were becoming

Christian, the teaching (catechesis) of the new believers was bound to be speedy and selective. In Rwanda, as in most countries, most Western missionaries "did not include the peace witness as an important part of their presentation of the gospel."[7] When does mission end? Some theologians of classical mission, such as the Catholic theologian Pierre Charles, have proposed that mission ends when it reaches its goal with the establishment of the church in a society. When Christendom is achieved, mission ceases to be a function of the church.[8]

The Christendom Origins of Classical Mission

Where did the type of missionary activity that we call "classical mission" come from? As we shall see in chapter 7, it did not come from the early church. The pre-Christendom church of the first three centuries was growing rapidly, despite disincentives, even though Christians practically never talked about mission or evangelism and had very few official missionaries. "From St. Paul to the conversion of Constantine, there are only two missionaries that we can name."[9] When the early Christian writers used the word *missio*, they used it theologically to refer to the Father's sending of the Son and not to refer to human efforts to attract people to conversion to Christ and new life in the church.[10] Nevertheless, for many early Christians, mission was their lifestyle, and the faith grew by "a process of constant fermentation."[11]

In the first half of the fourth century, things changed. In 312 Emperor Constantine I had a vision and began to align himself with the Christian church. He and later emperors replaced disincentives with incentives, and Christianity came to be associated with the Roman state and the imperial upper classes. At the end of the fourth century, Emperor Theodosius I made Christianity the only legal religion, and in the sixth century Emperor Justinian I made Christian baptism compulsory.[12] So in the Roman Empire of late antiquity, Christianity spread by coercion as well as voluntary conversion. Beyond the boundaries of the Roman Empire, Christianity spread by the action of missionaries, often monks, who at times were backed up by military power. The goal was the establishment of a unitary Christian society that from the seventh century onward called itself "Christendom."

In Christendom countries, notably in Europe, the entire populace was Christian; with the exception of Jews, membership in the church was the same as membership in the society at large. For many centuries, in European countries baptism was required by law; so also was attendance at worship services—although most people, even though they attended eucharistic services, took Communion infrequently. The Fourth Lateran Council required every Catholic Christian to communicate once per year; in eighteenth-century Lutheran Leipzig, where Catholic regulations had no authority, a believer as devout as the composer J. S. Bach took Communion only once or twice per year.[13] In Christendom societies, the church and state were in symbiosis: ecclesial and secular authorities supported each other. The state protected the church's spiritual ministries that provided "cure of souls"—the ministry of word and sacraments—to all the people.

And the church, for its part, was careful to justify the position and policies of the civil government. Bach wrote cantatas for use in the churches of Leipzig that celebrated the ministry of "the authorities" (*die Obrigkeit*); his Cantata 29 prays God's blessing on "those who rule us, who guide, protect, and lead us," as well as on "those who are obedient."[14] To carry out the church's activities, a large corps of religious professionals was required: ordained priests and ministers, musicians, members of religious orders. The majority of Christians, on the other hand, were nonspecialists, "laymen" who were expected to attend the weekly services organized by the clergy—and to pay for these services by means of the clerical tithe, a tax that from the sixth century onward was required of all citizens who were, of course, also church members.[15]

How did mission fit into the world of Christendom? It was present at Christendom's outset, as missionaries extended Christianity into the less Christianized regions of the countryside and into neighboring territories. But after the sixth century, when all the inhabitants of a society were baptized, mission largely disappeared from Western Christendom.[16] The church's purpose was not to spread the faith to new lands; it was to ensure the eternal salvation of people already Christian and to buttress the orderly functioning of Christendom societies. The theological faculty of Luther's university in Wittenberg in 1652 issued its "Opinion," which denied that the Lutheran Church had any missionary calling. Only the state could carry out missionary activity, converting pagans "through martial law."[17]

At times, to be sure, mission did take place. From the twelfth century onward, Roman Catholic religious orders actively propagated

Christianity beyond the confines of Christendom territories; and in the sixteenth century the founder of the Jesuit order, Ignatius of Loyola, for the first time used the word *missio* to describe these activities, in which many missionaries served in a vulnerable, costly way.[18] In the sixteenth and seventeenth centuries, Catholics sent missionary priests to China, Japan, India, Africa, and Latin America. Although the nonconformist Anabaptists of the Reformation era had been missionally active in sixteenth-century Europe,[19] it was only in late Christendom—the eighteenth to twentieth centuries—that the major Protestant bodies became involved in mission. Pietist renewal produced the Moravian missionary efforts of the eighteenth century, and these were followed, in the 1790s in England, by Baptists, Anglicans, and Reformed Christians who founded missionary societies dedicated to fulfill the "Great Commission" of the Matthean Jesus to "*go* into all the world" (Matt 28:19, our italics). In the nineteenth and twentieth centuries, missionary societies sprang up in other countries and were the vehicle for enthusiastic Protestant volunteers who went as missionaries to many places. The Catholic Church, especially after 1800, continued to send missionaries to many countries. This was "classical mission."

Classical Mission in Late Christendom

However, most Christian clergy in Christendom countries, both Catholic and Protestant, spent the bulk of their time with worship, not with mission. They were preoccupied not with missionary efforts but with liturgical and pastoral ministry—the "cure of souls." As the movement for foreign missions gained momentum in Protestant countries, it was enthusiastic laypeople—disproportionately women—who were its instruments.[20] As academic theology developed in the West, the theological disciplines developed as isolated specializations, and most theologians were uninterested in mission. According to David Bosch, "Mission was something completely on the periphery of the church and did not evoke any theological interest worth mentioning."[21]

When in the late nineteenth century mission finally emerged as an academic discipline in its own right, it had the lowest prestige of any theological discipline. No doubt this was because mission had to do with efforts to promote the faith not within Christendom but beyond Christendom. Gustav Warneck, the first Professor of Mission at a European university (Halle), introduced the distinction: Christians propagating the gospel far from their home cultures were engaged in *mission*, but Christians advocating their faith closer home were engaged in *evangelism*. And evangelism did not involve a critique of the worldview, structures, and mores of society in light of the gospel, but urged conversion that strengthened adherence to shared social norms.[22] In Christendom, few theologians—even missiologists—pondered the interaction of the gospel with their own cultures. They did not reflect on the inculturation—unconscious and therefore overconfident—that had happened and was continuing to happen in their own societies, often at the cost of domesticating the Christian good news. The result was what Bishop Lesslie Newbigin called an "illegitimate alliance with false elements in culture."[23]

As a result, when missionary initiatives proliferated in the nineteenth and twentieth centuries, they were often associated with dominant Christendom values. Many Western missionaries were remarkable people, sensitive students of the cultures to which they went, and servants of their people. But at times the missionaries were less admirable. Programed by Christendom assumptions, they sometimes became instruments of the national policies and colonial ambitions of their native countries. Julius Richter, a leading German missiologist during World War I, urged German missionaries to be true to the Christian values that were uniquely embodied by the German culture and not to surrender German-controlled mission areas to the English, whom he characterized as "greedy shopkeepers."[24] Many missionaries related comfortably to foreign merchants and colonial administrators. In 1907 a Methodist missionary to China described the foreign missionaries' impact on the country as being a "walking advertisement" or a kind of "sandwich man" in the interests of promoting Western imports into the country.[25] At the end of World War II, General Douglas MacArthur counted on this tradition when he called for American churches to send "thousands of missionaries" to the recently conquered Japan.[26] Karl Rahner's judgment is severe, but it contains more than a grain of truth: "the actual concrete activity of the Church in its relation to the world outside of Europe was in fact . . . the activity of an export firm which exported a European religion as a commodity it did not really want to change but sent throughout the world together with the rest of the culture and civilization it considered superior."[27]

Within Christendom the missionary movement was always marginal. The eminent church historian Owen Chadwick proved that
it was possible to write a two-volume history of the nineteenth-
century English church without once mentioning the missionary
movement.[28] But, as Andrew Walls has pointed out, the missionary
movement was unleashing underestimated but powerful forces; it
was "the detonator of the vast explosion of the demographic transformation of the Christian church."[29] Especially in the latter half
of the twentieth century, often after the Western missionaries had
gone home, Christians in the global South appropriated the Christian faith that missionaries had brought them and translated it into
the local cultures and vernaculars. As Jehu Hanciles has argued,
"Contrary to the popular evangelical conception, the phenomena
of growth of Christianity in the non-western world owe a lot more
to indigenous initiatives than to western missionary agencies."[30] So
Southern appropriations of Christianity often look very different
from the Christendom Christianity that the missionaries brought.
As the Southern appropriations proliferated, world Christianity
grew not only in numbers but also in cultural variety and richness.
This variation and growth occurred at the same time that Christian
observance in Christendom's heartlands was waning. Significantly,
it was at the very time of Christendom's recession in the West that
a new vision of mission emerged—the mission of God.

THREE

Mission After Christendom: The *Missio Dei*

The decline of Christendom in the West has been a long process that is not yet complete. No doubt it began with the Protestant Reformation. National churches, breaking with their Roman Catholic mother, attempted to realize the Christendom vision in their own territories, with varying success. The Radical Reformation intensified this process by founding voluntary churches that separated themselves from the society-encompassing Catholic and Protestant churches. In central Europe, the seventeenth-century Wars of Religion fragmented things further, and in many places urbanization and the emergence of denominations led to the crumbling of Christendom institutions. By the nineteenth century, many European countries relaxed requirements that restricted admission to universities or the assuming of political office to members of the established churches.

Church attendance in many places plummeted. By the 1930s and 1940s, theologians and church leaders began to sense that Christian faith and practice were in retreat in Christendom. The shattering effects of World War II made this sense all the more acute. A prophetic exponent of this view was the Cardinal Archbishop of Paris, Emmanuel Suhard, who in the 1940s controversially began to speak of France, a country that had seemed to be at the heart of Christendom, as "A Country of Mission."[1]

It was at this very time, as the recession of Christianity within Christendom was becoming apparent, that theologians began to articulate a new view of mission. In 1932, at a missionary conference in Brandenburg in Germany, the great Swiss theologian Karl

Barth commented that, in the early church, the term *missio* did not have to do with sending missionaries to other countries; instead, *missio* was "an expression of the doctrine of the Trinity—namely an expression of the divine sending forth of the self, the sending of the Son and the Holy Spirit to the world." And he added, "Can we indeed claim that we can do it in any other way?"[2] Mission, in other words, was not a human activity; it was an action of the divine sender, the triune God. After World War II, in 1952 at a missionary conference at Willingen in shattered Germany, the theologian Karl Hartenstein refined Barth's idea and for the first time used the term *missio Dei*—the mission of God.[3]

Six years later, German missiologist Georg Vicedom wrote a full-length treatment of the subject that was soon translated into English—*The Mission of God: An Introduction to a Theology of Mission*—that developed the term and popularized it.[4] In 1966 J. G. Davies, ever attuned to new ideas, in his *Worship and Mission* adopted the *missio Dei* and called it "a revolution in thinking about the Church and mission."[5] Soon the term spread from ecumenical Protestant thinkers to other traditions. The fathers of Vatican II espoused a *missio Dei* theology in their encyclical *Ad Gentes*.[6] Mennonite missiologists such as Wilbert Shenk have given special articulation to *missio Dei* theology.[7] Evangelical Protestants at times have been critical of *missio Dei* theology, but many of them also have made it their own. The Lausanne document of 2005, "Reconciliation as the Mission of God: Faithful Christian Witness in a World of Destructive Conflicts and Divisions" begins with the sentence "The mission of God in our fallen, broken world is reconciliation."[8] The most thorough biblical rationale for a *missio Dei* theology, by a theologian of any Christian tradition, is that of evangelical missionary exegete Christopher Wright, in his 2006 *The Mission of God*.[9]

All these movements and thinkers, in a post-Christendom world, confess that mission is not human work; it is God's work. It grows out of God's overflowing love for the world. Stephen Holmes has recently insisted that mission is not simply a work of God; it is an expression of "the eternal inner-triune relationships of love which Father, Son and Spirit share, and in which the church is called to participate." For this reason it is appropriate to call God "missionary."[10] Holmes goes on to comment that "a church that refuses the call to mission is failing to be the church God calls it to be just as fundamentally as a church that refuses the call to be loving."[11]

In this book we will not generally use the word *missionary* for God. The reason is simple. In many circles, *missionary* has come to have overtones of cultural imperialism; further, *missionary* often connotes the cross-cultural and long-distance dimensions of God's mission (for example, Korean Christians who are sent to Zambia). In both of these ways, the term *missionary* restricts and limits our understanding of God's reconciling work, which sends all Christians, wherever they are, into their own lives as bearers of the good news of reconciliation in Christ. But, since we find it fruitful to think of mission as "a reflection of God's own nature and character, reflecting who God is from all eternity," we will refer frequently to God as "the missional God."[12] We agree with Chris Wright that "missional" is a useful adjective denoting something related to the sending character and activity of God.[13] And we are convinced that the word *missional*—as distinct from *missionary*—is proving its worth today as many churches in post-Christendom discover their vocation to take part in God's mission.[14]

Missio Dei: The Bible's Grand Narrative

The *missio Dei* approach develops like this: The triune God created the cosmos in love. Genesis 1 portrays God creating the cosmos to be "good," even "very good." God's creation was full of shalom, marked by relationships that were comprehensively, multidimensionally right. God's love was self-emptying and nonviolent; in love God would not coerce worship or require obedience. The result was painful. The humans chose autonomy and disobedience. God had created them, male and female, to be in fellowship with God, to be in right relationship with each other, and to be the stewards of creation. But they chose not to ascribe worth to the God who had created and loved them. Their "fall" led to brokenness and alienation. This caused anguish to God. God in love has been pained by the marring of his relationship with humans, by the crippling of humans' relationships with each other, and by the blighting of creation that resulted from human disobedience. God in love is determined to make things right, to counter the fall and to restore shalom, and in the fullness of time God will accomplish this. This is God's mission; as some liberation theologians put it, it is "God's project."[15] As Chris Wright has argued throughout his book, the mission of God is the Bible's "grand narrative."[16]

The goals of the *missio Dei* are huge. God's mission is to bring God's kingdom, God's redemptive reign. God's mission is creation-encompassing; it is to recreate creation, to bring new creation (Isa 65:17; 66:22; Gal 6:15). God's mission is to make all things new (Col 1:20; Rev 21:5)—humans with "hearts of flesh" in a right relationship to God (Ezek 36:26), humans reconciled to their bitterest enemies (Isa 19:23-24), and the whole creation restored as a place where justice is at home (2 Pet 3:13). In all these dimensions—humans with God, humans with other humans, humans with creation—God's project is shalom, an all-comprehending wholeness (Col 1:20). God's mission is peace. Throughout the Bible, prophets and seers tried to explain this, and they used a variety of visual images. We will explore two of these.

Wolves and Lambs

The first image is the reconciled creation. In his eleventh chapter, the prophet Isaiah graphically depicts this reconciliation—this *impossible* reconciliation—between predators and victims. The spirit of the Lord will rest upon the descendant of David ("a shoot . . . from the stump of Jesse") who delights in the fear of the Lord and righteously judges the poor. Astonishing things will happen. "The wolf shall live with the lamb"—a counterintuitive thought—and many other reconciliations will happen as well: cows and bears, nursing children and snakes—"and a little child shall lead them." According to Hans Walter Wolff, this is an "unprecedented ecological peace."[17] It is a vision of a transformed future in which the lethal alienations of the present have been overcome by "the knowledge of the Lord." This is the direction, says Isaiah, that God is taking history. It is a destination without hurting or destroying; it is a destination of comprehensive, humanly impossible shalom.

The power of this vision was clear to the nineteenth-century American artist Edward Hicks (1780–1849). Hicks was a Quaker sign painter who was deeply distressed by the conflicts between two Quaker groups—the Biblicist Orthodox Quakers and the more liberal Hicksite Quakers—which seemed likely to lead to a fissure between them. Between the two factions, Hicks had his own preferences, but his deepest desire was for reconciliation between them. He expressed his desire—he *prayed* his desire—by painting the Isaiah 11 peaceable kingdom no fewer than one hundred times, of which sixty-two renderings have survived.[18] In this astonishing array of variations on a theme, two motifs recur. One is the reconciled relations between natural enemies, especially the wolves and the lamb, and the child and the snake. A second recurring motif in many of his paintings is a depiction, in middle distance, of Quakers and Algonquin Americans smoking the pipe of peace as they ratify a treaty. This, for Hicks, represented an imperfect, halting anticipation of the reconciled creation that Isaiah 11 promised. Hicks always separated it from the reconciled creation by a chasm. "We're not there yet," Hicks seems to be telling his Quaker friends, "but this is the direction that God is taking history; and the destination can guide our behavior now."

A Feast for All People

The second image is the banquet for all nations. In Isaiah 25 the prophet anticipates the day when the Lord of hosts, on his mountain, will make "for all peoples a feast of rich food, a feast of well-matured wines." As people feast at this banquet, the Lord will destroy the death shroud that is cast over all the peoples and will "swallow up death forever." This feast for all peoples, says Isaiah, is the salvation of our God, and it is worth anticipating with active waiting (Isa 25:6-9).

Early in his public ministry, this vision sprang to the mind of Jesus when a Roman centurion interrupted him and implored him to heal his servant. Jesus was moved by the centurion's appeal, and he offered to go to the man's home to cure his servant. For a Jew, this home—a Gentile household and a Roman barracks—represented threat and ritual pollution. The centurion confidently refused Jesus' offer, for he understood Jesus' authority and believed that Jesus could heal without sight or touch. At this, Matthew reports, Jesus was "amazed." Never in Israel had Jesus seen such faith. Jesus then began to speak of the banquet: "Many will come from east and west and will eat with Abraham and Isaac and Jacob in the kingdom of heaven" (Matt 8:5-11).

The image of the banquet for "all peoples," for "many," functioned in Jesus' thought as the image of the peaceable kingdom functioned in the imagination of Edward Hicks. God's determination is to bring impossible reconciliation, shalom, between enemies—even between Roman soldiers and the Jewish people living under Roman occupation. The apostle Paul is in this tradition. In Colossians 1:19-20, he ends his christological hymn by celebrating the comprehensive peacemaking of Christ:

For in him all the fullness of God
was pleased to dwell,
and through him God was pleased to reconcile
to himself *all things*,
whether on earth or in heaven,
by making peace through the blood
of his cross. [our italics]

For Paul, as well as for Isaiah and Jesus, the mission of God is to make peace, multidimensional shalom. It is to bring impossible reconciliation.

The Means of God's Mission: Sending

But what means does God use? From the beginning of the Bible's narrative, God's means is not force; it is not compulsion. After the fall as well as before it, God is self-limiting. God will not coerce worship or force obedience. Instead God's strategizing and action are characterized by sending. Sending (*missio*), not compelling, is God's *modus operandi*.

- Sending Abram and Sarai to leave security in Mesopotamia to be a blessing for all the families of the earth (Gen 12:1-3).
- Sending the people of Israel to be a "priestly kingdom and a holy nation" (Exod 19:6) and to be a corporate participant in God's mission.
- Sending the prophets, who offer a vision of a servant who will announce, and enact, the gospel of peace (Isa 52:7).[19]
- Sending, in the fullness of time, Jesus of Nazareth. Anointed by the Holy Spirit, Jesus as second Adam obediently recapitulates the story of Adam, embodying the vision and making peace by his life, death, and resurrection.[20]
- Sending the Holy Spirit upon the disciples and the church, empowering them to be corporately sent by the resurrected Jesus.
- Sending the church to be a light to the nations, to bear witness to Christ and the kingdom, and to be the primary instrument of God's mission.
- Sending all Christians, energized and gifted by the Holy Spirit, to incarnate and enact the way of Jesus in the world: "Peace be

with you. As the Father has sent me, so I send you. . . . Receive the Holy Spirit" (John 20:21-22).

Sending: this is the means of the God of mission. It is the sending, the *missio*, of God. How risky it all is; how vulnerable the work of a God who entrusts the healing of his broken creation to fallible humans—and who takes flesh that humans can torture and crucify. As Darrell Guder has commented, "It has always been possible for humans to encounter God's Word and work in history and to ignore it, to reject it, to distort it, or to manipulate it for selfish ends. . . . God respects the freedom of the creation but mercifully does not treat us the way we treat him."[21] And through it all, and in untold ways that will transcend it all, God is working to bring his kingdom of reconciliation and joy.

So, what is the *missio Dei* like—this post-Christendom vision of mission? Let us reexamine the areas we mentioned in chapter 2 when we discussed classic, Christendom mission.

Characteristics of the *Missio Dei*

Sender

In the *missio Dei*, the sender is not the church, as in Christendom; the sender is God. Some mission workers may have a sending church, or a group of supporters, or a parachurch agency to which they relate. But it is God who is the true sender. God is at work, not simply when people are designated "missionaries," but in all kinds of situations, in innumerable places. God is at work among people who are not consciously part of the church or God's family; God is at work in places of darkness and danger; God is at work among people who do not know how to name God. At their best, Christian missionaries have always discovered that God is at work before they get there. And this is the task of all Christians who participate in God's mission: to expect to find God at work and to be intensely alert to what God is doing.

In the Gospel accounts, Jesus was like this. He looked at the centurion or at the Syrophoenecian woman or at the Samaritan woman in Sychar and saw God already at work. The Johannine Jesus stated this vision with reticent beauty: "Very truly, I tell you, the Son can do nothing on his own, but only what he sees the Father doing" (John 5:19).

Mission, Jesus affirmed, is God's activity, and God sent Jesus to enter into what God was doing; and then, later, Jesus said that he was sending his disciples to do what he did—to enter into the work of the God who is already working (John 20:21). Paul underscored this approach, stating that his friends are God's coworkers (*synergoi*) (1 Cor 3:9) and coworkers in Christ (Rom 16:3, 9). Manuscript traditions differ.[22] But according to one early tradition Paul—in one of his passages most beloved by pastoral theologians, Romans 8:28—stated this yet again. The meanings of the verse in two manuscript traditions are intriguingly different, and wise commentators urge us to listen to both.

> Romans 8:28
>
> KJV/NRSV   We know that all things work together for good for those who love God, who are called according to his purpose.
>
> RSV   We know that in everything God works for good with those who love him, who are called according to his purpose.

Countless Christians across the centuries bear testimony to the comforting truth of the former reading. But the second reading is also true and may be preferable.[23] It is striking how perfectly it states the vision of the *missio Dei*: in all things God is at work, together with people who love him, for good! The *missio Dei* vision always ascribes the initiative to God, but allows for collaboration on the part of God's people. The church, led and empowered by the Holy Spirit, has a unique part in God's mission (Eph 2:22; 3:10).

Territory

In the classical, Christendom model, missionaries were sent abroad, "out there," to "regions beyond" Christendom, to heathendom. The classical text of mission in late Christendom was Matthew 28:19: "Go therefore and make disciples of all nations." Many Christian groups still do emphasize the imperative *Go!* even though in the original text *go* is not an imperative but a participle of attendant circumstances—*as you go.* As Chris Wright emphasizes, "Jesus did not primarily command his disciples to go; he commanded them to make disciples."[24] But many people, rightly, still do go, in all directions. In 2005 19,500 people went as missionaries from the United

Kingdom to other countries; 115,700 went out from the United States. However, missionaries are also going in other directions. Today half of all Protestant missionaries in the world come from non-Western countries, and they go from many countries to many other countries—including to the United Kingdom and the United States. In 2005 there were 15,800 Christian foreign missionaries in the United Kingdom and 35,100 in the United States, in addition to Islamic, Hindu, and Buddhist missionaries.[25] The West is "a new frontier of global Christian expansion."[26]

After Christendom, missionary sending no longer follows imperial patterns. It no longer goes from Christendom to heathendom; it goes, as Samuel Escobar has put it, from everywhere to everyone.[27] So the central mandate for mission has shifted in post-Christendom, from the Great Commission in Matthew to John's version of the commission: "As the Father has sent me, so I send you" (John 20:21). As Escobar points out, "Here we have not only a mandate for mission but also a model of mission style in obedience to the loving design of the Father, patterned by the example of Jesus Christ and driven by the power of the Holy Spirit."[28] And this is the point: in the *missio Dei* understanding, mission is more a matter of stance, rooted in the vulnerable, nonviolent, nonimperial example of Jesus Christ, than it is of sending people to foreign territories. For God's mission is at work along the Silk Road but also in rural Illinois and in inner-city Toronto. Indeed, the missional God is at work in all kinds of places, among the most surprising people. God's mission takes place everywhere people are out of relationship with God, everywhere reconciliation between humans is necessary, everywhere humans commit acts of rapine on God's creation. This means that God's mission, the *missio Dei*, is potentially everywhere!

Agents
In the Christendom tradition, missionaries were special people: priests, nuns, clergy, full-time Christian workers. But the *missio Dei* vision is not clericalist. It includes all who are in Christ. The missional God sends all Christians to be agents of God's mission. Mission is something that God is doing, and God calls all Christians to be involved in it. Indeed, in a *missio Dei* understanding, Christian baptism is baptism into mission. Through baptism with water and the Spirit, believers are in Christ, caught up in Christ's work, which

the Spirit impels. As Davies put it, baptism is "a missionary sacrament enabling us, through the Spirit, to share in the divine love for the world and so in loving service to all mankind. Baptism is therefore an instrument, used by God, to equip us for mission."[29] All Christians find their place in the world as they come to see their lives as carrying out God's mission. Mennonite ethicist Ted Koontz has found this liberating: he no longer thinks that "this world is in a mess and I need to fix it"; instead he knows that "God is moving in history to do something, and I can join in."[30] God may send some people to the other side of the world; but God sends all of us into our own lives—our lives of work, leisure, community life, and retirement. *Missio Dei* thinking rightly places great emphasis on what we Christians do with our everyday lives, especially our lives of work. This makes us aware of the pain of the world, in every area of our experience. And it sends us into the struggle of the world, aware that God is at work in the struggle before we get there and that the struggle can lead to suffering. The cross of Christ reminds us that at the heart of God's mission there is suffering—divine suffering and the suffering of those who participate in God's mission.

Goal

In the Christendom understanding, the mission's goal was to save souls and build the church. This has been incredibly important. Thanks in part to evangelistic work begun by Christendom missionaries, 70 percent of the world's Christians now live in the non-Western world.[31] But God's mission is bigger than saving souls; it is bigger than building the church. To get a sense of mission's colossal expanse, we return to biblical images: the impossible reconciliations of Isaiah 11, leading to a "peaceable kingdom"; or the Isaiah 25 banquet for all people, involving Roman occupying troops as well as oppressed Jews. We could look at other biblical images, for example the "new creation," which is one of the organizing themes of the New Testament; or at "a new heaven and new earth, in which justice dwells."[32] However we view the goal, it will involve "the entire renewal of the cosmos" in which God's people work as God's coworkers toward multidimensional shalom and impossible reconciliation.[33] In this collaboration, the church bears witness to the justice, peace, and joy of God's kingdom (Rom 14:17) and embodies it in a way that anticipates the kingdom in our life together.

Mission involves worship. The goal of mission is worship.[34] In Philippians 2, Paul's great hymn ends with every knee bending in worship and every tongue confessing that Jesus Christ is Lord (Phil 2:9-11). In Revelation 7:9 a great, numberless multitude stands before the throne and the Lamb; it comes from "every nation, from all tribes and peoples and languages"—improbable people, miraculously reconciled; and it engages in ceaseless worship, falling down before God as it sings songs of blessing and thanksgiving in the shalom of God's reign.

Nicholas Wolterstoff has put the *missio Dei* vision with poetic economy:

> *Shalom* is both God's cause in the world and our human calling. Even though the full incursion of *shalom* into our history will be divine gift and not merely human achievement, even though its episodic incursion into our lives now also has a dimension of divine gift, nonetheless it is *shalom* that we are to work and struggle for. We are not to stand around, hands folded, waiting for *shalom* to arrive. We are workers in God's cause, his peace-workers. The *missio Dei* is *our* mission.[35]

Implications of *Missio Dei* Thinking

- Mission is central to theology. Many Christendom approaches to mission have enabled people to regard mission as an appendage to theology as a whole, a seedy subdivision of pastoral theology. In contrast, the *missio Dei* invites us to see mission as central to the entire theological enterprise. It is central to all areas of theology, because all have to do with God, whose nature, whose passion, and whose determination is mission leading to the reconciliation of all people and things in Christ. It is also central to the life of every church and every Christian. As Jürgen Moltmann has put it, "The whole congregation and every individual within it belong with all their powers and potentialities to the mission of God's Kingdom."[36]

- Shalom is central to God's mission. Christendom missionaries often made peace with God central to their evangelism, but they rarely mentioned the many facets of biblical shalom and the centrality of reconciliation to God's purposes. Now, after Christendom, the *missio Dei* restores peace in its many dimensions to the heart of all reflection about evangelism. More than that, it also sees God's shalom-making in all areas of life, where God is active and invites the collaboration of God's people.[37]

- The *missio Dei* integrates mission with life—all aspects of life. In Christendom, mission was a specialized activity, carried out by special Christians in behalf of ordinary Christians. Further, most people saw mission as having especially to do with the relationship of humans to God, so mission and evangelism were often used as interchangeable terms. After Christendom, in *missio Dei* understandings, evangelism is as necessary as ever—God still invites people to be at peace with the God of love. But the God of love is also the God of mission. And God's mission is broader than evangelism. There are other areas—for example, reconciling between estranged enemies, restoring justice, building community, caring for the earth, ending the arms trade, growing and distributing wholesome food, providing safe and ecologically modest transport, healing bodies and minds—that are also issues of God's mission. Mission is broad, as broad as the Creator's concern, as broad as the creation of which Jesus Christ is Lord. As we realize this about God, we will join Andrew Kirk in affirming that "the life of work is for almost all Christians the primary missionary frontier."[38] A product of *missio Dei* thinking is that, after Christendom, the workplace may be filled with Christians who decide what they do, and do what they do, in a distinctive way because they know they are participating in God's mission. And not only work, but also retirement, which can either be self-indulgent or a participation in God's mission.

- Discernment is necessary. The *missio Dei* approach may make mission seem so all-encompassing as to be meaningless. As Stephen Neill once commented, "If everything is mission, nothing is mission."[39] Neill's objection is a serious one. *Missio Dei* thinking can be vague and slippery.[40] There are areas of God's action that some advocates of the *missio Dei* are tempted to view as old-fashioned, and some Christians who are committed to conflict mediation are intolerant of evangelism and church planting.[41] Other advocates of the *missio Dei* are overeager to construe sociopolitical movements as expressions of God's mission. Eusebius of Caesarea's sense of realized eschatology in the accession of Emperor Constantine I to the Christian faith has recent parallels in some Western Christians who enthusiastically embraced the Chinese Communist Revolution as "the foreordained answer to devout Christian prayers."[42] It does not follow that something is an expression of the *missio Dei* simply because it is novel and politically potent. Further, it does not follow that something is an expression of God's mission simply because it calls itself "Christian." Alas, some Christian phenomena—including some forms of missionary activity—have been impediments to God's mission. Remember, Jesus was scathing when he spoke about Jewish missionaries who "traverse sea and land to make a single proselyte" whom they made "a child of hell [*Gehenna*]." And it was in the very citadel of Jewish cultic life that Jesus became thoroughly angry and began to throw things about (Matt 23:15, RSV; Mark 11:15ff.). So it is vital that we trust the Spirit to help us discern well what the missional God is doing and what human actions collaborate with God's work. In contrast, it is crucial that we discern what God is not doing and what human actions are violations of God's mission.

Criteria for Discernment

We suggest three criteria for discerning God's actions and whether, as a result, human actions are compatible with the *missio Dei*.[43]

Jesus Christ

God's actions today are compatible with the person, teaching, cross, and resurrection of Jesus. Jesus was God's sent one; he was the paradigmatic embodiment of the *missio Dei*. Jesus told his disciples that he was sending them "as the Father had sent him"; that is, he was sending them in the same spirit and manner as the Father had sent him (John 20:21). Jesus showed us the Father, who was constantly at work. Jesus expected to see God at work, not least in surprising people, and was willing to let God interrupt him. Jesus said that he could do only what he saw God already doing (John 14:8). Jesus' involvement in God's mission embodied alertness to God's action. It was humble and compassionate to the outsider. And it rejected violence, coercion, and domination. God's missional action today has the same character as God's missional action in Jesus. So in our commitment to God's mission, we will discern what God is doing today by immersing ourselves both in the life of our times and in the Jesus of the Gospels, by listening to him, watching him, and apprenticing ourselves to him. We will evaluate our own collaboration with God by what we are learning from Immanuel—"God with us."

The Metanarrative
God's actions today are in keeping with the whole story of God, with the Bible's missional metanarrative, which points toward God's reign of comprehensive reconciliation. As would-be participants in God's mission today, we will discern God's activity by asking how something that someone proposes as God's work fits in with God's shalom-making activity throughout the Bible. And we will evaluate our own collaboration by asking how our actions point toward the reconciliatory banquet and healing of creation that God has promised as the culmination of the story (Matt 8:11).

Freedom from the Powers
God's actions today, as in the Bible, are in conflict with the false gods, idols, principalities, and powers that mar relationships and deprive humans of the "freedom of the glory of the children of God" (Rom 8:21). God today is acting as God did in the exodus and in the incarnation in Jesus—to set people free. This leads today to God acting in conflict with the "strong man" (Mark 3:27). As people who want to discern God's missional activity so that we can be useful participants in God's mission, we will ask the Holy Spirit to show us where God is unmasking and undoing the "benefactors" (Luke 22:25), the inevitable sensibilities and structures that "for our own good" (and even for the gospel) shackle people, prevent reconciliation, and pervert shalom. We Christians will find our missional calling as we enter into the work that God already is doing that, nonviolently, sets people and creation free.

An Exemplar of the *Missio Dei*

So, what does someone involved in the *missio Dei* look like? Chapter 2 dealt with mission in late Christendom, and we began it with our friends Don and Dorothy, who went to China. To close chapter 3, which deals with mission after Christendom, we could cite many Christians whose lives and work—within their home countries and around the world—embody the *missio Dei*.

Recently we read George Monbiot's 2007 book *Heat: How to Stop the Planet from Burning.*[44] Monbiot calls for Western cultures to make radical changes in their lifestyle, to cut carbon emissions so that humans can inhabit their environment peaceably. As we were reading Monbiot's discussion of a public transport system that will "smooth the passage of the car," we suddenly found him devoting seven pages to the work of the economist Alan Storkey.[45] In his *Guardian* article of December 5, 2006, Monbiot called Storkey "a visionary economist." We were pleased to read this about Alan, who like Don and Dorothy is a friend of ours. In his book Monbiot carefully exegetes Alan's meticulously thought-through proposal of a transport system for the United Kingdom based on long-distance coaches traveling from coach stations on the edges of urban areas.[46]

What Monbiot doesn't point out is where the vision that undergirds Alan's "visionary economics" comes from. He doesn't mention that Alan has a deeply considered Christian worldview, about which he has written extensively, or that Alan's imagination is sparked by the gospel of shalom.[47] So Alan's participation in God's mission is substantive but reticent. In all of this, Alan is quite unremarkable; he is one of many examples of believing, worshipping, thinking Christians who are caught up in God's mission. Other Christians, equally thoughtful, are involved in forms of evangelization that explicitly seek to enable humans to be reconciled to God. But note that all four characteristics of the *missio Dei* are evident in Alan's experience.

- *Sender*: God is the sender; God's mission involves the creation and the human practices and policies that affect creation.
- *Territory*: God sends people to countries close and far, including their own; Alan, who lives near Cambridge, is as deeply involved in God's mission as if he lived in Cambodia.
- *Agent*: God sends people into their own life and work as God's missional agents; Alan's immersion in the Bible as a disciple of Jesus gives him distinctive perspectives about public policy.
- *Goal*: God's Spirit animates humans to work toward God's goal of comprehensive reconciliation—with creation as well as with God and with other humans.

Where will Christians such as Alan Storkey find the perspective to discover their place in God's mission? More broadly, where will entire communities and congregations of Christians find the insight and inspiration to participate in God's mission? This can happen in many ways. But we believe that the setting within which the missional God renews the imagination of God's people is the faith community gathered for worship. Worship is the environment within which God's people learn to discern what God is doing and are sensitized to recognize the inbreaking of God's reign. Worship is the clarifying air that God's people breathe, enabling them to detect idolatry and to repudiate facile solutions.[48] All of this happens in Christian worship because in their worship services Christians tell and celebrate the story of God and give thanks and praise to the One who is continuing that story.

FOUR

Post-Christendom Worship: The Recovery of Narrative

H ow does the *missio Dei* affect our acts of worship? What does mission have to do with our weekly gatherings?

We have seen that our worship is authentic when it ascribes worth to the missional God, whose passionate project is to restore all things in Jesus Christ, and whose mission is to bring about impossible reconciliation. This God—the God of both testaments of the Bible—has promised to make all things new and to usher in all-encompassing shalom. Our worship services have integrity when they attune us to God's project and when they align us with God's mission, so that our lives as individual Christians and as Christian communities are invested in who God is and what God is doing. Further, our acts of worship ascribe worth to God when we allow the God we worship to transform our allegiances, behavior, and priorities in light of God's character and mission.

To put it simply, worship is telling, celebrating, and continuing the story of God. When we do this, as individuals, families, congregations, and communities, we ascribe worth to God. We tell God's story when we gather; we tell the story also when we get involved in it. We become more than cheering onlookers as the story unfolds; we become committed participants in it, taking part in "the overflow of mutual blessing of God and humanity."[1] And as we tell the story in which we, by God's grace, are involved, God draws us into praise, worship, and joy.

The Power of Story

Stories are so important![2] All preachers know that a lethargic congregation sits up when it hears "let me tell you a story." Stories trigger interest.

Stories also have the power to shape identity. They shape us as individuals. They even determine what we, deep down, actually believe. We truly "find ourselves" when we discover "the story or narrative in terms of which one's life makes sense."[3] We know that when we are under pressure, our personal and community stories shape our reflexive responses; they determine our behavior far more than the principles that we hold.

Stories shape us as communities. Stories tell us who we most deeply identify with, who our people are. Robert Pinsky, the American poet laureate at the end of the last century, observed that "a people is defined and unified not by blood but by shared memory"; further, "deciding to remember, and what to remember, is how we decide who we are."[4]

This is true of the stories that shape our national identities and get citizens to behave in certain ways.[5] When we first went to England in the 1960s, we were mystified by the curious behavior of children in early autumn, sitting with a grotesque effigy and begging "a penny for the guy"—until we learned about the 1605 saga of Guy Fawkes, a Catholic gentleman who had conspired to blow up Parliament.[6] As we talked with friends, we also discovered powerful memories of British troops escaping from Dunkirk in 1939 and Spitfire pilots engaging in dogfights during the battle of Britain. Scottish friends reminded us of the battle of Culloden and the exploits of Robert the Bruce. It would be worth pondering the effect of these stories on English and Scottish identities and behavior.

As primary school children growing up in the United States, we were told the story of George Washington and his hatchet. As recounted by Mason Locke Weems, rector of the Washington family's parish in Virginia, the story tells of a youthful George who went about brandishing his hatchet and "chopping every thing that came in his way." On one occasion when his father was absent, George cut down a "beautiful young English cherry-tree," which was a favorite of his father. When the elder Washington returned to his plantation, he saw the tree stump and inquired "with much warmth" who had cut down the tree. George bravely cried out: "I can't tell a lie, Pa; you know I can't tell a lie. I did cut it with my hatchet." To which his father replied, "Run to my arms, you dearest boy. . . . Glad am I, George, that you killed my tree. . . . Such an act of heroism in my son [in refusing to tell a lie] is worth more than a thousand trees, though blossomed with silver, and their fruits of purest gold."[7]

Why, we may ask, do teachers tell this embroidered story to generations of children in American primary schools? What does the story tell us about the first president of the United States and, by derivation, about the appropriate attitude U.S. citizens should have to the truthfulness of subsequent presidents? Or about the attitudes to the care of the earth—and the cutting down of trees—that generations of American schoolchildren have imbibed?

What is true of national communities is also true of faith communities: their identity and behavior are deeply shaped by narratives. Our denominations and congregations have fabled founding figures, who at times peer down at us from portraits on the wall. We also look back on exoduses and great treks, revivals, persecutions survived, and years of faithful presence and stability. The stories that we tell and how we tell them have an effect on us. When twenty-first-century Mennonites tell the stories of sixteenth-century Anabaptist martyrs, we may be inclined to think that Catholics are dangerous; but if Mennonites tell the story of a church in Kansas that lost its building in a tornado and was welcomed and given a place to worship by the local Catholic parish, the sixteenth-century stories take on a different coloration. When Christians tell stories of common projects—collaborating with others to save a local school building from the wrecker's ball, or to provide clothing, shoes, and back-to-school kits for needy children, or to write letters on behalf of Amnesty International prisoners of conscience—the ecumenical resonances are clear.

The Stifling of Story in Christendom
In the Bible, storytelling flourishes when God's people are aware of their dependence on God. Storytelling atrophies when people are living independently. As we shall see, it was people newly liberated from slavery who told the story of the exodus and whose psalms narrated acts of concrete deliverance. But as the people

became settled and secure, their songs of praise became general, concentrating on God's attributes (glory, beauty, might) and ignoring God's actions (liberating the oppressed, judging and humbling the mighty).[8]

The classic example of this is the marginalizing of the exodus story. According to Exodus 12, God commanded the Israelites every year to recall the exodus in the Passover. But after the advent of kingship and the building of the temple, the Israelites for centuries ignored this storytelling rite. According to 2 Kings 23, only when the book of the Law was rediscovered under King Josiah was the Passover reinstated: "The king [Josiah] commanded all the people, 'Keep the passover to the Lord your God as prescribed in this book of the covenant.' No such Passover had been kept since the days of the judges who judged Israel, even during all the days of the kings of Israel and of the kings of Judah" (2 Kings 23:21-22). Religious bodies that are strong, secure, and in control do not need—or do not want—exodus stories. Their worship loses memory and hope. Their worship becomes static.

In the history of the Christian church, a similar development is evident. In early Christian worship, especially in the rite of baptism, there was a strong concentration on God's liberating, exodus-like action. As Christendom developed, however, story atrophied and stasis flourished. As J. G. Davies pointed out, classical collects, such as those in the *Book of Common Prayer*, pray for the church and its members rather than God's action in the world.[9] Instead of giving life to the biblical narrative, many preachers in the Protestant traditions have spent months preaching through a Pauline epistle, verse by verse, or they have concentrated on stating and defending systematic theological truths. Classic hymns concentrate more on God's sovereignty or beauty than on the story of God's actions. How welcome it is to find a hymn that tells the story of God's mission:

God is working his purpose out as year succeeds to year.
God is working his purpose out, and the time is drawing near.
Nearer and nearer draws the time, the time that shall surely be,
When the earth shall be filled with the glory of God as the waters
    cover the sea.[10]

We would be delighted to sing the same theology in contemporary worship songs, which often mine the psalms for texts about God's attributes and ignore the psalms that tell the story of God's actions.

The stories we tell shape us more profoundly than the ideals we formulate. The type of stories we tell, and the extent to which our faith communities tells these stories, shapes our communal values and reflexes. If we are to be God's missional instruments in the world, we must be a storytelling people. The past, internalized through story, provides guidance for the community's next steps. Our storied past gives us a sense of what our future will be and where history is going. How we tell the story will determine what we can hope for, indeed whether we can hope at all. It is supremely in worship that we tell, indeed dramatize, the story of God.

God's Story: A Five-Act Drama

In 1991 N. T. Wright first offered the image of biblical history as a five-act drama, and he has repeated this image in other works.[11] Like many others, we have found Wright's image helpful.[12] A recent example is *The Drama of Scripture* by Craig Bartholomew and Michael Goheen, who have added complexity to Wright's fifth act.[13] We also give a distinctive shape to Act 5, which we believe alters the way the church worships God. Our emphases are somewhat different from theirs. Here is history's five-act drama as we conceive it:

History as a Five-Act Drama
Act 1: Creation
Act 2: The Fall
Act 3: God with Israel
Act 4: Jesus' life and teaching, passion, resurrection
Act 5: Pentecost and beyond
        Scene 1—the New Testament Church
        Scene 2—the church throughout history
            (including our denominations, our
            congregations, and the church's missional
            expansion)
        Scene 3—
        Scene 4—future history
New Creation: the *eschaton*, Christ's coming, judgment and
            cosmic reconciliation, messianic banquet

In our presentation of the fifth act, we have added scene 2, which deals with the history of the church between the New Testament church and our own time; also scene 4, which comprises the future history of the church and world. And we have spelled out slightly the play's conclusion: the advent of God's kingdom in fullness, with Christ coming and God making creation new and completing God's project of reconciliation, healing, and shalom.

In the midst of the fifth act, we have placed scene 3 and left it blank. This is *our scene*. This is the unprogrammed place in which we, Christians living today, play our part. We will play it in light of the story of the past as we narrate it and in light of the future as we anticipate it. As Wright puts it, "The church would then live under the 'authority' of the extant story, being required to offer an improvisatory performance of the final act as it leads up to and anticipates the intended conclusion."[14] Our task is to improvise our part in act 5, scene 3, but not willfully; we improvise in light of the past that we remember and the future that we hope for.

Worshipping God in the Present, Between Past and Future

Between the past and the future, between history and hope—that is where we live and worship. In Revelation 1:8, John the revelator, worshipping God on the island of Patmos, hears the voice of God: "'I am the Alpha and the Omega', says the Lord God, who is and who was and who is to come, the Almighty."

John is worshipping God in the *is*, the brief present; he is worshipping in light of the *was*, the history that has led up to the present; and he is worshipping toward the *is to come*, the future that God has promised. We today, like John, worship God in the brief present, between memory and expectancy. In this way we locate ourselves within God's mission. When we are in tune with God's purposes, our worship is worthy; it ascribes worth to the God of mission and promotes God's purposes of reconciliation, healing, and hope. On the other hand, some acts of worship are idolatrous—they misread the past and get in the way of God's future, impeding us and others from collaborating with our missional God. Of course, our worship services, no matter how misguided they may be, cannot stop God's mission. We can frustrate God's mission, but "the zeal of the Lord of hosts" is determined to accomplish it (Isa 9:7).

Our acts of worship take place in the brief present, the *is*. When we gather to ascribe worth to God, we meet God in the moment. This, the evanescent present, is brief, transitory, and infinitely precious. It is here that we enter into God's holiness, experience God's beauty, and lose ourselves in God's timelessness. Orthodox writers speak of "the eternal now"; Pentecostal worship leaders speak of the "transcendent moment."[15] "O, that *today* you would listen to his voice!" the psalmist exclaims (Ps 95:7, our italics). It is in this brief parenthesis between past and future that we take off our sandals as we respond to the living God in fear and love. This can be a moment of revelation; as the psalmist says, "[I did not understand] until I went into the sanctuary of God" (Ps 73:17). This also can be a moment of ecstasy; indeed, there can be a sense of the static about the ecstatic—time stands still and we forget to check our watches. It is here that God orders our deep affections and our abiding dispositions. Pentecostal theologian Steven Land calls this "orthopathy," right feeling.[16] We may plan our cultic activities, but the God we worship is sovereign—wild. So in fascination and fear, in the presence of the Holy One, we take off our sandals. In this place, between yesterday and tomorrow, God addresses us with love and judgment, comfort and commission. For this reason, we believe that there must normally be a space for unpredictability in the liturgies of God's people. Because of the *now*, our services must, like the Christian liturgies of the first three centuries, normally have spontaneity as well as structure, freedom as well as form.

So worship and the mission of God relate in three time dimensions. We encounter God, in trembling and thanksgiving, in the brief present; there we recall what God has done in the past and there we receive God's empowerment to collaborate in the future in what God is passionately committed to—the *missio Dei*, leading to the reconciliation of all things in Christ. Our scene—act 5, scene 3—occurs in the midst of the entire drama, the biblical metanarrative. This is why narrative is so important in biblical worship. The entire Bible is "relentlessly narratival."[17] So it is not surprising that biblical worship is narratival as well.

The Past: Acts of Worship in the Bible Tell the Story of God

When we stop to consider acts of worship that the Bible records, it is striking that these acts of worship, in both testaments, are narrative in character.

Old Testament

- The first worship service in the Bible, the "Song of the Sea" in Exodus 15, tells the story of the exodus and celebrates God's exploits: "horse and rider he has thrown into the sea. . . . Your right arm, O Lord, shattered the enemy. . . . Who is like you, majestic in holiness, awesome in splendor, doing wonders?" (Exod 15:1, 6, 11).[18]
- The first ritual in the Bible, the Passover stipulated in Exodus 12, recounts, plays, and practices the exodus. This is a means of recalling and replaying God's liberating act in such a way that children are intrigued and want to learn the story: "And when your children ask you, 'What do you mean by this observance?' you shall say, 'It is the passover sacrifice to the Lord'" (Exod 12:26-27).
- The first religious artifact described in the Bible is the manna jar of Exodus 16. Moses ordered the people to put manna in a jar and place it in the tabernacle, "that they may see the food with which I fed you in the wilderness" (Exod 16:32), and remember the story. God feeds the people, graciously, equally.
- The historical psalms—poetic narrative songs—were used at festivals and in temple worship. Their function was to give an interpretive, memorizable reading of God's work with his chosen people, the Jews. Why have historical psalms? One of the longest of them, Psalm 78, replies, "that the next generation might know" the story (v. 6) and not be like their parents, forgetful of the story, who did not trust God and who instead trusted in wealth and weapons.

New Testament: For Christians the Story Goes on

- The New Testament sermons—such as those of Peter on Pentecost, Stephen before his accusers, and Paul in Pisidian Antioch—were almost entirely narrative, telling the story of what God has done in the Messiah Jesus (Acts 2, 7, 13).
- Meetings of early Christian assemblies were occasions at which eyewitnesses and storytellers recounted the story of Jesus.[19] Out of these narrative events came the four New Testament Gospels.

New Testament rites

- The Lord's Supper was a meal in which the community told, reenacted, and replayed the stories of Jesus. "Do this in remembrance of me" (Luke 22:19; 1 Cor 11:25).
- Footwashing was a ritual event in which the Master washed the feet of his disciples and three times urged them to wash each other's feet (John 13:14, 15, 17). Jesus' instructions to his disciples to emulate him in replaying this rite were directive: "If I, your Lord and Teacher, have washed your feet, you also ought to wash one another's feet. For I have set you an example, that you also should do as I have done to you."

Narrative Worship that Tells an Odd Story

Why was it so important to the biblical writers for worship services to tell the story of God? Not just because stories give people a sense of their identity and destiny. It is also because God's story is a challenging story—an odd story. Precisely because of its oddity it needs to be told and retold; if it is not frequently rehearsed, easier stories—conventional stories—will overwhelm it.

The cultural worlds of the ancient Israelites and early Christians were filled with dominant stories. Since these stories accorded with common sense, they were very attractive. The biblical writers knew that when people indwell these ordinary stories and do not challenge them, they marginalize God's story, privatize it, or forget it. And if they and their communities forget their foundational stories, with all of their angularity and oddity, they and their communities will become conventional and dead. And so, when God's people are tempted to adopt ordinary stories that are permeated by self-evident wisdom, God invites them to "switch stories."[20] In other words, God invites them to be "restoried" into a community that believes that another story is truer than the dominant stories and that things can be different.[21] God calls people to be socialized into a society shaped by the Bible's story, in which the odd story lives as good news.

In what ways is the Bible's story odd? First, it has values that are upside down. God works not primarily through kings and superpowers but through marginal people and an insignificant nation. In God's work there is a reversal of status, which Hannah celebrates in her song as Mary does in her Magnificat (1 Sam 2:4-8; Luke 1:52). When we get to the climax of the story, in the life and teaching, death and resurrection of Jesus, we encounter oddness in an extreme form. As theologian Stanley Hauerwas commented in the *Time* magazine issue that was published immediately after September 11, 2001, "If Christians really faced up to the facts of Jesus' story, they would be shocked." Hauerwas continued: "Through his ministry and death, Jesus offered humankind a radical vision of forgiveness and freedom from revenge.... An omnipotent God incarnate ... relinquishes his power and dies an ignominious death in order that human beings might 'have life and have it more abundantly.'" This sounds impracticable and upside down, and it was not what ancient people saw on their televisions or we see on ours. But, said Hauerwas, this odd, upside-down story is the story that Christians are to bring to all nations.[22]

Second, the story of the Bible is odd because it assumes that God is present and active in the world. The Bible's story is one of a God who intervenes in human history with unpredictable displays of surprise and miracle. This divine intervention conflicts with the dominant assumptions of the establishment and of Enlightenment and post-Enlightenment cultures. In many of the churches in the prosperous West, Christians do not expect God to be alive and active, capable of answering prayer and actually doing something. Jonathan Bonk calls this attitude "subliminal agnosticism."[23] According to Christian Smith and Melinda Lundquist Denton, the religion of most contemporary Americans is "moralistic therapeutic deism,"[24] which is far from the faith of Christians of the early church and of many contemporary Christians in the global South. Their God is a force to be reckoned with.

Third, the Bible's story is odd in that it makes claims on those who tell it. The biblical writers told the story believing that it transforms the values and behavior of those who hear it. God acts, and God requires the people who worship him to act in response. The story of the exodus, which God's people tell in worship, is meant to form an exodus people.

At the heart of the exodus people's life is what biblical scholars call the "motive clause." According to the motive clause, "particular moral demands are predicated on a reminder of the gracious saving deeds of God."[25] The Deuteronomic law stipulated, "You shall not deprive a resident alien or an orphan of justice; you shall not take a widow's garment in pledge. *Remember* that you were a slave in Egypt and the Lord your God redeemed you from there" (Deut

24:17-18, our italics). In this and many other Old Testament passages, the motive clause is rooted in God's liberation of the people in the exodus, and it transforms the compassion and hospitality of the worshipping people. People who remember that God has set them free will have unconventional approaches to immigrants and people who are poor.[26]

In the New Testament, Jesus repeatedly used the motive clause in his teaching: "I forgave you. . . . Should you not have had mercy?" (Matt 18:32-33; see also Luke 6:36; John 13:34). The story of Jesus that the church tells and retells in worship similarly functions as a motive clause, calling the hearers of the story to be shaped by the One whose story they hear. New Testament writers recurrently use the motive clause, and they expect that God's liberation and forgiveness of the people through Jesus' life, death, and resurrection will bring about a liberating and forgiving response on the part of the worshipper.[27] As John admonished his friends, "We know love by this, that he [Jesus] laid down his life for us—and we ought to lay down our lives for one another. How does God's love abide in anyone who has the world's goods and sees a brother or sister in need and yet refuses help?" (1 John 3:16-17).

Similarly, Paul wrote to the Ephesians, "Be kind to one another, tender-hearted, forgiving one another, as God in Christ has forgiven you" (Eph 4:32). As Christopher Marshall has argued, "Because Jesus personally incarnates the moral and political message he proclaims about the inbreaking of God's justice, simply to hear the story of Jesus is already to receive moral instruction, while to emulate the example of Jesus is to imitate God."[28] The odd story, told in worship, forms people and communities whose odd values and behavior are shaped by the story that suffuses their acts of worship.

So it is in worship that we tell these stories. We get the sweep of the biblical narrative, from act 1's creation story through the New Testament church of act 5, scene 1. And at nodal points in the sweep we get the stories of the exodus and of Jesus. These are the generating stories—the origin stories—of both testaments. They are designed to function as motives in our lives. As we live our lives between the past and the future, we remind ourselves of a story line that is odd, upside down, and that reveals a God who is alive and active. This is a metanarrative that is not oppressive but liberating. And we know that as we enter into this dramatic story with freedom and allow it to shape our lives it will endanger our conformity to conventional values and transform our lives and our communities. It will also enlist us in God's mission.

Ways of Telling the Story

How then do we tell the Bible's great story—and the individual stories that comprise it—in our worship? Worship tells the story of God's mission, the *missio Dei*. So who is God? What has God done? What is God doing? Where are things going? What is the God-plot? How do we tell the story of history's five-act drama in worship?

Sermon

Preachers tell the story of God. The most important function of their sermons is to enable the worshipping community to know God's story and to understand it with the imagination. Preachers articulate God's voice, which calls all hearers—Christian and non-Christian—to find their part in the story. Preachers hold the hearers accountable to the story. Some emerging churches have left the sermon behind and use other modes of teaching and learning. Whatever the storytelling mode, "When we submit our lives to what we read in Scripture, we find that we are not being led to see God in our stories but our stories in God's."[29]

Children's Time

Churches and communities that have a special "children's time" will find that these are occasions in which the children learn that life is about God's big story. Children also will see the connections: the little stories of the Bible are part of the big story that will include their own stories too.

Bible-Reading

Worshipping communities will give significant time to listening to Scripture, including continuous reading of longer narratives. The person introducing the reading chooses a few words to place the reading in its bigger context in the story.

Song

Narrative worship songs are important. But they are not very popular today. Christmas hymns are an exception. In their succession of narrative verses, they anchor the story of the incarnation in our memories. The same narrative power is present in some passion hymns. But how about Jesus' life? Pete Ward, an astute observer of worship in Britain, has called for leaders who "encourage song writers to begin to focus on the historical Jesus."[30] In a similar vein, missiologist Eddie Gibbs has called for "a new genre of contemporary songs in the form of ballads that tell the biblical stories." Without this, he observes, "we will have a generation that is biblically illiterate."[31] So why not commission multiple-stanza songs recounting, for example, the broad sweep of the exodus saga, the storms of the kings and prophets of Israel, or the conflicts and compassionate actions of Jesus? Song-choosers for worship can look for hymns that outline the shape of creation and redemption, or that carry a personal message with strong biblical allusions. Excellent examples are classics such as "Guide Me, O Thou Great Jehovah," "The God of Abr'am Praise," or the more recent "Passover God."[32]

Lord's Supper
The greatest missed opportunity to tell the big story of God's mission in many churches is the thanksgiving prayers at the Lord's Supper. Liturgical scholar Gail Ramshaw has suggested ways to strengthen the thanksgiving by restoring an improvisational character of prayer, similar to pre-Christendom Christian practice. Citing Justin Martyr's injunction to the presider to "offer up prayer and thanksgiving, as much as he can" and Reformation patterns of "prayers from the heart," Ramshaw calls for a style of free praying based on a trinitarian outline. Such a prayer praises God for creation, thanks God for salvation through Christ, and honors the transforming work of the Holy Spirit.[33]

James McClendon reminds us of the kind of remembering that Jesus called for:

> [This was] not a memorial of his death alone, and not of his death and resurrection, though these are central, but a meal "in memory of *me*", that is, of Jesus himself, and thus of the larger story that frames his life: the divine-human story of creation, and the election of Israel, and its existence as a people, and the birth of Messiah Jesus, his life and ministry, and the great signs from God that have followed.[34]

In contrast, how bare, if eloquent, are many eucharistic prayers. More is at stake at the table than memorializing and reenacting the events of the Last Supper. Two dimensions that need to enter our praying in Communion are

- *Ecology*: Denis Edwards suggests that "when Christians gather for the Eucharist they bring creation with them." So the prayer at the table should reflect an ecological theology and be "a memorial of God's marvelous deeds that include creation as well as redemption and the promise of final transformation." According to Edwards, the eucharistic prayer is always "a lifting up of the whole creation."[35]
- *Nonviolence*: Emmanuel Charles McCarthy proposes that the prayers in the Lord's Supper should specifically mention the nonviolent means that Jesus used in his conflicts. So he suggests modest but significant additions to the eucharistic prayers, true to the gospel story, that shape the character of the worshipping community. Instead of praying simply "on the night before he died, he broke bread," McCarthy proposes that the president should pray: "on the night before he died, rejecting violence, loving his enemies, and praying for his persecutors, he bestowed upon his disciples the gift of a New Commandment: Love one another. As I have loved you, so you also should love one another." How, McCarthy asks, can one remember Christ's command to break bread in memory of him while "religiously ignoring" his nonviolent struggle and his new commandment?[36]

Collects

These brief prayers, though short in compass, can embrace a wide view of God's purposes and reign across time and place. As J. G. Davies pointed out over forty years ago, of eighty-six collects in the *Book of Common Prayer*, eighty-two "are concerned solely with the Church and its members, and four alone have any reference to the world."[37] It is worth monitoring collects in more recent service books to see whether they ask God, who has acted in saving ways, to empower God's people to be involved in God's mission.[38] For example, from a contemporary Anabaptist prayer book:

> Gracious God, you sow your storied word in us with compassion. As this day breaks upon us, may we remember your mercy and extend it to others as we live for the sake of your reign. In hope we pray: Our Father . . .[39]

The same concerns apply to Christian traditions that pray extemporaneously. Do they praise the God of mission; do they ask the God whose mission is to bring all-embracing reconciliation and shalom to equip the praying community to be coworkers with God?

Lord's Prayer

This rich resource for worship is a gift from the Lord Jesus himself. It occupies the central place in the Sermon on the Mount. The Lord's Prayer expresses succinctly a sense of who God is and what God most passionately cares about. Truly the Lord's Prayer is a missional prayer. Praying this prayer together draws Christians into the heart of the mission of God—the coming of the fullness of God's reign. This is why Jesus commanded his disciples to pray it: "Pray then in this way" (Matt 6:9). Some free-church congregations think praying this prayer is "vain repetition." But there is a difference between vain repetition and life-giving repetition.

Drama

Bible reading can be multivoiced. The simple casting of different voices can enliven the reading of biblical passages and heighten their communicative power. Dynamic dramatization of biblical themes or stories can also be useful and can suggest contemporary applications in today's idioms. Mime and improvisational drama are also effective ways to open imaginative connection with the great narratives.

Visuals

The visual environment of the place where the church meets speaks without words. Is the entrance beautiful? What do we ponder visually during the worship service? Is it simply aesthetically beautiful or does it "speak" with symbolic language of the truth and values of the gospel? Does it, for example, give visions of reconciliation and restoration, of creation and humanity at peace with God in our world? One church we know has filled one entire wall with a breath-taking, humbling photo of the earth as viewed from space. Many artists are profound theologians whose works in a variety of media convey the heart of biblical stories and themes with imaginative immediacy. These works are more than decorative; they can be integral to the total proclamation of God's message. Time and again we return to the works—especially the drawings—of the great Dutch artist Rembrandt (d. 1669), who interpreted biblical stories insightfully and provocatively. Projected during worship, his works always engage the imagination of the congregation. The resources of the worldwide church—such as the works of the Chinese painter He Qi, or the Jesus Mafa paintings, which contextualize the story in Cameroon, or the annual Misereor hunger cloths—are also useful in worship.[40] Many emerging churches are alert to the power of the arts and integrate the work of poets, artists, sculptors, photographers as well as musicians.[41] They earth the biblical narrative; they contemporize it and globalize it.

The Liturgical Year
The development of the liturgical year took place especially in the fourth century and so is a phenomenon of early Christendom. This "historicizing of worship" is an important contribution that will continue to enrich the worship of the church after Christendom. In the pre-Christendom centuries, the great feasts of the year were "synthetic"; that is, they conveyed the weight of the whole biblical story. Easter Day celebrated the entire story of salvation, not just Christ's resurrection. Every Sunday was a little Easter, and so week by week the church celebrated the whole story of redemption. In the course of the fourth century, the church picked the story apart and assigned particular episodes to specific dates throughout the year—Christmas, Epiphany, Maundy Thursday, Good Friday, and the rest. There are good reasons to value the historicizing effect of the liturgical year. It ensures that the specific stories are told within the compass of the overarching narrative. Each bit is told, savored, and pondered every year, so that people's lives are shaped by this story rather than by competing stories. But it's important not to lose sight of the narrative sweep. Every time the church worships is the time to celebrate the whole story of the mission of God that brings restoration and reconciliation. Every Sunday is a little Easter.[42]

Testimony
Christians should find occasion to connect their own stories with the biblical narrative. As we do this with imagination and insight, we learn to speak of it aloud in testimony. The Bible isn't just a collection of cautionary tales or inspiring dramas. The Bible's sto-

ries are like beacons that illuminate our own lives. Peter warming himself by the courtyard fire is more than a tale of sad betrayal. As we read the accounts of his denials we, too, are in that courtyard, challenged by the maid's question, "Surely you, too, were with him?" And so with Jacob, wrestling in the fearsome dark; with the persistent widow, nagging the powerful judge until he gives her justice; with Ruth, widowed and directionless; with Paul, blinded and stripped of his Damascus mission and awaiting the new thing. We allow the Bible's stories to illuminate our own stories, and in worship we tell our experiences of illumination and overlap with vulnerability, gratitude, and joy.

All these worship acts equip us Christians to find our place in the narrative of God. They help us to play our part in the great drama. Act 5, scene 3 is our scene! But to play our part well, we Christians in worship also need to attend to the post-biblical past and to the future. In our next chapter, we will see how a multidimensional, historical sense, expressed in worship, equips us to participate in God's mission.

FIVE

Narrative Resources for Worship: Hoping the Past, Remembering the Future

Telling the great story of the Bible is at the heart of Christian worship. But there are other stories that we remember as we worship: act 5, scene 2, the story of God's work between the New Testament and today; and act 5, scene 4, the part of the drama that is yet to be played. In this chapter we will explore how we can draw on these other narrative resources in worship.

Hoping the Past

To draw resources from the past, we must recognize that history is always ambivalent. It has its ups and its downs, and it is always a matter of interpretation. For Christians, the story of the church is a parallel to the experience of the Jewish people after the exodus. Church history can function, in Christian worship, as the Old Testament experience functioned in the historical psalms. Psalm 106, for example, records not only God's fidelity but also human inconstancy. At times, when the people recalled the exodus and Torah, the people "observed justice and did righteousness." At times they "believed his [God's] words; they sang his praise" (Ps 106:3, 12). But at other times the people forgot God's mighty acts and failed to remember God's steadfast love. As a result they engaged in grumbling and idolatry. Psalm 106, like Psalm 78, reminds God's people in worship of the entire story, with its good bits and bad bits, with a God of faithfulness and resourcefulness, and with humans who often forget the story and lose the plot. The historical psalms remind us that, as we gather to worship and as we seek to participate in God's mission, we are profoundly shaped by our past, including our recent past.

For many Christians, the two thousand years of church history are "gap years."

- Some Christians have no sense of what happened between Acts 28 and the year 2000. They ask, "Doesn't the New Testament provide enough guidance for us today as we recreate the church from scratch? Why bore ourselves with church history?"
- Some Christians have no sense of what happened between the end of the New Testament and dramatic events at which "meaningful" church history began—with Martin Luther's ninety-five theses, Calvin's *Institutes*, the Anabaptist baptisms in Zürich, the hearts strangely warmed in Aldersgate Street, or the Azusa Street revival. Some of these Christians, who are loyal to their own denominations, may develop a sense of continuous peoplehood through their denominational origin stories.
- Some Christians today, in a postmodern way, are attracted to selected bits of the past. They construct a pastiche of Christianity from the early church, Celtic stories and prayers, Catholic spirituality, and various Protestant phenomena, including Pentecostalism. At times they call their approach "Ancient-Future" Christianity.[1]
- Some Christians, rightly alerted to the abuses of Christendom, are tempted to sweep much of Western Christian history, including the Middle Ages, into a garbage can of forgetfulness.
- Some Christians—most Western Christians, in fact—are oblivious to the remarkable history of the Christian traditions of the East, in the Persian Empire and beyond.[2]
- Some Christians have had very painful experiences in churches and are inclined simply to block these out of their memories. These people may seek "a new experience of the Lord," which somehow excuses them from the tasks of remembering, thanking, repenting, and forgiving.

Drawing on the "Gap Years"

We believe that God's Spirit was moving throughout the history of the church in ways that help believers to participate in God's mission today. Inspiring and instructive things took place in the past two thousand years that can be useful to us as we improvise our part—act 5, scene 3. The various Christian traditions have rich stories. The Spirit of the missional God was always at work, even in parts of the Christian story for which we personally may have least empathy. For example, during the time of the Renaissance papacy, which some of us find repellent, renewal movements were taking place in monastic communities that influenced the early Anabaptists and can be resources for many Christians today.[3] As people involved in the *missio Dei*, we must, whatever our Christian tradition, accustom ourselves to listening to God among the "other." Further, through this wider listening, we come to be open to God's work of building a community—a peoplehood—that transcends time and place, ethnicity and class.

There is something unhealthy about repressing painful experiences or blocking out the past. A recent sample of this, China's unwillingness to have its history textbooks deal with the Cultural Revolution, is dangerous.[4] A failure on the part of Christians today to face the more sordid parts of their own histories is similarly dangerous. Some congregations are in denial about their own past, and there are times when Western Christians refuse to be candid about the sins of prideful dominance that were committed in Christ's name during the period of Christendom or, in many countries, by Western missionaries. The past—whether that of the Cultural Revolution or of the murkier side of Christendom or of the bleaker episodes in the experience of all Christian traditions—is always there, even when it is repressed. If we don't study our past, repent of it, and allow God to transform it, it will come back and haunt us. The repressed past impedes God's mission.

God calls us to remember the post-biblical past. Not everything from the past will be useful to us. Some things we must recall with repentance and discard as "baggage" that weighs us down. But other things we will recall with gratitude and appropriate as provisions that will nourish us on our journey.[5] There are many stories that can inspire us to collaborate with God's work—for example, seventh-century missionaries of the Church of the East walking for 250 days from Persia to Western China; William Wadé Harris preaching across West Africa in the early twentieth century; the Anabaptist "martyr synod" of 1527.

So we need to remember the past, but we also need to hope the past. To participate in God's mission in our time, we need to believe that there is wisdom in the past, not just in the biblical past but in the history of God's people, that can point ways forward for us today. God has "provisions" for the church's missional future that come from the church's past. How can we appropriate these provisions in worship?

Saints of the Church
Every Christian tradition has its saints, its founders, inspirers, and exemplars. Every local congregation and parish has its own "cloud of witnesses" (Heb 12:1)—pioneers, role models, and servants—who were bearers of God's mission in their time. If a parish in the Anglican and Catholic traditions has a "patronal festival," it may have a saint already, but many parishes could research the saint's special charism and see how this can challenge their life and mission. It could be that the congregation's saint is very distant and that there are more immediate saints that are also worth pondering. Every congregation—on saints' days—has the opportunity to honor their memory and tell their story. The congregation that we now belong to has a formidable founding figure, John Funk.[6] Every year in April our congregation honors "saint John Funk" with a weekend that helps us concentrate on one of the themes of his life: mission, mentoring, music, or migration. We call this the "Funk Fest," and we wear special T-shirts to celebrate it. Our congregation's future depends on our reappropriating the DNA of his creativity and vision. Why not have fun while doing so?

Church Anniversaries
Many Baptist churches annually celebrate the birthdays of their founding. "Church anniversary Sundays" recall the congregation's origins. Church anniversaries can also recall the beginnings of new programs and the transformative initiatives that counter dominant currents of society. Photos, films, and dramas can help members enter into the story. As young people in churches do research and present the narratives, they feel bonded to the community in

new ways. All these can help Christians enter into God's story and to ask useful questions: What does God call us to cherish as "provisions"? What does God call us to offload as "baggage"?

A Community's Story in Ballad Form
John Bell has pointed out that in some societies "the purveyors of history did not simply recite texts, but set them to music."[7] Congregations can use this medium to tell their stories, not only to remind themselves of their history and identity but also to pass on the story to the next generation. Littlemore Baptist Church, a small congregation on the edge of Oxford in England, has determinedly stayed alive for two hundred years and now, early in this century, is experiencing renewed vigor. Its members have written a ballad to recall the ups and downs of their history: "And God will lead us on." Some of the words are cryptic, incomprehensible to outsiders—"and the apple tree was dead." But the song is not written for outsiders. For the congregation's growing community, the song expresses their inner energy, rooted in their belief that God has been faithful and is beckoning them to a significant future. As the ballad recounts the congregation's narrative, a simple refrain recurs:

> God has brought us to this place,
> Given hope, encouragement:
> In dark times he gave us strength,
> And he will lead us on![8]

The Keepers of the Memory
Some churches recognize one or more members who know the story of the church very well. When decisions are being made, the keepers of the memory can speak of the original call and charism of the church's founding; they can remind the church of its distinctive DNA; they can tell stories that have contemporary application.

Drawing on the Immediate Past: "Reports from the Front"
God's actions are not confined to the Bible or church history; they continue in our immediate past. Act 5, scene 2—the church throughout history—contains God's actions in the distant past, but also in the recent past. The worshipping community not only remembers the distant past; it also reports God's deeds that are fresh and new,

pondering them, praising God for them. As it does so, it enters into the realm of testimony.

Testimony is a term that bores some people and alarms others. It bores people because at times testimonies are oft-repeated stories about long-ago conversion experiences. The result is testimonies that become "an ever-more-distant memory from the past that has less and less impact on the circumstance of the moment."[9] Testimony in worship alarms people when the stories become embarrassingly personal. No one wants to listen to an inappropriate testimony.

But if God is at work today as God has been throughout history ("My Father is still working, and I also am working" [John 5:17]); if God's mission continues unabated in the present as in the past; and if we want to enter, as Paul puts it, into God's actions as "God's coworkers [*sunergoi*]" (see 1 Cor 3:9), then it is necessary to provide data about the ongoing story of God. Week by week, new chapters of the story are being written in lives, communities, and nations around the world. The Holy God is alive and at work. When we gather for worship, we take notice of God's passionate and compassionate actions and celebrate them. If the word testimony seems shopworn, we can perhaps call these "reports from the front." Why do we give reports from the front?

Scriptures Validate the Use of Testimony in Worship
Testimony has deep roots in Scripture. Walter Brueggemann sees the Old Testament documents as examples of the genre of testimony, in which participants in a law court state their experiences and perceptions of the action and character of God.[10] The psalmist, in Psalm 40:9-10, states, "I have told the glad news of deliverance in the great congregation. . . . I have not concealed your steadfast love and your faithfulness from the great congregation." In the early Christian community, the apostles Peter and John, under pressure, assert, "We cannot keep from speaking about what we have seen and heard" (Acts 4:20). The sense, in both testaments, is this: God's work is ongoing, and God wants people to talk about it, wonder at it, and admiringly praise it. Or, when God seems not to be at work, when injustice appears immovable and broken relations seem to be beyond repair, God invites the people to cry out in the testimony of lament: "Have mercy upon us, O LORD, have mercy upon us, for we have had more than enough of contempt" (Ps 123:3).[11]

Reports from the Front Form a Living Tradition
What are they about? Individual conversion stories are important. Living congregations encounter these as people find forgiveness, deliverance, and redirection through Jesus Christ. But these stories must be supplemented by the continually fresh stories that reflect the ongoing work of God. For many churches, this is not easy. Roman Catholic theologian Gerhard Lohfink has observed that "in our liturgy and our community assembly, we no longer relate the deeds of God in the present or recent past; we no longer tell of God's leadership, God's signs and wonders. Things like that are embarrassing. We leave them to outsiders or fringe groups. We [Catholics] no longer even have the words to shape such a story."[12] Catholics are not the only contemporary Christians to struggle with this. To recover the possibility of giving reports from the front, many Western Christians today—unlike many of our worldwide Christian brothers and sisters—need to develop the conviction that God is at work in our world, the expectancy that we can discern God's action, and the vocabulary and practices necessary to enable testimony to take place in our worship services.[13]

The Dangers of Not Having Testimony
If we receive no reports from the front in our congregations, we are in trouble. Without testimonies we experience a drought, a nutritional deficit for healthy Christian living. And the dominant cultural narratives take over. God seems powerless and inactive. And Christians who do see evidence of the missional activities of God in our time may only whisper about it in the church's hallways or discuss it during the week in house groups or on the telephone—but not in worship services.

Early Christian Use of Testimony—and Its Disappearance
In the New Testament church in Corinth—and in congregations for a century and a half thereafter—it was not like this. There was a connection between the communal meal, at which Jesus was remembered and worshipped, and the after-dinner conversation (symposium) in which believers shared songs, prophecies, and testimonies. As we shall see in chapter 6, 1 Corinthians 11–14 deals with a unified meal in which the table and the mutivoiced word were both essential; this was still present in Tertullian's Carthage almost two centuries after Jesus.

We shall also note how this interconnection disappeared, leading to the disappearance of testimony. It's understandable: liturgical controllers in large congregations found it all rather difficult. By AD 200, congregations grew larger. To combat heresy and disorder, church leaders began to restrict the freedom that the earlier church had known in worship. In the second half of the fourth century, liturgical writing emerged to ensure orthodox speech and order in worship.[14] There was no longer room for speaking about what God had recently done in the lives of believers. When basilicas superseded house churches, a vital aspect of mission became almost impossible.

Reports from the front: these grow out of congregations that cultivate alertness to God's work. Where will we see this? Especially in areas in which people are vulnerable and out of control of their situations.

- *Stories of provision*: People report that God has provided safety, protection, housing, finance, or breakthroughs in neighborhood relationships. There is a freshness to their experiences that invites others to join in celebration. In inner-city Baltimore: "I used to be living in a rat-infested hole. There were shootings. [But now] this neighborhood is blessed."[15]
- *Significant milestones*: "I didn't think I could make it through an entire year without a drink, but AA has helped keep me sober. The Lord has protected me."
- *Lament*: The United States spends more on its military than the rest of the world together, and we need the money to bring decent schooling to our community. And we cry out, "How long? How long do we suffer? How long until you vindicate our cause? 'Rouse yourself! Why do you sleep, O LORD?'" (Ps 44:23).
- *Significant political events—local or global*: In May 2007 in Northern Ireland, the Ulster Volunteer Force leader Gusty Spence gave a press conference in which he announced that the Protestant paramilitaries had put their weapons beyond use and the leaders had encouraged all volunteers to "show support for credible restorative justice projects."[16] Imagine: restorative justice instead of the threat of guns in Northern Ireland! And the church responds, "Lord, it took so long, but

your hand is in this. We praise you!" The Christian community confesses: God does perform wonders, and we celebrate these. They are beautiful in themselves, and they are foreshadowings of God's shalom-ful reconciliation of all things in Christ.

Testimony: Benefits and Risks
According to Ugandan church leader Kefa Sepangi, "A religion is true if it works."[17] We suspect that the same is true in the post-Christendom West. People are drawn to churches that are involved in God's mission and in which, because their members are aware of God's work and able to talk about it, there is a sense of hope and expectancy. Churches like this, week by week, collect evidence of God's action. In worship the church brings reports from the front, ponders God's acts, and praises the Actor. So, as church members prepare for their weekly worship services, they develop the spiritual discipline of asking God, "Where have I seen you at work in the past week? How can I share this with the great congregation? Is there a good time to tell my friends or a small group?" The task of the worship leader is to ensure that these stories cohere with the character and plot of God's great drama. As in the Corinthian church (1 Cor 14:29), there needs to be discernment and on occasion correction. There are risks inherent in this approach. However, if God's people let God's actions go unnoticed and uncelebrated, the dangers are greater. The people sink into self-protective immobility and disbelief. It is people who can give reports from the front about a living God who has done astonishing things who can attempt risky, radical things. Their lives overflow with hope (Rom 15:13).

Remembering the Future
The five-act drama is not complete. As we have seen, we play our part in act 5, scene 3 in light of the story of the previous acts—not only the biblical drama of act 1 through act 5, scene 1, but also the post-biblical narrative of act 5, scene 2. The story of God and God's people is our primary story. We tell this story, and the story shapes us, but the story is not complete.

There is a future history that takes place in act 5, scene 4 and that precedes the conclusion of the drama. We do not know how long this scene will be. We listen, as Christians have listened for two thousand years, to the One who says, "Surely I am coming soon" (Rev 22:20). But we know that this "soon" could be tomorrow or thousands of years from now. So we must prepare to play our part in the drama that is ahead of us, however long or short it may be. How we play our part depends not only on the way we, in the present, tell the story of the drama's past acts; it also depends on the way we remember the future.[18]

The Loss of Hope

In the West many people have forgotten the future. In the Christendom centuries, a tendency to equate God's kingdom with the established Church sapped hopeful expectancy. Instead of hope, there hovered a fear of the last judgment, depicted on countless "dooms" painted on church walls, in which the future was associated with threat and terror. The nineteenth-century liberal Protestant theologians also lost a hopeful vision; as Ernst Troeltsch put it, "The eschatology office is mostly closed."[19] The materialistic self-absorption of recent Western culture has also exacted a price. When he returned to Britain in the 1970s after many years in India, Bishop Lesslie Newbigin noted the absence of expectancy. When asked, "What is the greatest difficulty you face in moving from India to England?" he replied, "The disappearance of hope."[20] In the West, people have had consumer goods, comfort, and healthcare beyond the imagination of their grandparents. Technology has enabled Westerners to exercise unprecedented control over many aspects of life. But most people in the West have lost a vision for the future. In our controlled comfort, we simply want to keep things as they now are. As Jonathan Bonk observes, "The great purpose of [modern] life ... is ... to move from birth to death as comfortably as possible."[21]

When people in many contemporary Western cultures speak of hope, it is often a weak, negative hope: "a desire that certain bad things *not* occur."[22] We are uncomfortably aware of big threats to our way of life: the certainty of climate change, the threat of pandemics and terrorist attacks, the likelihood of nuclear war, and the immediate reality of job losses and shriveling investments. How do people respond to these threats? Often by repressing serious thought about the future; with a vague sense of dread; or with a combination of calculation and risk management. Our approaches to the future are either forgetful or defensive. If we think about the future, we tend to think about damage limitation.

Many Christians have made their peace with this generalized hopelessness. Their view of the future is limited to an escape from this world, a "flight of the soul, at death, to an invisible world of eternal reality."[23] They do not want God's kingdom to come "on earth as in heaven," because the new creation would be disruptive and would have unpredictable consequences. How much better, they think, to have a "rapture" that would whisk them neatly out of their gas-thirsty vehicles to celestial bliss, leaving behind a world that God has given up on and will destroy with fire. A bumper sticker crisply expressed this point of view: "When the rapture happens this vehicle will be driverless."

Regaining Hope

In contrast to this negative vision, the Bible's vision of the future is expansive and imaginative. So we propose to think about the future in terms of hope. We believe that God will work in act 5, scene 4, to establish shalom and to bring an all-encompassing rightness of relationship.

As the prophets, Jesus, and the New Testament writers keep reminding us, God intends a future for the earth. According to Richard Bauckham and Trevor Hart, the Bible offers us images of the future of this world that "transcend the boundaries of the present." These images "go beyond the given." They stretch "outwards and forwards, in search of something more, something better, than the given affords us."[24] This expansive vision is the gift of the God who says, "I am about to create new heavens and a new earth. . . . The wolf and the lamb shall feed together. . . . They shall not hurt or destroy on all my holy mountain" (Isa 65:17, 25).

God's promises beckon us to the future, not when we repress thought about it and not when we attempt to control it, but when in worship we remember the future. How can we Christians dare to remember the future with hope? In light of the worsening economic and ecological crises and the spreading troubles in Central Africa and the Middle East, how can we take the lion and lamb passage from Isaiah 11 seriously? Edward Hicks, the American Quaker artist we mentioned in chapter 3, was caught up in the tensions that were tearing nineteenth-century Quakerism apart. Hicks coped with these tensions by painting multiple versions of "The Peaceable Kingdom." He painted soulful lions reconciled with safe prey; he painted Quakers making peace with Algonquins. Hicks was unwilling to do anything but remember the future. He was fixated by the future. In our time, can we allow the Isaiah 11 passage to speak to us as it did to Hicks—or the equally hard-to-imagine future sketched out in the "swords into ploughshares" prophecy of Isaiah 2:2-5?[25] These passages anticipate things that seem counterfactual, as do prophecies of a God who will bring a "new creation" and "make all things new." How can we hope for a future that seems beyond belief?

Anticipations Little and Big

When we gather for worship, we report little events, happenings that we do not read about in newspapers but that are "kingdom sparklers" to the faith community. The life of a broken person is healed; a house in a poor area is renovated and is home to a family; a child from a deprived neighborhood gets an advanced education. God, we confess, is at work. Or the bigger facts: Goshen, Indiana, where we grew up, was one of thousands of "sundown towns" whose ordinances in the 1950s still forbade blacks from sleeping within the town overnight; in 2007 Goshen was served by an elected black city councilor.[26] In Berlin, the Wall—feared, lethal, monumentally imposing, evidently eternal—is gone, smashed by the nonviolent power of marching people. In South Africa, there is a majority government that was achieved without ethnic war. In Northern Ireland, there is a power-sharing executive, with Protestant Unionists and Catholic Nationalists working together.

In the lifetime of all of us reading this book, impossible things have happened. Christians confess that these things happened by God's grace, at work through risk-taking and courageous people. These events, little and big, are anticipations, down payments of new creation. Each of them is a miracle, and some of the miracles are huge—to observers, utterly astonishing. To the worshipping community they point toward the conclusion of history, toward the *eschaton*, the New Jerusalem. The church bears testimony to these miracles in what Brueggemann calls "reportage as anticipation."[27] In this we acknowledge God at work toward the completion of God's mission; we stop, take notice, and praise God. Together with Jesus, who worked with his Father who was "still working" (John 5:17), we in worship say, "God, we praise you for your work, which exceeds our anticipation; show us how to work with you."

But the world seems bent on self-destruction, and humans relentlessly make the millions of wrong decisions that prevent a change of lifestyles and policies. The disciples of Jesus seem utterly inadequate to the crisis. We lack imagination and energy. What reason do we have for hope?

The resurrection. We are Christians because, along with the earliest believers, we confess that God has raised Jesus from the dead. Among improbable events, the resurrection of Jesus must have been the hardest to anticipate. But the early Christians confessed that God raised Jesus by God's astonishing intervention, not by human imagination and prowess. The Creator of life brought new creation to his Anointed Son. This intervention reminds us that the completion of God's mission is God's work. The comprehensive reconciliation that God has promised, in which there will be peace with God, peace between humans, and peace with the creation—this will involve natural processes and costly human effort. But ultimately it is God whose sovereign action will bring about the promised reconciliation. Things will not become new in evolutionary fashion; it is God who will make all things new (Isa 66; Rev 22). We humans cannot engineer the future; it will be God's gift of surprise and grace. The new heavens and new earth in which justice is at home may come about only through purging fire (2 Pet 3:13). But we can longingly enter into the birth pangs of the new creation (Rom 8:23); we can pray for God to bring new creation to completion; and we can invest our lives as co-laborers in the work of new creation because, as disciples of Jesus the Resurrected One, we are committed to living toward God's future. This is what missional people do. As Jürgen Moltmann put it, "The whole body of Christians is engaged in . . . the Christian mission of hope."[28]

Long-Sighted Christians

To live in this way requires what John Howard Yoder called being "long-sighted." Short-sighted living concentrates on the problems and impediments of the immediate situation; this kind of living leads to decisions that are prudential and self-protective. Long-sighted living, in contrast, enables Christians to keep the Bible's big anticipation in mind and equips us to make decisions to follow Jesus with courage and imagination. History is not changed by human calculation, Yoder contended. It is changed by God, who uses hopeful people. We trust in God's promises in light of the cross and resurrection of Christ, and we act in light of our trust.

"Significant action," Yoder wrote, "is accomplished by those whose present action is illuminated by an eschatological hope."[29]

In our acts of worship today, we become people of the big story, from creation to new creation. The practices that burn this story into our imaginations—strong preaching, the Scriptures well read, the sacraments, testimony, song, art—are potent ones. We live in the present moment, and in the present moment we worship God. In this brief moment, both precious and evanescent, we hope the past. We retell the story of God's acts, believing that the story is true and thanking God for the ways it has enabled us to orient lives to God's mission of reconciliation. And we remember the future, the future that God has promised, committing ourselves to living toward that future as disciples of Jesus Christ.

SIX

Early Christian Worship: Multivoiced Meals

The church is a community that hopes the past and remembers the future. It is a community that experiences anticipations of the fullness of God's reign breaking into the present. It is a community that points toward the completion of God's mission in which Christ will be all and in all, and all things will be reconciled in him. How does a community like this engage in acts of worship?

For many years, scholars assumed that the New Testament would tell us. They assumed that from the outset there was a pattern of worship that united the scattered Christian communities. Drawing from various New Testament passages and early patristic writings, the Swiss Reformed exegete Oscar Cullmann constructed what he called "the early Christian service of worship" with its basic components of preaching, prayers, and Lord's Supper.[1] Similarly Anglo-Catholic liturgist Dom Gregory Dix believed that from the earliest days there was an essential uniformity. He discerned a classical "shape" of the liturgy: the service of the word, rooted in the synagogue service, followed by the Eucharist, rooted in Jesus' last supper with his disciples.[2] Cullmann and Dix agreed that there was a pristine uniformity of early Christian worship that Christians later refined and developed as the church spread into different settings.

But did a standard template for early Christian worship actually exist? Scholars of early Christian worship have come to doubt this. Drawing on Jewish scholarship, Paul Bradshaw and others have noted that first-century Judaism was a varied reality, that the extant Jewish sources date from centuries after the New Testament era, and that before the third century there may not have been a form of regular Sabbath liturgy in the synagogues. They have also observed that in the early Christian communities there was a variety of meal practice, both in words and actions. So Bradshaw, followed by many others, has posited that the early Christian communities worshipped in many ways. Early Christian worship was not uniform but "pluriform."[3] Only later, when Christendom dawned in the fourth century, did a "homogenization" of Christian worship take place.[4]

Since we will never find a standard template for worship in the New Testament era, we must be modest in our claims. We accept that there was probably a wide variety of early Christian models. But we also can explore the implications of one of these models, which the apostle Paul presents in 1 Corinthians 11–14. In these four chapters, Paul provides a dense cluster of writing that deals with the theology of worship and gives directions about how to practice it. The liturgical practices of the Pauline community in Corinth may or may not have been characteristic; there was bound to have been a wide variety of worship practices in Christian communities scattered across a huge geographical area.[5] The messianic communities radiating out from Palestine and Syria, which retained a strong Jewish identity, very likely worshipped in ways that were different from the communities founded by Paul, in which the Gentiles figured prominently.

So these four chapters in 1 Corinthians are not valuable to us because they provide us with a master template for early Christian worship; they are valuable because they provide a lot of detail about one community. In these chapters Paul gives specific suggestions to a particular congregation about how it should order its life of worship. Further, these chapters are precious because Paul has the church's evangelistic mission in mind. In a book on worship and mission, these chapters from 1 Corinthians are bound to figure largely because they are the one place in the New Testament in which worship and mission explicitly come together. We will therefore give what readers may consider a surprising amount of attention to these chapters, to their significance throughout history, and to their potential for today.

To be sure, throughout the Christendom era, Christians have cherished isolated bits of 1 Corinthians 11–14. Scholars have written at length about the verses in chapter 11 (23-26) in which Paul provides the "words of institution"; these have been the warrant for the eucharistic theology and practice of many Christian traditions. However, scholars have paid less attention to Paul's warning to the Corinthian Christians in the same chapter about the problems they faced at the table. If, as Paul says, these problems were so severe that they can keep the church's meals from being "the Lord's Supper" at all (11:20), every generation must wrestle with these texts.

Further, scholars have shown little interest in the text's strong implication that the Corinthians worshipped in the context of a real meal. Until recently, that is. There is now a widespread stirring of interest in the way that worshipping and eating went together, in both Jewish and Greco-Roman settings.[6] Finally, scholars have rarely paid attention to the way Paul's writings to the Corinthians about worship fit together; they have not seen that 1 Corinthians 11 moves inexorably toward one of the New Testament's most overlooked chapters: 1 Corinthians 14. In these four chapters, Paul presents not disjointed teachings but a coherent, integrated presentation of a unified act of worship that took place at table, in homes.

Why have writers missed these points? Possibly because they have had a Christendom mindset. As we will argue in chapter 7, when the church is not involved in mission, but is a society-encompassing institution that exists to foster acts of worship that support a dominant social order, a connection among these chapters is unclear and 1 Corinthians 14 appears irrelevant. But as Christendom crumbles, these chapters come alive. They suggest possibilities for Christians who are investing their lives in God's mission today.

Inculturating the Gospel

Paul, a theologian and a pastor, was primarily a missionary. The heart of the missionary's calling is translating the message, embodying it, and expressing it in words and rituals that are comprehensible to the people of the culture that they are addressing. Because Jesus is Lord of all, his message can be translated and applied to all cultures.[7] So, sensitive missionaries ask, How does the good news of Jesus Christ and of God's mission of all-encompassing reconciliation apply to each cultural situation into which it comes?

This task of expressing the gospel in a culture requires Christians to be alert and discerning. They must engage in something more profound than *enculturation*—an unconsidered adaptation to the characteristics and norms of a culture. Instead they will engage in *inculturation* which, as missiologist Andrew Walls has taught us, is an engagement with culture that is both embracing and questioning. People who practice inculturation value their own culture and the other cultures that surround them, but do not sell out to them. Instead, they seek to be both at home in a culture and critically alert to its dangers. As Walls has argued, in every setting, as the good news enters a culture, two principles are simultaneously at play:

- The *indigenizing* principle: the gospel expresses itself within the understandings and customs of the culture. It finds things in the particularities of the culture that point toward God's reign. In every culture Christians are residents.

- The *pilgrim* principle: the gospel critiques the culture, pointing out ways in which it contradicts God's reign and impedes God's mission. And it suggests alternatives that both challenge the culture and are comprehensible to it. The inculturated gospel provides ways for Christians to be at home in the culture, but not fully at home. In every culture Christians are resident aliens.[8]

There are other ways of describing the challenge of inculturation: "parallel and alternative," "relevant and resistant," "welcome and critique," "graced and disgraced." In the words of Stuart Murray, all these terms ask of all aspects of culture and human behavior, "Is this creative and sensitive contextualization or irresponsible syncretism?"[9]

Applying the indigenizing and pilgrim principles requires cultural alertness and discernment. The New Testament writings provide precedents, theological principles, and questions for us, but they cannot supply formulas for worship today in the wide variety of cultures in which Christians find themselves. Dynamic inculturation in our cultures will parallel but not neatly reproduce what happened in first-century Corinth, which was only one of a number of ways that the scattered, early Christian communities worshipped.[10]

Inculturating Worship in Corinth

What was going on in Corinth? In 1 Corinthians 11–14 we get a glimpse of Paul, the missionary church planter, as he inculturated the gospel in a Greco-Roman city. Paul carried with him a memory and passed along a "tradition," which gives us a glimpse of Jewish

Christian sacred meals "held with regularity in the gatherings of early Christians during the first years of the movement."[11] The form of meeting of the Corinthian church, undoubtedly made up of a mixture of Jews and non-Jews, becomes clear in 1 Corinthians 11–14. This form was familiar in first-century Greco-Roman culture: a meal shared in a home, in which eating was followed by additional convivial activities. This was how associations, clubs, and families organized their gatherings. At everyday meals, the men sat; on special occasions they reclined on couches; and social inferiors "would sit on the end of the men's couches, or on chairs or low benches."[12]

The Christian meetings in Corinth were apparently in this tradition. They depended on the hospitality of a patron or host; they were situated in dining rooms, which might overflow into courtyards; they were centered on shared food; and they were augmented with conversation and ritual.[13] This was the indigenizing part: for their meetings of fellowship and worship, Christians adopted a familiar cultural pattern.

As always the pilgrim part was more difficult. Paul's reactions and recommendations helped the Corinthian Christians to adapt the familiar forms of their culture so that they would express values and meanings that were distinctively Christian.

A typical Greco-Roman banquet, in simplest outline, had two parts: part 1 was a meal, followed by part 2, an entertainment called a "symposium."[14] In 1 Corinthians, Paul gives us a glimpse of worship in a Corinthian house church. It took place at a meal "within the wider context of banquets in contemporary culture," and especially of the symposium, the meal's informal, conversational conclusion. Indeed, in Corinth the "Lord's Supper" may have been a variant of the banquet resembling a potluck, to which participants brought substantial quantities of their own food.[15] For many Christians, the common meal practice may have carried memories of Jesus at a variety of shared meals, formal and informal.

The way Paul dealt with the Greco-Roman meal tradition that he encountered in Corinth is instructive. He attempted to inculturate the Christian community's meals so that they would be both indigenizing and pilgrim. He took the banquet practices and ideology of the Greco-Roman banquet in three areas—social bonding, social obligation, and social stratification—and altered these so they could express the values of the Christian message.[16]

- *Meals created social bonding.* The banquet was a "community-creating ritual" that formed a sense of family.[17] In Galatians Paul asserted that in Christ there was no distinction between Jew and Greek, slave and free, male and female (3:28). Likewise, in his first Corinthian letter, Paul emphasizes that in the one Spirit all had been "baptized into one body—Jews or Greeks, slaves or free" (12:13). It was inconceivable that these, whatever their ethnicity, gender, or social status, would not eat as one. For in Christ they were all bonded together, and they all praised as one, "with one voice glorify[ing] the God and Father of our Lord Jesus Christ" (Rom 15:6). "Almsgiving and care for the poor had little place in Greco-Roman society, where the destitute were largely ignored."[18] But Paul's rebuke to the Corinthian church shows his keen concern for equity at the table.
- *Meals symbolized social obligation.* In his first Corinthian letter Paul encouraged unity and especially edification. "All things," he stated, must "be done for building up" the community and for strengthening relationships within it (14:26).
- *Meals expressed social stratification.* In the midst of a hierarchical society in which formal meals expressed power ranking, Paul fostered a contrasting society that emphasized meals in which all members of a unified body ate the same food, all "were made to drink of one spirit," and each one had a contribution to offer to the community's worship (12:13; 14:26). In this community there would be a diversity of gift but not of status.

Paul did not develop his theology as an intellectual exercise. He always thought in the context of mission, in which the communal meals played an essential role in the life of the communities that embodied and displayed the gospel that he was proclaiming. After all, Paul was a disciple of Jesus. Isn't it possible that he would have known the traditions that told of Jesus' remarkable table manners, his habit of teaching at mealtimes, and his willingness to confront social norms? If this Corinthian meal-worship was to be called the Lord's Supper, it must reflect the character and actions of the Lord himself.

1 Corinthians 11–14 Is All One Piece

Much of Paul's first letter to Corinth deals with worship. In chapters 5, 8, and 10 he refers to matters of food that had been offered to pagan gods. Chapters 11–14 taken together address matters of the church's assembly, its practices, theological meanings, and the behavior of participants. Of these passages, 1 Corinthians 11:17-34 has been the most important in the history of Christian worship. It recounts Jesus' last meal with his disciples and includes the standard text that the Christian liturgical traditions (with emendations) have used as warrant for the church's central rite, the Eucharist.

But it is not only 1 Corinthians 11 that deals with worship. Paul's discussion of spiritual gifts in 1 Corinthians 12–14 also has to do with the community's worship life. In the view of a growing number of scholars,[19] Paul is talking not about two separate worship occasions (a eucharistic meal in chapter 11 and, in chapter 14, another meeting of free charismatic worship) but about one assembly. Note the recurrence throughout both chapters of the expressions "come together," "assembly," and "body."[20] All these terms have to do with the gathered Christian community, not with isolated individuals.[21] It seems likely that all these activities were part of the same event, and all took place at table.[22]

1 Corinthians 11—The Meal

The meal Paul describes in 1 Corinthians 11 was a community meal in which food was eaten together and sharing was practiced. John Howard Yoder says it simply: "In short, the eucharist is an economic act."[23] How the Corinthian Christians practiced the meal would be their most articulate form of witness.

In a culture in which meals created social bonding, expressed social obligations, and indicated social ranking, Paul was concerned to inculturate the good news so that the meal would contribute to the mission of God—so it would be for good and not "for your condemnation" (11:34).

Paul spoke severely to the church, naming distortions and abuses in Corinthian meal practices. But he also made specific suggestions on how they might reform and realign their meetings to conform to the character and mission of the God they worshipped.

What scandalized Paul about the worship of the Corinthian Christian community was the injustice, specifically at table, of its communal meal. The problem lay in the Corinthians' behavior, which uncritically conformed to Greco-Roman patterns of social stratification and exacerbated divisions within the community. Instead of bonding all members together, the Corinthians' way of eating divided members along class and economic lines which, Paul contended, expressed "contempt for the church of God." Instead of honoring all those whom God had called from many social origins to be one in Christ, the Corinthian meals "humiliate[d] those who have nothing" (11:22). Some people, the wealthier, were eating first; the poor, who evidently had to work longer, came late and were hungry, by which time there may have been no food at all ("those who have nothing" [11:22]). This was worse than secular banquets. Contemporary authors observed that at least "leftovers belonged to the slaves."[24] Further, it is possible that the wealthier members reclined to eat in the house's dining room, while the poorer members were crowded into the less comfortable open courtyard.[25]

Of course, this mealtime behavior of the Corinthian Christians was a form of inculturation. But from Paul's perspective it was so indigenized in a stratified society that it had lost its pilgrim Christian content. It simply was "not the Lord's Supper" (11:20). It did not ascribe worth to the God of the Lord Jesus. Indeed the church's behavior at table interfered with the *missio Dei*, which was to bring shalom and justice for all. Paul was incensed, for he was convinced that there could be no authentic worship if the relationships between the worshippers were unjust.

So, what was the way forward for the Corinthians' worship? First, Paul urged the Christians in Corinth to "discern the body" (see 11:29). These words have been extensively discussed and may contain a multiplicity of meanings.[26] What was indisputably in Paul's mind is that "the body" to which he refers in this text has to do with the Christian community, which is the body of Christ (10:17; 12:12-20, 22-25, 27, etc.).[27] This community—this body—included members who were poor as well as rich, slaves as well as free, women as well as men. But its meal practices, though conventional in Corinth, were abhorrent to Paul's understanding of the new creation in Christ. The meal could not be the Lord's Supper unless the body of Christ that participated in it was Christlike, with a life that manifested equality and justice before the God they worshipped. The Corinthian Christians, who were in trouble at table, needed to discern the body.

Second, Paul urged the Christians at Corinth to reorient themselves by recalling the story that had given them life. He reminded the Corinthians of the "tradition" that the Lord had passed on to him (by unspecified means), which Paul has already passed on to them (11:23-25):

> For I received from the Lord what I also handed on to you, that the Lord Jesus on the night when he was betrayed took a loaf of bread, and when he had given thanks, he broke it and said, "This is my body that is for you. Do this in remembrance of me." In the same way he took the cup also, after supper.

The way forward for the Corinthians, in trouble at table, was to remember the Lord Jesus at table. The Corinthians were to remember him at table in the Last Supper; very possibly to remember him at table in other meals[28] and to remember him as crucified Savior "until he comes" (11:26). The way to the future was to remember the past. In Yoder's words, "the poor man Jesus continued to call people to follow him, which meant sharing bread and condemning social stratification."[29]

Paul refocused the attention of the Corinthians on Jesus. He did not spell out precisely how the commemoration of Jesus, and particularly the memory of Jesus' behavior at table, pointed a way forward for the Corinthians. But he did give them some practical advice that he evidently thought would ensure that they, as the "body," would be eating "the Lord's Supper" (11:33-34). The wealthy should not eat first, but should "wait for one other." Further, if members were too hungry and unable to wait, they should eat at home and not sully their corporate meals with evidences of inequality. By proceeding in this way, they would share (literally make a *koinonia* of) the blood of Christ and the body of Christ (10:16). The Corinthian Christian meal should not be a conventional stratified meal; it should be a meal that bonded the body together: "we who are many are one body, for we all partake of the one bread" (10:17). In this unusual meal and in the after-dinner interaction that followed it, the body of Christ, although diverse and varied in its composition, would display the new creation to the world: "For in the one Spirit we were all baptized into one body—Jews or Greeks, slaves or free—and we were all made to drink of one Spirit" (12:13). Injustice, which privileged an elite, undercuts the way a Christian community is called to anticipate and prefigure God's reign of justice, peace, and joy. Paul called the Corinthian Christians to be true to God's story and to God's mission. Otherwise their worship would be not "for the better but for the worse" (11:17).

In summary, we note in Paul's assessment of the communal meal and his vision for it:

- There is something about the meal, whatever it is called (Lord's Supper, Eucharist, Communion, Agape, Mass), that is grace bearing. When Christians eat it, Christ is present there in his body. For this reason, Christians from the third century onward have referred to the meal as a mystery or sacrament.
- In this meal, God forms the body of Christ with unique efficacy and grace. The Christian liturgical traditions have recognized this and made the celebration of the meal central to their worship. Christian traditions that observe the Lord's Supper infrequently or not at all have much to consider here.[30]
- The Eucharist/Agape meal, like any other Christian worship practice, can be unjust, cause conflict, be out of tune with the story of the Lord whose name it claims, and be an impediment to God's mission. When communities eat "in an unworthy manner," without "discerning the body," they endanger the very life of the church and its members (11:27-30).
- At its best, the Christian Eucharist/Agape meal is an instrument of God's mission. It tells and enacts the odd story of God in order to enable the worshipping community to participate in it. It is here, in the meal, that Christians can be reoriented by the story; it is here that the worshippers, surrounded in the rest of their lives by conventional values, are "restoried." From a Roman Catholic perspective, Fr. Bob Hovda in 1983 reminded a Catholic Worker community in New York City of the unique characteristics and potential of the Eucharist:

Where else in our society are food and drink broken and poured out so that everybody shares and shares alike, and all are thereby divinized alike? Where else do economic czars and beggars get the same treatment? Where else are we all addressed with the proclamation of a word we believe to be God's, not ours, and before which we all stand equal? Where else are we all sprinkled and bowed to and incensed and touched and kissed and treated like *somebody*— all in the same way? This is playing the reign of God. This is an alternative in contradiction, in sharp distinction, to our status quo. This classless society is the way things ought to be.[31]

1 Corinthians 14—The After-Dinner Conversation

In chapters 12 and 13 of 1 Corinthians, Paul laid the foundation for his discussion in chapter 14 of what happens after the shared meal. In chapter 12, he presented his vision for the church as the Spirit-gifted body of Christ in which all members were indispensable and the weaker were accorded special honor. In chapter 13 Paul gave poetic praise to love (*agape*). This was an equivalent to an after-dinner speech at a Greco-Roman banquet, which conventionally might have dealt with friendship or *eros*.[32] But for Paul, *agape* was to govern the way that Christians behave at table and speak in worship: "speak in tongues of mortals and of angels . . . prophetic powers . . . patient . . . not boastful or arrogant" (13:1, 2, 4). In John Koenig's phrase, Paul encouraged good "table manners" for the meal and symposium.[33] These admonitions were necessary, for, as Paul demonstrated in chapter 14, the Christian community "played the reign of God" and contradicted the status quo by means of their post-meal activities as well as by means of the meal.

In ordinary practice, after the people had eaten, the dishes were cleared away. Then, following a libation or toast, the diners enjoyed conversation or entertainment. Philosophical clubs prided themselves on elevated conversation in which every guest could bring a contribution.[34] Again, the Christian community in Corinth inculturated its gatherings in the meal practices of the local culture. From Paul's perspective, the after-meal entertainment and conversation had great potential. He may have recalled Jesus' practice of teaching after meals (for example, Luke 14:7-24). In the world of Pauline Christianity, this was a time for those who had "all drunk of one Spirit" to pursue *agape* love and exercise the spiritual gifts (1 Cor 12:4-7, 13; 14:1).

Paul's Objections: Disorder and Incomprehensibility

Paul had serious reservations about Corinthian Christians' post-meal activities. The problem with the meal was injustice, but the problems with the after-dinner entertainment (symposium) were also serious: disorder and incomprehensibility. In chapter 14 he critiqued the practices of the Christian symposium, because it was inculturating too uncritically, marring the body of Christ and frustrating the mission of God. Instead, he proposed a way for the Corinthian church to worship God more truly, a way that would inculturate the after-dinner session in a constructive, pilgrim way.

The first problem was disorder. Spiritually gifted members at times exercised their gifts in ways that were not conducive to the life of the entire body. Some of them spoke in unintelligible tongues without interpretation; some engaged in competitive spiritual pyro-technics. Paul did not criticize the church for having after-dinner sessions; he assumed that this was a normal practice. But he knew that the competitive chaos did not edify the believers. It did not shape individual believers to be Christlike; it did not build up the community corporately. Further, a second problem emerged: the Christians' behavior baffled and confused the outsiders and unbelievers who came to their meals. In light of what the Corinthian spiritual athletes were doing, the outsiders might conclude that the Christians were "out of your mind" (14:23); that is, the outsiders might mistake Christian worship for an orgiastic session of one of the mystery cults.[35] The Corinthians' behavior dishonored God.

Paul's approach to disorder at Corinth was not drastic. He did not conclude that the after-dinner session was intrinsically disorderly and tell the Corinthians to suppress it. Instead, he saw its potential. When practiced in an orderly way as an act of worship of the "God of peace," the symposium could build up individual Christians and the Christian community as a whole to be instruments of the *missio Dei*. The Greek word *oikodome*, literally "the act of building the house," recurs repeatedly in this chapter.[36] This significant word expresses Paul's vision for individual Christians as well as the Christian community. In chapter 11, it was unequal eating that did not do justice that distorted the meal; here in chapter 14 it was competitive chaos that did not build up the Christians that distorted the symposium. The Corinthian Christians misused the spiritual gifts, especially uninterpreted tongues, in ways that Paul considered neither decent nor orderly (14:40). He favored the use of tongues in the Christian gatherings, but he required that someone interpret them (14:5, 28). Further, he vigorously advocated the exercise of prophecy, which built up, encouraged, and consoled individual Christians and the congregation, and convicted unbelievers of their sins.

We do not know with certainty what these prophetic utterances were like. They may have come as Spirit-inspired admonitions to the community to be true to its convictions. Around AD 150 the prophet Hermas was moved to speak, possibly with considerable emotion, to his congregation in Rome:

> Listen to me, and "be at peace among yourselves" and regard one another and "help one another" and do not take a superabundant share of the creatures of God for yourselves, but give also a part to those who lack. For some are contracting illness in the flesh by too much eating, and are injuring their flesh, and the flesh of others who have nothing to eat is being injured by their not having sufficient food and their body is being destroyed. So this lack of sharing is harmful to you who are rich, and do not share with the poor.[37]

But prophecies in the context of worship could also be lower-key: "spontaneous, intelligible messages, orally delivered in the gathered assembly, intended for the edification or encouragement of the people."[38] Paul did not give the prophets carte blanche; he required them to behave in an orderly fashion, to take turns and to sit down if another member received a revelation; and he required the community to "weigh what is said" (14:29).

Throughout these four chapters, Paul's main concern was with edification. How did the actions of the church gathered for worship affect individual Christians and how did they affect the Christian community? In chapter 11, although Paul did not use the word *oikodome*, his concern was similar. How did the way that the Christians shared their common meal affect their equalization of status, their social bonding, and their care for one another? His worry was that the church's worship was not building up the community into a just and harmonious body.

In chapter 14 Paul again expressed these concerns, using the word *oikodome*—build up, edify—seven times. An early example is verses 4 and 5: "Those who speak in a tongue *build up* themselves, but those who prophesy *build up* the church. Now I would like all of you to speak in tongues, but even more to prophesy. One who prophesies is greater than one who speaks in tongues, unless someone interprets, so that the church may be *built up*" (our italics).

Paul here used the term *oikodome* in two ways—to build up the individual believer and to build up the corporate body of the church. In chapter 14 he used the term three times to refer to the building up of individual Christians (vv. 3, 4, 17); three times to refer to building up the body of Christ (4, 5, 12); and in one crucial verse (v. 26), he used *oikodome* in a way that seems to have applied both to individuals and to the entire Christian community: "When you come together, each one has a hymn, a lesson, a revelation, a tongue, or an interpretation. Let all things be done for *building up*" (our italics).

Paul could hardly be more emphatic than this. His primary criterion for evaluating worship was whether it *built up* the individual Christians and especially the Christian community. He knew that when their worship "builds the house," when it strengthens individual Christians and joins them in love and care, it also leads them to participate positively in God's mission. The believers gather, collectively, as a "contrast society" whose corporate life is intriguing; then they scatter, as individuals whose distinctive behavior poses questions.[39]

Outsiders Are Present

Corinthian Christians met for worship in homes and at meals, and these were occasions of missional outreach.[40] Paul indicates that there were outsiders and unbelievers who were present after dinner (14:16, 24), and these must have been present at the meal as well.[41] We know that the participants called the meal "the Lord's Supper"; and we know that, according to chapter 14, the outsiders were especially moved, not by the meal itself, but by the orderly, but free, shared worship in the symposium that took place after the meal.

What, however, did the outsiders and unbelievers observe? Paul, as a sensitive missionary, was worried that the competitive chaos was problematic. For at its worst the Corinthian community's after-dinner behavior not only failed to build up the members and their corporate life, it also mystified and misled the community's guests. Paul had three concerns:

- *The language was unintelligible.* The outsiders, Paul feared, would be put off by a flow of words that, although moving to the tongue speaker, would be incomprehensible to the outsiders. He asked, "How will anyone know what is being said?" (14:9).
- *The unintelligible words stifled the outsiders' capacity to participate.* When tongue speakers uttered blessings in the spirit, Paul was sure that the outsiders, unable to understand the words, could not take part in the service by joining in the "Amen" (14:16).
- *The overall impression given by the worship was chaotic.* This was the most serious problem, because it gave the outsiders the wrong impression. "If, therefore, the whole church comes together and all speak in tongues, and outsiders or unbelievers enter, will they not say that you are out of your mind?" (14:23). As many commentators have noted, the Greek word that the NRSV has translated "out of your mind" does not refer to dementia or mental illness. Paul is rather alluding to the worship of mystery religions—the emotionally charged pagan cults—with which the contemporaries often categorized Christian communities. He was concerned that visitors would watch the Corinthian Christians as they worshipped after their meal and would conclude that their goings-on were just like the gatherings of adherents of Cybele, Mithras, and Serapis.[42]

So the way the Corinthian Christians behaved and the way they worshipped excluded outsiders and prevented them from understanding the Christian message. Indeed, the outsiders' impressions distorted the Christian message and misled them about the church— and about God. Paul welcomed inculturation and was happy for the Corinthians to have a symposium. But the chaotic Corinthian symposium did not edify the believers in either of the ways that were crucial to Christian witness: it neither built up the individual believers to be Christlike nor the community to be the body of Christ. Further, the indecent and disorderly Corinthian symposium did not communicate a clear message to the outsiders because it resembled other cultural forms with which the inquirers would have been familiar—the orgiastic worship of the mystery religions.

Paul's Vision for Table and Word

In this setting, Paul developed a vision for the worship of the Corinthian community at both the meal and the symposium. In chapter 11 he had stated a way forward for the community at the meal table: the believers were to remember Jesus, discern the body, and wait for one another; if they were hungry they were to eat at home. Similarly, in chapter 14 he stated an ideal practice for the symposium. This practice took Paul's concerns seriously—his concern for edification of the members of the body and of the body itself, and also his concern for the outsiders. Dealing with these concerns would be possible in the house and tenement churches that he knew in many cities, in which the believers shared meals at table, could easily look into each other's faces, and hear each other's voices.[43]

What might this worship have looked like a generation later in the mid-first century? Depending on the location and the surrounding culture, the early Christian worship gatherings must have varied considerably. The Johannine communities, meeting in Asia Minor, like the Pauline community in Corinth, had a meal followed by an extended conversation (John 13–17), but it differed in that its rituals may have included footwashing as well as sharing bread and wine.[44] We can only speculate what Christian communities' worship would have looked like in areas where the *diaspora* Jewish background predominated, such as Damascus or Edessa. But in the Pauline communities, we observe the following components:

- *There was a shared meal.* It was eaten in reverence and justice, an event that remembered the story of Jesus, especially his meals and his great meal "on the night when he was betrayed." It also looked forward in hope to his coming again. There may have been a liturgy, either drawing on Jewish models or spontaneously generated, that depended on the traditions of the community and the charisms of its leaders and members.
- *Outsiders were present.* We cannot be sure, of course, whether they took part; 1 Corinthians 11 doesn't say, but in 1 Corinthians 14 it is clear that they are present and able to participate. By the late first century, when the *Didache* was written, the nonbaptized were not to partake (9:5); and Justin Martyr's *First Apology* of the mid-second century indicates that those

who were not baptized did not take part in the eucharistic meals.[45]

- *There was wide participation.* Worship in the Pauline communities such as that in Corinth was marked by freedom. Paul knew that "all were given the one Spirit to drink" (1 Cor 12:13 NIV). So it is not surprising that he assumed that "all [will] prophesy," not a few (14:24); and that "each one," not just the leaders, will have "a hymn, a lesson, a revelation, a tongue or an interpretation" (14:26). The worship of the community was the product of the entire community; indeed Paul wanted to encourage participation of this sort because it built community (14:26).
- *The worship was orderly.* It was not formless, but it had its courtesies and conventions. According to Paul, many members could take part, but they should take turns and not interrupt each other (14:29-31). If anyone spoke in a tongue, the number of tongues speakers should be limited to "two or at most three," who would speak in turns and be followed by an interpretation. Paul insisted that "you can all prophesy one by one, so that all may learn and all be encouraged" (v. 31). But under the specific conditions in Corinth it might be best if only two or three prophesied, after which others weighed what they said. In Paul's vision, there was a synergy between speaking, listening, and discerning. This is what he viewed as orderly worship.

The most widely quoted verse in 1 Corinthians 14 in the Christendom centuries is verse 40: "all things should be done decently and in order." It is legitimate to emphasize this phrase, provided that we read it in the context of the verses that precede it and recall that it referred to worship that was multivoiced and sensitively deferential. In this worship that was decent and orderly, each worshipper was able to make a contribution of some sort (v. 26). They participated according to an etiquette of participation (vv. 27-32), a kind of free liturgy, in which people took turns, in which members spoke freely, deferred to each other, and discerned what God had said; further, they brought hymns, teaching, and revelations. Paul gave similar directives to believers in Colossae who apparently also worshipped domestically in a meal-symposium event:

> Let the peace of Christ rule in your hearts, to which indeed you were called in the one body. And be thankful. Let the word of Christ dwell in you richly; teach and admonish one another in all wisdom; and with gratitude in your hearts sing psalms, hymns, and spiritual songs to God. And whatever you do, in word or deed, do everything in the name of the Lord Jesus, giving thanks to God the Father through him. (Col 3:15-17)[46]

When this happened, Paul was convinced, the Holy Spirit could speak through anyone, and through the cumulative effect of the contributions.

- *The content of the prophecy and other contributions must have varied.* The prophets and teachers often brought words of encouragement or insight. They also no doubt reflected on the work of God as they encountered it in their lives and the life of the entire community. If this is so, they were in the tradition of the early Jerusalem Christians who, in worship, received the report from Peter and John about the way the religious leaders had threatened them under interrogation (Acts 4:23).[47] In the domestic setting the contributions, even the teaching, would have the character of conversation rather than speech making. Edifying teaching, reportage, and prophetic utterance intermingled, as the congregations encountered new evidence of the missional God at work enabling people to live through pain and joy as God brought the future into the present.

- *This form of worship ascribed worth to God by exegeting the character of God.* Paul believed it was relational worship—multivoiced rather than monovoiced—that best expressed the character of God as "a God not of disorder but of peace" (1 Cor 14:33). "God of peace" (*eirene*) is a characteristic Pauline term, which to Paul expressed the multidimensional wholeness of the Hebrew word shalom.[48] He called the Corinthian community to a state of shalom, to right relationships in which all were flourishing. Worship of this sort was the product of relationships. It built communities; it edified individuals; it formed them all into the character of the God of peace.

- *Something holy happened.* When the community was gathered after a meal for prophetic speaking and listening, God's power broke forth. The members of the community had together remembered the Lord Jesus at table and had "tasted and seen that the Lord is good" (Ps 34:8); they had celebrated and experienced his presence. Now they brought hymns, a reading, a teaching, a prophetic utterance, a revelation, or a "report from the front." Such multivoiced worship built the community and aligned it and its members with the ongoing story of God. The community—at dinner and after dinner—re-membered the body of Christ; its worship "stitched it together" again.[49] And, as Paul said repeatedly, it edified them—it built them up as the body of Christ.

- *Witness occurred.* As the believers were being built up, the outsiders and unbelievers at the table, or in the courtyard, watched it with wonder. As the insiders were worshipping, the outsiders and unbelievers were impressed not by the grandeur of the liturgy, or by the eloquence of the speakers or the cultural accessibility of the songs, but by the Spirit's work in the entire meal event. And in the outsider's inner being, God's voice spoke. The outsider, according to Paul, was "reproved by all and called to account by all. . . . The secrets of the unbeliever's heart are disclosed" (1 Cor 14:24-25). We cannot know what these secrets were, but they must have been varied: sexual abuse and preoccupation; a struggle with occult powers; economic desperation and physical hunger; fear of personal violence; a desire for the healing of a sick child; all of these "secrets" revealing a hunger for God.[50]

Somehow, Paul was convinced, the Holy Spirit used the words of the worshippers to address the inarticulate cries of the outsider. And the outsider, he stated, fell down in wonder-struck awe, declaring the real presence of God: "God is really among you" (14:25). This is the only time, in all his letters, that Paul uses the New Testament's most emotive term for worship, *proskynēsis*. In the living presence of God, worship and mission come together.

SEVEN

After Christendom: Multivoiced Worship Returns

For several centuries before the advent of Christendom, multi-voiced table worship such as Paul describes in 1 Corinthians 11–14 seems to have been normal for many churches. This is not surprising. The Christians had inculturated their worship in the meal traditions of Greco-Roman society. As time passed, the Christians, responding to needs, made changes in the symposium. In the course of the first two centuries, the table activities of many churches began to include the reading of passages of Hebrew Scriptures and Christian Gospels as vehicles of praise and as a means of passing on the story. Homilies, probably conversational, also emerged as a development of prophecy; these exhorted the people and at times applied the Scriptures to their lives. Elders (*presbuteroi*), whose authority was independent of the household, began to take leadership in the domestic churches.[1] Another early change, crucially important for the churches' mission, was their decision to bar outsiders from their meetings. In AD 64, Emperor Nero instigated a severe persecution of Christians in Rome. In subsequent decades, as a measure of self-protection, the churches began to prevent unbaptized people from entering their assemblies—no doubt in differing times and ways from place to place.[2] Nevertheless, even though the outsiders could not observe their worship services, the churches grew rapidly.

Why did the churches grow? Not least because the meal-based, multivoiced worship services were instrumental in forming the Christians to be distinctive people, whose lives and worship intrigued the non-Christians. Significantly, the rumors that polytheists circulated about the secretive Christians had to do precisely with their behavior at meals. As the pagan Caecilius put it around AD 200, "Their form of feasting is notorious; it is in everyone's mouth."[3] More or less at the same time, Tertullian, the father of Latin Christian theology, describes a Christian worship service in North Africa that was clearly a meal plus symposium:

> Our dinner shows its idea in its name; it is called by the Greek name for love (*agape*) . . . We do not recline at table until we have first tasted prayer to God. Only so much is eaten as satisfies hunger; only so much drunk as meets the need of the modest. They satisfy themselves only so far as men will who recall that even during the night they must worship God; they talk as those would who know the Lord listens. After water for the hands come the lights; and then each, from what he knows of the Holy Scriptures or from his own heart, is called before the rest to sing to God; so that is a test of how much he has drunk. Prayer in like manner ends the banquet. Then we break up; but not to form groups for violence nor gangs for disorder, nor outbursts of lust; but to pursue the same care for self-control and chastity, as men who have dined not so much on dinner as on discipline.[4]

But even as Tertullian was writing, describing worship that took place in the evenings, with meals followed by free worship and conversation, changes were afoot. Recent scholarship has indicated that practice varied from place to place and that change happened gradually. As a result, the meal-centered worship that we have seen in Paul's writings was still functioning in Carthage in Tertullian's time but withered in the third century. By the late fourth century, the classical form of morning Eucharist had superseded it everywhere, although the persistence of local Christians in practicing the meal-based agape continued to cause discomfort to some bishops.[5]

The Disappearance of Multivoiced Table Worship

Why did the multivoiced table worship disappear? There were several reasons.

- *Persecution*: In some areas, such as in early second-century Pontus under the governorship of Pliny, pressure from the imperial authorities—who were fearful of private associations (*collegia*) in general—forced the Christian communities to cancel their evening meal services in which multivoiced worship had been possible.[6]

- *Scale*: As people converted to Christianity, the Christians not only had a larger number of domestic churches, but their gatherings for worship also grew in size. The kind of worship services Paul was advocating in Corinth might have worked for communities of forty to fifty at maximum.[7] But in the third century, Christian assemblies in many places were growing rapidly and needed to remodel domestic buildings to accommodate larger congregations.

- *Time pressure*: Christian worship transferred from evenings to mornings, "from dinner to breakfast."[8] This took place gradually. In the early third century, many North African Christians still had their main meetings on Saturday evenings, in which eucharistic evening meals preceded symposium-style free worship. In Rome, on the other hand, the Christian assembly Justin Martyr described (about AD 150) seems to have met in the morning. Of necessity, the services in Justin's church would have been much shorter than those in Tertullian's. The evening meal services could sprawl in time, lasting over two and a half hours;[9] but the leaders of the morning services, which took place before people went to work, needed to keep the services relatively brief. Homilists at the morning services, Justin records, were limited to speaking "as long as time permits" (1 *Apology* 67); there would have been little time for congregational participation in the prayers; and the meal, which now came after the sermon at the end of the service, was evidently a eucharistic liturgy with only token food and drink. There were many house churches in Rome, such as Hermas', and some of these may have continued the Pauline practices that were so resilient in North Africa.

Nevertheless, the service, which Justin described for the first time and which probably took place in the morning, provided a template that became dominant in the Christendom traditions. The morning service was not only shorter than the earlier evening worship, it was also sparer and more fully under clerical control. Notably, it transposed the sequence of elements in the service: word-preceding-meal replaced meal-preceding-word. To restate the change: instead of the early practice, in which an actual meal was followed by the communally uttered word in the symposium, in Justin the clerically uttered word was followed by a symbolic meal. The churches of both East and West gradually made the Sunday morning liturgy standard, a pattern that for centuries was virtually universal (but that some emerging churches today are querying). Liturgical theologians have come to call this pattern of word plus ceremonial meal (sacrament) "the *ordo* of Christian worship."[10]

- *Issues of power and control*: Bishops (overseers), who were emerging as accredited congregational leaders, at times became involved in power struggles with the wealthy families who hosted the gatherings in their large houses, as well as with spiritually gifted members. Issues of control were inevitable, and an evening meal with symposium was harder to control than a morning service.
- *Changes in charismatic practice*: In the Pauline churches, the gifts of the Spirit seem to have operated primarily in worship at table.[11] But as time passed, the work of the Spirit became less immediate. No doubt in many areas, especially in periods when the churches were relatively safe, there was a "cooling off" of Christian worship. Charismatic worship, in which prophecy figured significantly, was central to many early Christian traditions but seems to have become rarer in the second and third centuries. In the 240s, the theologian Origen, writing in Caesarea in Palestine, referred to memories of the Spirit's gifts and "traces" of the charismata.[12] In some areas, however, notably parts of Asia Minor, the gifts of the Spirit evidently remained a vital part of the church's life into the fourth century. The Testament of Our Lord, a late-fourth-century church order probably from Asia Minor, is saturated with references to the Holy Spirit and charismata. In it, churches still met on Saturday evenings, and the bishops prayed that their people might have spiritual gifts to which Paul referred in 1 Corinthians 12 and 14: "Sustain unto the end those who have gifts of revelations. Confirm those who have a gift of healing. Make those courageous who have the power of tongues. Keep those who have the word of doctrine upright."[13]

- *Issues of doctrine*: Orthodoxy of theology became the paramount concern of the developing catholic tradition; there was an understandable (and well-based) fear that unvetted prophecies could lead to division and heresy.
- *Christianity as the imperial religion*: According to Andrew McGowan, in the fourth century, after Emperor Constantine adhered to Christianity, the "process of attenuation or abbreviation of the meal into a food ritual—still retaining certain trappings of ancient banqueting practice—was related to the emergence of the church as an imperial religion." This church now began to meet, not in domestic dwellings, but in public buildings such as basilicas—ecclesiastical adaptations of the imperial audience hall. The effects of the shift from house to basilica were far-reaching, and proceeded at different paces. In certain areas, these effects were underway well before Constantine, while elsewhere, as we have seen, they were deferred into the fourth century.[14]

During the first half of the third century, in many places—especially urban centers—the meal was becoming stylized. Of course it remained very important, for it was a source of spiritual power. In Tertullian's day, North African Christians in the morning tasted eucharistic food—which probably had been consecrated the previous evening's Eucharist/Agape—before they ate anything else.[15] A century later, North African martyrs asserted, "We cannot go without the Lord's Supper," which by then was probably a eucharistic service in the form that was to become classical.[16]

In summary, in the course of the third century, in most churches the morning word and table displaced the freer evening table and word Eucharist/Agape, and the real meal gradually disappeared. With it dwindled the multivoiced exercise of spiritual gift and testimony, which had characterized the symposium of Paul's communities and the churches of the early centuries.

1 Corinthians 11–14 in Christendom
In the course of the fourth century, as Christendom emerged, things changed further. Constantine I was eager to bring the populace into the churches, and his successors generally shared his concern. From 321 onward, Sunday was a public holiday, so the number of people

attending increased and services could last much longer. So an "amplification" of worship took place[17] in two areas. First, in the preached word: sermons could now become longer, and at their best they became impressive rhetorically and profound theologically. Second, in the ritual of the service: the splendor of the services increased, as liturgically alert clerics developed new rites and made old rites beautiful and awe inspiring. The words of institution in 1 Corinthians 11 became all-important and were central to the eucharistic prayers that churchmen began to write down, not only for themselves but also for others; by the fifth century, written eucharistic prayers had largely replaced the extemporaneous prayers that up to then had been the normal practice of churches East and West.[18] A late fourth-century church order, the *Apostolic Constitutions*, used significant phrases: it likened the church to a ship, in which the clergy were the "mariners" and the people were "passengers," and it assigned to the deacons the tasks to "watch the multitude, and keep them silent."[19] A general "homogenization of worship" was taking place.[20] But Christians rarely called to mind Paul's concerns in 1 Corinthians 11 and 14 that worship services should be expressions of justice, equality, and reconciliation, and that "all" and "each" should be empowered to contribute their gifts to the worship of God.

These forgettings are hardly surprising. Already in the fifth century, theologians were increasingly concentrating on the holiness of the consecrated elements as the body of Christ and losing sight of the importance of reconciled relationships between worshippers as the body of Christ.[21] Many people, terrified by the awesomeness of the rite, stopped taking Communion altogether.[22] By the late fourth century, when John Chrysostom harangued his congregation in Antioch, the multivoiced, domestic symposium of 1 Corinthians 14 was a distant memory.

You see, in its first days the Church was like heaven: the Spirit led the people in everything, moving and inspiring each of those who presided. But now we possess only tokens of these gifts. . . . Even now, two or three of us speak by turns, and when one begins another remains quiet. Yet these are only signs and reminders of those earlier gifts. This is why, whenever we begin to speak, the people reply, "And with your Spirit," to indicate the way preachers used to speak of old, inspired not by their own wisdom but by the Spirit. . . . Formerly, private houses were churches, but now the church is like a private house, or, rather, it is worse than any house. At least in other houses one can find things all in order. . . . But in the church there is great commotion and confusion, no different from a tavern.[23]

Chrysostom was of course exaggerating, but it is not hard to detect in him a wistfulness for the interactive, Spirit-inspired world of 1 Corinthians 14. Throughout the Christendom centuries, church leaders rarely cited this chapter. And when they did so, it was not to search for possibilities but to impose limits. They quoted two parts of the chapter most frequently: 14:34-35, which included the injunction that "women should be silent in the churches;"[24] and 14:40: "all things should be done decently and in order." So this chapter, which is unique in the New Testament in its explicitness concerning worship and mission, has had little authority in the Christendom centuries in determining the way Christians worshipped God. In textbooks on worship and liturgical theology, 1 Corinthians 14 rarely appears. And why should it? It literally comes from another world— the vanished world of pre-Christendom, in which Christians were marginal, met in small-scale settings, and the Spirit could inspire "all" and "each" to contribute to the worship.

Multivoiced Worship: Bubbling to the Surface

Of course, during the Christendom centuries, traces of the vanished world at times bubbled to the surface. In 1521 Martin Luther evoked it in his anti-Catholic polemic, "The Misuse of the Mass." Pointing to 1 Corinthians 14, he asserted: "Paul says that they can all prophesy, and in an orderly way, one after the other. . . . Christ has made you and everything that is yours subject to everyone. He has given everyone the right and power to weigh and decide, to lecture and preach."[25]

Luther later had second thoughts about this.[26] But the Radical Reformers in Switzerland, the Swiss Brethren, in a document of 1590 entitled "Concerning Separation," were happy to cite the early Luther to validate their own understanding of 1 Corinthians 14. This was the chapter that they cited to explain their refusal to go to parish churches in which the clergy presided over monological worship services. "When one comes into the congregation and hears only one person speaking and the listeners are all silent, neither speaking nor prophesying, who can . . . confess that God is dwelling and working among them through his Spirit and gifts?"[27] The Anabaptists also appealed to 1 Corinthians 14 to present a multivoiced vision of normal Christian common life. In the 1540s the civil engineer-theologian Pilgram Marpeck wrote:

> My beloved ones, let us be aware of the High Priest Christ in our hearts, and of his anointing of us, with the oil of gladness, comfort and peace. This anointing gives us all learning, wisdom, understanding, and comprehension, and then we may understand what is best and most pleasing to the Father of our Lord Jesus Christ. We should . . . diligently discern what God the heavenly Father has conferred upon and given to each for the service of building up the body of Christ. The gifts in every single member must be heard and seen. There can be no unendowed member who has not been given something of the treasures of Christ.[28]

The early Baptists were at home with a multivoiced approach to reading the Bible; so were others in the radical English Christian tradition.[29] The Quakers gave greater attention to multivoiced worship than most people in other Christian traditions.[30] The Wesleyan tradition, the Salvation Army, and the holiness revival tradition all gave voice to the people through the practice of testimony. The Plymouth Brethren were particularly committed to having worship services in which spontaneity at the table would be normal. None of these traditions has found the multivoiced worship to be problem-free. As Paul knew well, the kind of worship he describes in 1 Corinthians is not always easy to control, and it is susceptible to the opposite danger—routine and even predictability, with the same people offering the same "spontaneous" prayers in every service.

Churches After Christendom

Does this matter? Yes, of course it does. In the Christendom centuries, the churches were respected parts of the landscape, institutionally secure, and relatively well attended. So Christians could coast along on autopilot. They had no sense that their lives were connected to the biblical narrative, and they had no expectation that God would act in their own lives or in the wider world. Without a sense of providence and eschatology, many Christians became functional deists; their God was a cosmic clockmaker who was uninvolved in human events and would not intervene in history disruptively, creatively, hopefully, to bring about impossible reconciliation. As a result, many Christians were docile, tractable participants in the status quo of a society that was, after all, "Christian."

But in our own time things are changing. In many places, the institutions and assumptions of Christendom, which have long gone unchallenged, are crumbling; in most Western countries it is evident that society is not "Christian" but pluralist. In many places, attendance at church services is plummeting, and the values and lifestyles of church attendees are much the same as those of people who do not attend church. How can it be otherwise, when the catechesis provided by advertising and the media is relentless and sophisticated, and overwhelms the church's resources to form its people?[31] Christians feel harried and pressured. Even observant Christians give only a fraction of the time to worship, prayer, and acts of service that they give to work and free-time pursuits. The global threats to shalom—military, economic, ecological—exude an impressive sense of inevitability. Many Christians settle for the comforts of religion while making their peace with cosmic hopelessness.

"It is for the sake of the hope of Israel that I am bound with this chain" (Acts 28:20). So Paul, who had just arrived in Rome, testified before the local Jewish leaders, and so we testify in post-Christendom. We Christians today are a people of countercultural hope. And we will grow in hope as we connect our lives to God's story; as we become aware of what God has done for us in Christ, forgiving us and shaping us as members of a community with a distinctive identity; and, as we become alert to ways in which God is real, active, and at work in our own time and experiences.

This is where worship and mission meet. In the worship that we offer God, God builds us up to be the kind of people who—whatever is happening in the world—are alerted by the Holy Spirit to ways that the missional God is at work. As God moves history toward the impossible reconciliation that God has promised, God builds us up in worship to be God's collaborators through our prayer and efforts.

Paul's Vision of Meal and Word for Today

Paul's vision of worship in 1 Corinthians 11–14, which we have examined, offers a resource for a people who can see and participate in the mission of God in our time. It is a vision of meal and word— God's people encountering God as we gather at table to remember and reenact the story, and God's people encountering God as we experience and express the word as it breaks newly into our lives.

The Meal

The liturgical churches have kept 1 Corinthians 11:23-26 central to the Christian vision, a eucharistic gift that has been precious to many Christians. In many Christian traditions in the West, the twentieth-century Liturgical Movement was of immense importance. Many churches began to celebrate Communion more frequently, and many worshippers who had been content merely to watch the eucharistic action from afar began to communicate more frequently. The Liturgical Movement brought the meal portion of the Pauline vision alive in a new way. But the renewed eucharistic life often failed to connect with real life. Many Christians struggled to relate their own stories to the story that the meal retells and represents. For the Eucharist always poses questions for worshippers and our communities. Are we, who gather to remember and feed on a broken Savior, willing to conform our lives to his? Are we willing to let him break and shape our bodies into sacrificial, interdependent, eucharistic communities?

For churches today, of whatever size, the meal can be central. Whether it is called the Lord's Supper, Agape, or Eucharist, the meal has been the heart of Christian worship from the outset. It was at the heart of the life of the pre-Christendom churches as well as the churches of Christendom. Those Christian traditions that do not regularly celebrate the Eucharist have a work of retrieval to do. We believe this is urgently necessary, and for good reasons. Theologically, the Eucharist is what James Wm. McClendon III called a "remembering sign."[32] The meal, as Paul knew and emphasized in 1 Corinthians 11, is a primary and profound way for the church to remember Jesus and to reorient itself by his story so it can embody and carry on his mission. We join with Nicholas Wolterstorff in the conviction that we need a balance of Eucharist and word to "overcome the tragedy of liturgy in Protestantism. . . . For this is the great feast in which we hold in remembrance Jesus Christ and in which we look forward to the coming of his Kingdom of *shalom*."[33]

In the contemporary West, the family meal table has lost its central place. Many families rarely eat together. Many people rarely invite guests to gather at their table. Some homes have no dining table. Some families report that they eat together only on Christmas Day or at motorway rest stops. We believe that the ritual meal culture in our churches, expressed with joy and mystery, can begin to feed people like these and to satisfy a hunger that they do not know they have. It also can provide a connection between the church's meal and the members' many tables, potentially transforming all of the members' eating practices and training them to expect to find Jesus mysteriously present at their many meals.[34] Restoring the centrality of the meal to our churches' worship will require many of us to change. In many free-church traditions, we will begin to celebrate the Lord's Supper more often. In nonconformist and liturgical churches alike, we will celebrate the ritual meal in ways that more closely resemble a real meal. It is not surprising that many emerging churches today have evolved the Eucharist to a real meal table and made it central; as Doug Pagitt puts it, "It is communion, not the sermon, that is the centerpiece of our time together."[35]

The Word
Some radical nonconformist traditions, unlike the liturgical churches, have kept 1 Corinthians 14 central to their worship. They have taught us anew that God is still acting and speaking, and is doing so as Christians gather for worship not only at the meal table but at contemporary equivalents of the symposium. From their origins over a century ago, the Pentecostals have been a tradition in which "worship becomes a participatory democracy in which the Spirit moves sovereignly upon persons who perceive themselves to be liberated agents and no longer victims."[36] Likewise, in parts of the worldwide Christian church, including African Initiated Churches, there has been an expectancy in worship that has given a voice to many worshippers.[37] Christians in a variety of countries today are following the Pentecostals and the African Initiated Churches in encouraging multivoiced worship. Not least, they are giving new attention to testimony, a practice that was central to the prophetic life of the Pauline communities and that can be life-giving to Christians today.

This, of course, raises questions about the sermon. In the worship of many Protestant traditions, the sermon has been the primary sacrament. Worldwide, countless Christians testify that "by the Spirit, God meets us in the preaching of God's word."[38] As the "word" in the service of word and sacrament, it has conflated into itself the various ministries Paul discusses in 1 Corinthians 14: teaching, prophecy, revelations. This combination gives the clergy considerable responsibility and power.[39] It is therefore appropriate for liturgists and homileticians to give tremendous attention to the sermon, and there are numerous periodicals and websites that provide preachers with resources and new ideas. When the sermon is functioning at its best, members experience God's presence and are inspired and empowered as well as instructed. Good sermons also edify the entire community and lead it in mission.

We are interested, however, in ways that the sermon can synergize with rather than displace multivoiced worship. Charles Pinches, drawing implicitly from 1 Corinthians 14:32, suggests that congregations find ways in which the message is "brought to bear, even tested, in the life of the assembled Church."[40] Opportunities to respond, or report back, could be constructive, for they indicate ways in which God's proclaimed word interacts with the congregation as it participates in God's mission. If this is to happen, when churches learn to incorporate elements of the symposium, pastors may need to recast their sermons. Because they have listened to the people's testimonies, they are able to help the people to relate their stories to God's story—to the *missio Dei*. And they may also need to make their sermons more dialogical.

Perhaps a way forward may be indicated by the way the sermon developed in the worship of the early Christian churches. As Alistair Stewart-Sykes has shown, the word *homilia* originally meant conversation; the homilies given as teaching in the early house churches led to discernment that was collective and conversational. As churches grew and became "scholasticized," the homily became an address, and "the dialogue became a monologue."[41] Nevertheless, for centuries the homilies, such as the *dia logou* that Justin Martyr mentioned, continued to assume responsive interaction with the congregations, and were still doing so as late as Augustine's time in the early fifth century.[42] It is worth noting that sermons in many churches worldwide are often dialogical. In New Guinea, for example, the Glory Hut congregation has "sermons-turned-pastoral conversations."[43] In the post-Christendom West, there are signs of a growing interest in recovering a form of preaching that invites response.[44] One of the gifts of the contemporary recovery of 1 Corinthians 14 is the opportunity for members to "say the 'Amen'" (1 Cor 14:16) to the preacher's message, not only as a liturgical response but also as "sermon responses" that tell how the message has connected with the hearers' experiences and the life of the congregation as a whole.[45]

So we contend that the Pauline vision of table and word is relevant for Christians in post-Christendom. But is it practicable? We believe that it is, in a wide variety of churches.

In Small Churches: Experimental

Today in the post-Christendom West, small churches are proliferating in wide variety, and they reflect a longing on the part of Western Christians for worship that is intimate and relational. Thirty years ago Jesuit spiritual writer Gerard Hughes expressed this longing:

> Today, why do we have to build large parish churches and live in presbyteries? In setting up new parishes, why don't we . . . live in houses in which the poorest in the city live, take part-time jobs to earn subsistence money and spend the rest of our time trying to build up a Church which does not possess its own buildings, but is a Church of people, a community, which celebrates its unity in Christ in house Masses and for larger occasions, hires a building?[46]

Many Christians today share Hughes's longing. Some are Christians who have gone out the "back door" of their churches, tired of assemblies in which they were simply looking at the back of other people's heads, but hungry for a common life that is authentic and responds to their culture and concerns. Some of these have joined together in gatherings of believers that call themselves "fresh expressions." Other new initiatives describe themselves as "emerging churches," whose members are aware of themselves as diaspora Christians who do not look wistfully back to Christendom.[47] Some are new church plants, such as the E1 Community Church in Wapping, East London, whose three distinctive characteristics are "peace church," "multi-voiced church," and "church at the edge."[48] Some are home churches, of which there are surprising numbers in the United Kingdom, North America, and Australia. Some have no self-designation, but are simply informal gatherings, in which

Christians meet in their homes for friendship, food, and conversation. Often these new initiatives are table churches, which meet in the evenings when people are relaxed and not pressed for time. Meals are central, and the participants are happy to see themselves as worshippers at table. Such churches find it easiest to remember Jesus when they are sharing their meals; some have developed table liturgies that specifically recall Jesus' table life and recognize his transformative presence.

At their best, these small, domestic churches meet the needs that many today express for simplicity and authenticity. Members find that they can invite friends who would never think of attending a morning service in a conventional church to an evening meal in a home, followed by conversation. Honest talk and real interchange can take place in a way that rarely happens over the post-service coffee hour. Members of domestic churches often have much to learn if they are to realize the potential of the multivoiced church described by Paul in 1 Corinthians 11–14. At times they need to think about the significance of the meal; writing table liturgies may enable them to put in words what they believe God is doing as they eat together. Further, at times they need to be explicit about the giftings and disciplines of multivoiced worship, and to experiment with these, if their after-dinner activities are to be expectant and Spirit-led. And often they need to give deliberate attention to ways in which "teaching" can happen so the story in which they meet can be transmitted from generation to generation. Those who participate in these house churches at times wonder whether what they are doing is "real" church. Some members sense that they must supplement their domestic meetings with the broader solidarities of larger congregations and global affiliations. If they are to survive, the house churches need a sense of catholicity—a sense of solidarity and accountability across time and space such as the networker Paul provided in the first century.

In Small Churches: Inherited

There are many small congregations, in both the United Kingdom and North America, that have memories of being larger and more secure. Some of these are conscious of lost glory and are simply holding on, hoping that the church will be there to bury them before the church itself dies. But other small congregations are buoyant. To their astonishment, they are discovering that there is virtue in smallness and that they can do things in new ways. So when they cease doing things according to a Christendom template—for example, perhaps giving up their buildings, simplifying their organization, and reallocating their resources—they sense opportunity rather than loss. They can experiment with new approaches to leadership, worship, and witness.

Already in the 1970s Anglican missionary theologian John V. Taylor observed that

> the essential unit in which the church exists must be small enough to enable all its members to find one another in mutual awareness, yet large enough for them to be an embodiment of the life of the Kingdom, which is a life of restored human-ness in action. . . . Little congregations . . . must become normative if the church is to respond to the Spirit's movements in the life of the world.[49]

Such congregations can become sensitized to the presence of the missional God, who is at work in and around them. They can learn to talk about God's work, bearing testimony to what they have seen, praying about it and giving thanks for it. And they can become expectant that God will change their lives—including their practices of hospitality and their service of others. In small churches, there can be infectious energy. Congregations like this are precious and increasingly common, and they have an important contribution to offer to their denominations as well as to their neighborhoods.

In Churches that Combine the Small with the Large

Some churches on both sides of the Atlantic, both Protestant and Catholic, have visions for their life that combine the small with the large. A creative example in the United Kingdom is St Thomas Crookes, an Anglican-Baptist partnership that is one of the country's larger churches. Set in the student area of Sheffield, it attracts large numbers of students and young professionals and has multiple activities alongside its main Sunday services. But pastoral support, mission, and discipleship are mediated by smaller gatherings. They have "clusters," midsized missional communities that engage with particular social networks in geographical areas of the city. And on a much smaller scale they have "huddles" for mutual accountability.[50]

A sample from the United States is Christ Community Church in Des Moines, Iowa. This Mennonite congregation of about 150 members does not own a church building, but meets in another church's building on Sunday mornings at 8:30 for a classic worship service, in which the service of the word with sermon is followed by the Eucharist. In the post-service coffee break, the members chat with each other before scattering to members' homes where their "house churches" meet. In these, the members welcome newcomers, study the Scriptures, share their experiences of the week and their concerns, help each other make decisions, and pray for each other before they share in delicious multi-cooked meals.

One way that U.S. Roman Catholics cope with the small and the large is by dividing their parishes, which are often extremely large, into "fraternities." For example, the Transfiguration Parish in Brooklyn, New York, has over a thousand people at its Sunday Masses; but it also has three hundred members who take part in its "fraternities," groups of ten to twenty who meet weekly to read and discuss the Scriptures for the coming Sunday, to review their lives together, and to pray and to eat together. Twice a year these groups go on retreat together. It is not surprising that this parish has a vigorous and varied ministry to some of New York City's most vulnerable people.[51]

In churches like these—clusters, house churches, fraternities— Christians who are not hemmed in by the historical developments and arguments of Christendom have developed a wide diversity of practices in tune with the New Testament. In many of these permutations, Paul's vision for table and word, which we have seen him advocating to the Christians in Corinth, is as relevant now as it was in the AD 50s. These churches are finding that the Pauline combination of meal and symposium is fresh and adaptable to a wide variety of settings. These churches are discovering that this approach edifies both the individual worshipper and the entire community; and they are learning that it is a means of ascribing worth to the missional God.

These churches are settings in which Christians can be at home. At home, better than in the basilica, the reality of the God of peace can be exegeted by the orderly practice of multivoiced worship. At home the Holy Spirit can intervene to demonstrate the undomesticable nature of God—in Walter Brueggemann's words "something potentially wild, unruly and dangerous."[52] But, as J. G. Davies in 1969 foresaw in a prophetic article, in all churches there must be "a recognition of God's action in the past *and* in the present. Worship, in other words, should be the meeting point of the past and the future in the present, thus liberating man [sic] to be a co-worker with God in fashioning the future."[53]

In Larger Churches

In larger churches, which meet in basilica-like buildings or state-of-the art auditoriums and are shaped by aspects of the Christendom vision, there are many blessings—the power of the music and liturgy, the careful preparation of sermons and prayers, and at times the beauty of art and architecture. For all the glories of these churches, it is harder in them to appropriate Paul's vision than it is in homes or humbler church buildings. But even in grand settings, it is not impossible to begin to do so. Indeed, when Christians begin to reinstate the second half of the meal—the symposium—new possibilities of creativity in missional worship open up. Chapter 14 of 1 Corinthians is still in the scriptural canon, and an increasing number of people are becoming aware of the price of excluding it.

Reinstating 1 Corinthians 14 in the thought and practice of Christians today will not be easy. The chapter was uncomfortable in Christendom, and it will be problematic in Christendom's wake, in which congregational members gather in large halls and in which clericalism's reflexes and mentalities are pervasive. As a result, the worship of many churches today may not exegete the character of God adequately. These churches have emphasized Paul's concern that God "is a God of peace" and that "all things should be done decently and in order" (14:33, 40), but they have forgotten that Paul wrote these phrases to rein in a Corinthian church, whose practices at the symposium were unpeaceable and chaotically undisciplined.

What would Paul say if he were writing to many churches today? Might he urge us, in order to exegete the character of the God whom we worship, to make our services less controlled and preplanned? Might he urge us to have services that are less monological, less predictable, and even to do things that some might see as unsafe, even "wild"? Many Christians think so. Evangelical worship scholar David Peterson has argued that "there should be some public opportunity for spontaneous and informal ministries as well as for the ordered and prepared."[54] The growing number of Pentecostal Christians in the West as well as in world Christianity would agree; the rehabilitation of the forms of worship that Paul prescribes in 1 Corinthians may be a gift from the Pentecostal traditions to the rest of the body of Christ. Of course, the Pentecostal and charismatic Christians at times need to be reminded that the Holy Spirit can move ahead of time, as clergy, liturgists, and worship teams craft words and services. But many Western Christians need to learn from the Pentecostals that the Holy Spirit is at work during the services, as worship leaders allow for spontaneity as well as structure.

For leaders who plan worship services, we propose the following principle: *plan for a least one unprogrammed space in which the Holy Spirit can do something unscripted, surprising, and grace filled.* Furthermore, worship leaders in the midst of a service, in response to the Spirit's promptings, should not be afraid to depart from the set order—to insert a prayer, change a hymn, or welcome an unanticipated testimony. Why? Because the "God of peace" (14:33), whom we worship, is the God not of peaceable orderliness but of shalom. And shalom is huge—it involves right relationships in every dimension of our lives; shalom is dynamic—it needs to be made; and shalom is being made by a God who inspires rather than stifles spontaneous utterances that build relationships. In all churches, even in larger churches, even in churches with a substantial legacy of Christendom practices and assumptions, even in cathedrals and megachurches, the liturgical and missional assumptions from Paul's letter to the Corinthians can begin to express themselves.

How? In what practical ways can this happen? We suggest the following.

Encourage Wider Participation, Even in Large Churches
Step by step, we can move beyond the clergy, beyond the specialists, to include lay voices. Paul's vision in 1 Corinthians requires that the worship of God's people be multivoiced because the body of Christ is multigifted. Spiritually gifted readers, prayers, singers, dramatists, and even preachers can emerge from the congregation to embody the reality that the worship of God's people is offered not by the clergy but by the Spirit-filled *body* of Christ. This may be especially important in the Roman Catholic tradition, in which theologians increasingly recognize that the strong emphasis on the consecrated bread as the body of Christ needs to be complemented by an emphasis on Christ's real presence in the people of God.[55] As Catholic liturgical theologian Jan Michael Joncas has commented, the recovery of the symposium in contemporary worship "might

allow more time for pondering God's Word and working through the implications of that Word for our common life than would be possible in a typically structured Liturgy of the Word followed by the Liturgy of the Table."[56]

Encourage Members to Exercise the Range of Gifts Paul Lists in 1 Corinthians 14
These gifts include hymns, teaching, revelations, tongues, interpretations, and especially prophecy. Some of these may be exercised in small-group or cell-church meetings. But let us not forget—Paul, in 1 Corinthians 12:7, had said that these manifestations of the Spirit were for "the common good." And it seems possible that prophetic words may be often directed to the entire congregation. According to Roman Catholic exegete Gerhard Lohfink, they may come "like a bolt of lightning to reveal the situation of those assembled, to clarify matters, or to indicate how to move toward the future."[57] Of course, as Pentecostal scholar Gordon Fee recognizes, the prophetic gift can be less dramatic than that: "Paul uses prophecy as representative of all other intelligible inspired utterances that are to be preferred to tongues in that setting."[58] As attentive readers of 1 Corinthians 14, Lohfink and Fee both realize that "the gift of discernment" is indispensable.[59]

In large charismatic and Pentecostal churches, at times members sense that God has said something to them for the encouragement and benefit of the entire congregation. If they sense this, before or during the service, the members customarily check their prophetic words or intuitions with the pastoral leaders. If the pastors discern that the message is authentic and from God, they make space for "the prophets" during the worship service. This process of confirmation by pastors is no doubt essential; unguided prophetic words can wreak pastoral havoc. But most churches should be aware of the potential price: domesticating prophecy, stifling testimony, and constricting the freedom of the Spirit who can move beyond clerical control. Symposium-like worship will flourish today only if there is a whiff of risk. If we cannot learn to take risks in our Christian assemblies, how will we ever become people who take the risks that are necessary to participate in God's mission in the world?[60]

Encourage Members to Engage in Testimony[61]
Testimony, as we have argued, is one dimension of prophecy.[62] Further, it is a place where the prophetic unpredictability that we believe is essential to Christian worship can happen. Testimony is essential, because in it Christians report what McClendon calls the "providential signs" that have "spared and directed their lives."[63] Testimony is where Christians collect evidence of God's generous interventions in their lives; this is where Christians lament God's apparent silence and absence; this is where believers make connections between the God of the Bible and the God who is alive in their daily life and professional experience. In all of this, humans are responding to the divine initiative, in which the Holy Spirit gives believers insights and words that enable them to talk about God and God's work. As Wolterstorff has said, "Liturgy is for giving voice to life, to lives of faith."[64] Especially in Western cultures, in which we are surrounded by principled secularism and spiritual anorexia, testimony renews Christians in the belief that God is alive and that God's mission of comprehensive reconciliation is moving forward in surprising ways. In short, reverting to the image of the drama that we used in the previous chapter, testimony emerges in the holy now—the brief, uncharted space between scenes 2 and 4 of act 5.

Testimony may take many forms. Where in the service should it take place? In churches whose worship is based on the ordo of sermon and sacrament, testimony may best take place after the sermon but before the prayers of the people, which it may inform, and the Eucharist.[65] In churches in which the sermon is the primary sacrament, we propose similarly that testimony take place so that it can feed the congregational intercessions. Ideally this will be after the sermon, so the testimonies can respond to it as well as to other events that have been important to members. In churches in the "praise and worship" tradition, testimony will be at home in the midst of praise—and will provide an impetus to further praise, lament, or exhortation. In the domestic church, testimony can take place naturally at table or in the after-dinner conversations.

Testimony: Three Ways

Whatever the worship tradition, we propose three ways in which churches of any size can open themselves to testimony.

Planned Testimonies and Interviews
A member tells her pastor, "Next Sunday I'd like to say something," and the pastor can discern whether it is an edifying contribution. Or a pastor approaches a member and says, "I've been impressed that what you're doing at work expresses your faith and is involved in God's mission. Would you be willing to tell us about it some Sunday?" Or a pastor says to someone else, "What you've recently experienced in your neighborhood is significant and would encourage many members and give them new ideas for their involvements. Would you be willing to share it with us all?"

Testimonies of this sort can be a means of bridging the gulf between members' life at work, their participation in a movement for social change, or their relationship to their neighbors and their life as church members; further, they can alert the congregation to the mission of God in its many dimensions. The pastors may also interview the member, eliciting the heart of the member's experience and at times reining in a member's expansiveness. The results can be life-giving: people learn from each other about their faith journey and are encouraged; trust is built; and the body is edified. A big church's worship cannot be like that of a small church. But in large assemblies, through taking the risk of candor and humble testimony, church members can help build the body. They begin to be able to talk about God.

A Testimony Series
Recently a mainline Protestant church in New England discovered that testimony was renewing its life and attracting new members.[66] In the congregation's annual stewardship emphasis, the pastor, Lillian Daniel, asked members to give five-minute talks explaining why they gave to the church. She called these "giving moments." And the members discovered that these were places where they, as reticent people, could find freedom to talk about God. Out of these "giving moments" grew "Lenten Reflections," and these then led to testimonies scattered throughout the church year. The church had one rule for these contributions: they must not be "Godless"—every story must explicitly refer to God at least once. The pastor made it a principle never to vet the testimonies beforehand. "Churches," Daniel commented, "can so easily become places where control and order shut out spontaneity." Instead, she joined others in waiting expec-

tantly for what the members would say. And the members responded by telling of God's work in their lives, often in ways that had brought them to the church. These testimonies, she discovered, were occasions in which the members of the church really listened. The testimonies led to conversations; they built community; they increased expectancy in worship. Daniel concludes, "Testimony transformed our church."[67]

There are of course numerous ways to have testimony. This bearing of testimony, New England-style, is orderly—there is form. But there are also elements of spontaneity, flexibility, and risk. Testimony makes a connection between the God of the Bible and the God who is at work in our lives. When this happens, God can speak through anyone.

Sharing Time
This is a term many North American Mennonites use. It designates a period after the sermon and before the pastoral prayer and Communion in which members, at a stationary or portable microphone, can make unscripted contributions. These can be spontaneous responses to sermons or prophetic words of perception and encouragement. Worshippers can also report ways they have seen God at work in the past week, and share concerns and requests for prayer. At times they lament developments in the life of the locality—"our local school is under pressure from new governmental regulations"—or in the life of the world. At times members report on their connections with the global family of faith: they have received emails from Christians in Kenya or Indonesia, for example, and they request prayer for them. On occasion, members celebrate and ask the congregants to join in their joy and gratitude. Or they want to share a song that has sustained them through a difficult experience and ask the congregation to sing it with them. Or they say how the sermon has connected with their own events and experiences. In all this there also needs to be reality—"the inclusion of 'testimonies of defeat' which in turn . . . render the 'testimonies of victory' more credible."[68]

Sharing time is never without problems. At times members' contributions can be hackneyed, maudlin, self-indulgent, or too explicit about medical issues. In some churches the extroverted few monopolize the microphone.[69] These problems are not surprising. The sharing time, like any practice, requires churches to develop spiritual disciplines and traditions that enable the members to know, as in Paul's Corinth, what edifies the body and what damages it. "Spontaneity requires discipline, to be free requires practice."[70] Pastors can train their people to discern what is edifying and how to share constructively. They also can propose parameters, for example, only so many people sharing per week; limit each person to one minute; ten minutes total for the entire sharing time.[71] Where people misuse their opportunity to share, they should be subject to pastoral correction, which the Quakers call "eldering."[72] Congregations can provide for personal prayer requests by designating space and time with a prayer team after the service. Seminaries can do their part by teaching pastors and priests how to introduce this practice in a congregation and how to guide it so it can develop in a wholesome way.

It would be useful to have a journal or website devoted to the multivoiced word. Wouldn't it be wonderful to equip congregations to have spiritually significant symposiums, to compare notes about what has been useful and to report ways that congregations have handled problems without diminishing the members? We can report that in many Mennonite churches in North America the sharing time has become a part of their regular Sunday liturgy. Many members anticipate this, especially the youth who often find this to be the place where unpredictability and reality break into the service. On one occasion, a Catholic nun visited a Mennonite church and observed a sharing time. Deeply moved, she turned to her host to comment that she had "seen the body of Christ."

These practices—planned testimonies, testimony series, and sharing time—when functioning properly, ascribe worth to God. They exegete the character of God and provide a vehicle for expressing it: "for God is a God not of disorder but of peace" (1 Cor 14:33). God is the God of shalom, who through Paul called the Christian community in Corinth to engage in common life in whose right relationships all members could flourish. Worship of this sort builds relationships; it builds communities; it edifies the believers who become witnesses to the world. It is an occasion for the eruption of the unanticipated. God's Spirit surprises people, and they can be moved.

Symposium-like Worship as a "New" Sacrament

Missiologist Andrew Walls, reflecting on the varying worship practices of the worldwide church, has commented: "I suspect in some areas of the world we are seeing what, in effect, are new sacraments emerging where the traditional sacraments have become misdirected." In these "new sacraments" the body of Christ is being enfleshed and demonstrated, and it results in "fellowship across the broken middle wall of partition."[73] The reality Paul described in 1 Corinthians 14 is evident in varied forms across church history, and today particularly in the life of many African Initiated Churches.[74] This may be a contribution—a *sacramental* contribution—from the contemporary worldwide church to the Christians of the post-Christendom West. And it may be a way of enabling Western Christians today to reappropriate something that had functioned with sacramental power in the pre-Christendom church that the Christendom churches had found uncongenial but that now, in post-Christendom, once again can be life-giving.

Inculturating Worship and Witness in the Post-Christendom West

Of course, we can appropriate Paul's meal and symposium practice today only if we inculturate it in such a way that it brings life in our cultures. If we try simply to reproduce first-century Greek cultural practices in our settings, it won't work. On the other hand, if we find analogies in our own cultures for the substance of what our first-century predecessors found precious, we will be enriched. Some people today—including not a few churchgoers—may find Paul's Corinthians vision of meal and symposium personally invasive or insufficiently awesome. But there are other people who have found traditional church culture arid and alien. These people are willing to eat with others. At table, they are willing to share life as well as food. In a domestic setting, they may well encounter the Holy Spirit's variegated work as they share bread and wine with other believers and as they talk about their struggles and joys as they seek to follow Jesus. At the end of a survey of Christian worship across two millennia, sociologist Martin Stringer observed that if "the meal and the Spirit . . . could ever be successfully reunited then Christian worship could be launched again in a new round of renewal."[75]

Why might many people today find this renewing? In contemporary Western cultures, people are harried and under pressure. People less and less gather around domestic tables but rather find takeout and fast food ways to get their calories while on the run. People are alienated from the meal. This seems to reflect a deep sense of unease, a longing for the table. It is clearly one reason why the meal dimension of the Alpha Course (born in England and exported to many countries) has appealed to large numbers of people. This is also why participants in the Alpha Course are grateful for the opportunity to hear the experiences of others and to discuss as well as to listen to authority figures. This may be why the meal-less, monological cultures of most churches are disappointing to many people who have completed the Alpha Course.

Inculturation requires cultural sensitivity. According to Thomas Stransky, it "works dialectically in a 'marvelous exchange': the transformation of the culture by the Gospel, and the reexpression of the Gospel in terms of that culture."[76] However we analyze our cultures today, we must make sure that the ways we embody Paul's insights in 1 Corinthians 11–14 address the hungers of the people of our cultures. We must be vigilant to ensure that our embodiments are pilgrim as well as indigenized and that they truly exegete the character of the God we worship. But the forms that 1 Corinthians 11–14 will take today will be many and will vary from culture to culture. In contemporary Western cultures, eating is problematic and many people are obsessed with calories and cholesterol. This is a wonderful time to find forms of redeemed communal eating that can become means of experiencing the presence and passion of God.

When worship services combine the meal and the symposium, outsiders are interested. In both parts of the service, God's presence is palpable and God's power can break forth. Worship is our offering of praise and thanks to God. God is there, and wants to be listened to. The meal and the individual contributions—the Scripture readings, the singing, the testimonies, the words of teaching and encouragement, the silence—all these can be vehicles for the Holy Spirit who addresses the outsider's deepest longings. The outsider will sense whether this community's worship has integrity. Is it real? If it is, the "secrets of the unbeliever's heart are disclosed," and he or she will ask, "What is going on here?" Somehow, the Holy Spirit uses the words and actions of the worshipping community to address the needs of the outsider. This is true witness: as the believers are being built up, the unbelievers will believe. They will bow down before God and worship God, declaring, "God is really among you" (14:25). As we shall see in chapters 12 and 13, in God's plan, edification and witness go together.

EIGHT

Worship Forms Mission I: Glorifying God, Sanctifying Humans

Many people today who are interested in worship and mission think that the chief concern of all Christians should be people who don't go to church. The outsiders: the woman from a Christian background who has not attended church in years, but is in a personal crisis and wants to give the church one more chance; the man of no religion who senses that there might be something real in God because he admires the Christian he knows at work; the teenager dragged along to a service by a friend. Certainly, this reasoning goes, these outsiders—whatever their reasons for coming to our worship services—ought to be our preoccupation. How can we get them to attend our worship services? What will they think of our worship? Can the preacher address their concerns and speak their language? Will they feel at home with the music? Will the worship be culturally comprehensible? Will it make sense?

Christians asking questions like these are hospitable and compassionate. They are attempting to lower what George Hunter calls the "culture barrier" that separates church-attending Christians from their non-church-attending neighbors.[1] And their assumption is this: if outsiders don't come to our churches, it's our fault. Our services are "culturally imperialistic." Our members are unwelcoming. If a church is to have a future, these people argue, its services and members must change for the benefit of the outsiders.[2] These are worthy concerns, and we will deal with them more fully in our final chapters.

137

Worship Edifies Attractive Christians

But it was the members, not the outsiders, that Paul was mainly concerned about in 1 Corinthians 11–14. As we have seen, Paul cared how Corinthian outsiders and unbelievers responded to the worship of the local Christians, but he gave his primary attention to the "building up" of the insiders. Did the community's worship edify the individual Christians and build up their communal life as the body of Christ? Was their worship in tune with the "peace" of the God whom the Christians worship (14:33)? It is striking that the New Testament writers don't urge the insiders to invite outsiders to worship services. But repeatedly the writers call for the churches' life and worship to edify the insiders so that they will be participants in the *missio Dei*. Jesus urged his disciples to build communities that would shine like light before others "so they may see your good works and give glory to your Father in heaven" (Matt 5:16). Peter admonished his friends in Asia Minor to conduct themselves honorably among the Gentiles so that they may "see your honorable deeds and glorify God when he comes to judge" (1 Pet 2:12). The important thing, to Jesus and Peter, was that Jesus' followers should live in a way that had integrity and distinctiveness, that was visible, and that flowed with God's mission.

This approach led to numerical growth. In the three centuries between Pentecost and Emperor Constantine I's adherence to Christianity in the fourth century, the pre-Christendom church grew rapidly.[3] This growth took place despite the fact that, from the persecution of Emperor Nero from AD 64 onward, many Christian churches barred outsiders from their services.[4] Deacons guarded their doors, allowing only baptized believers and people undergoing catechesis into the services of the word, and only the baptized into the Eucharists. By these means the churches excluded spies and rumormongers, but also people who might have had a genuine interest in the Christian faith. Why did the churches grow? Not because their worship was attractive to outsiders. The pre-Christendom Christians clearly did not believe that their churches' worship services were the right means of drawing outsiders to the faith.

Instead, early Christian writers repeatedly offered another explanation for the church's growth: the attractive lives of believers and their churches. "We do not preach great things," wrote an early Christian apologist; "we live them."[5] Christian apologists did not talk about their appealing worship services. Instead they claimed that the Christians behaved differently from other people.[6] The early Christian preachers did not urge their hearers to evangelize their friends; instead they urged them to obey Jesus' teachings and to "imitate" his way in their lives.[7]

The results of this strategy were intriguing. When the pre-Christendom Christians, individually and as communities of believers, lived the teachings of Jesus, outsiders were fascinated. Some of them were willing to go through the years of catechesis that the church required before they could be baptized. Then, after their baptism, at last they were able to worship with the Christian community. Throughout the early centuries, the catechesis and the worship services were crucial to the growth of the church. The catechesis trained the apprentice Christians to live as Christians; and the church's worship maintained the Christians' vision, fortified them when they were under pressure and gave them access to the "wondrous deeds" of the Holy Spirit.[8] So the pre-Christendom Christians didn't offer the world intellectual formulae or evangelistic methods; they offered the world a way of living rooted in Christ. It was a way of living that they claimed was fully alive and divinely empowered, and that was shaped by catechesis and worship.[9]

Things look different in post-Christendom. As we try to be true to God's mission in our time, fifteen hundred years of Christendom lie behind us. During these years, there were many glories. Pope Benedict XVI has pointed to two of these as primary evidences of Christianity's truth: "the saints the church has produced and the art which has grown in her womb."[10] But from the time of Constantine onward, as Christianity began to grow first by means of flattery and advantage, and then from the time of Theodosius I in the 380s by means of battery and coercion, the church's membership changed character. It was bound to. As people flooded into the churches, catechesis speeded up and lost its ethical focus.[11] Soon Christian preachers were complaining at the deplorable behavior of many people who called themselves Christian. In a world in which a byword for Christian was "hypocrite,"[12] it had become difficult for Christians to advocate their faith; they were no longer convincingly interesting or ethical. In the Christendom centuries, it was expected—indeed often legally mandated—that people should attend church, and mission, which had been central to the early Christian lifestyle, largely disappeared as a Christian concern.[13]

In late Christendom—depending on the area—churches and governments relaxed the pressures to conform, and people began without apology or shame to absent themselves from church. This was the time when evangelism became a primary concern of Christian leaders who wanted to attract the "backsliders" back to the church. The preferred vehicle of their activity was personal evangelistic encounter, but the secondary vehicle, in which the conversion was often brought to completion, was a form of evangelistic worship services called the revival meeting.[14] Revival meetings assumed that the people who attended, as members of a Christendom society, were latent Christians whose dormant faith needed to be revived or renewed. People needed to repent and come to a personal faith. So, from the Great Awakenings onward, revival meetings spread through Europe and North America, and at times these had great impact.

When Western Christians today think about worship and mission, they reflexively think, What is the effect of our worship services on outsiders? But in recent years, as attendance in the churches has fallen and as the alienation of many people from the churches has intensified, evangelistic services have become less effective. And Christians, whose lifestyles have been much like that of non-church-attendees[15] and whose church leaders have sometimes been morally compromised, have not been able to do what the pre-Christendom Christians did. They have not been able to point to the compassionate spirit and imaginative lifestyle of Christians as reasons why non-Christians should consider becoming believers.

In many places in the West today, Christians are in situations that are intriguingly parallel to pre-Christendom. Of course, there is great variety from country to country; the religious scene in the United States is different from that in, for example, Scotland. Furthermore, situations vary greatly within individual countries: the "Bible belts" are not like the inner cities. Nevertheless, if we are to participate in God's mission today, it will be helpful to us to rediscover what the early Christians knew or assumed—that worship affects the church's growth by building up the members so they will participate effectively in God's mission.

To be sure, after Christendom we have to contend with the weight of Christendom's legacy. A lot of people today perceive Christianity negatively. Many people are bitter at the churches. Their disbelief that life-transforming ideas can come from the Christians and their

Scriptures humbles us; we must listen attentively as they tell us that the last place they would turn for liberation is the Christian gospel. But, like the early Christians, we can make a case for Christianity. We can only make it, however, if we and our communities embody a message that is life-giving and interesting. When we behave in a way that outsiders listen to us and look at us and say, "I see what you mean," then we will be on the right track.[16]

Glorifying God, Sanctifying Humans

So, what is the role of worship in the mission of post-Christendom churches? Its primary purpose is not converting the outsiders; it is "the glorification of God and the sanctification of human beings."[17] Christian communities do not worship God simply to increase the numbers of members. Worship is not instrumental, a means to attain a statistically measurable goal. Christians bless and glorify God because God is worthy of all praise. We worship God because of God's saving acts, through Israel and preeminently through the life, death, and resurrection of Jesus Christ. We worship God because God has saved us from sin, disintegration, and despair. And we worship God because of our confident hope in the God who through the Holy Spirit is operating in distinctive ways to accomplish God's distinctive goal— the comprehensive reconciliation of all things in Christ Jesus. God is worthy of all praise. God—the God of the liberating metanarrative, of God's mission, of God's project—is good. Our worship is a free offering of joyful thanks and of unalloyed allegiance.

Worship, however, does not leave the worshippers unchanged. It touches us personally. As the psalmist pointed out, we become like what we worship (Ps 115:8). When we join the church of all ages in singing the hymn Paul quoted (Phil 2:6-11), we ascribe worth to Christ Jesus, who "emptied himself, taking the form of a slave . . . and became obedient to the point of death." And when we bow our knees to the glorified Jesus in anticipation of the time when "every knee should bow," then *we are changed*; then we are transformed so that we "let the same mind be in [us] that was in Christ Jesus" (Phil 2:5) so that we too are willing to be emptied and become God's slaves for the sake of the *missio Dei*. Such worship sanctifies us; it makes us holy. It conforms us to the image and mission of Christ. To use Paul's term, worship *edifies us*. Worship is God's gift to us, and in worship we receive God's forgiveness and grace. Such worship forms us, as forgiven people, and converts us to God's way of operating in pursuit of God's mission. Such worship gets us involved as grateful collaborators with God as we learn to live in keeping with God's mission. "Worship is the time when God trains his people to imitate him in habit, instinct, and reflex."[18] Such worship alters our impulses and makes them Christlike. Such worship rereflexes us.

Such worship also changes our faith communities. It forms us corporately. It shapes our churches into cultures that embody the reconciling *missio Dei* and that equip us with practices that question and transform the cultures that surround us. Where else, in contemporary Western culture, do people share wealth and wash each other's feet? Worship reminds us of the teaching and ways of Jesus, and gives us imagination to discover approaches to intractable issues—approaches that are rooted in him. Worship makes our communities visibly different from the rest of society—a people in the world "so that one can clearly see, by looking at that people, how God proposes that human society should be."[19] Our churches become known, not for their defensiveness and attempts to protect Christian privilege, but for their capacity to be provocative.[20] In worship, our communities develop a culture that, because it points to Christ and acts provocatively, poses questions.

The churches that worship in this way inculturate in their society, but they do so in "pilgrim" ways. They know that the indigenizing dimension of inculturation is necessary; people who worship God identify authentically and lovingly with their own society. They revel in its music, its art, its speech, its humor, its sports, its food. In every society there are things that are "graced," and the church will acknowledge these gratefully. These will affect its worship. A friend of ours who has frequently visited Havana reports, "In Cuba Christian worship sounds and looks like Cuba!" At the same time, the faithful church scrutinizes its local society in light of the gospel and is vigilant to note things that are "disgraced."[21] At these points the church must assert the pilgrim dimension of inculturation, which calls it to be countercultural.

Vigilance is especially necessary because every culture is gravitationally pulled toward conventional values that are ethnocentric and violent. Wherever the television and internet reach, there is the tremendous catechetical power of "global culture industries."[22] As Rodney Clapp has commented, "Advanced capitalist consumerism surely stands as one of the most powerful formational systems in our time, and perhaps throughout history."[23] Churches that meet in inner-city areas may be more aware than others of the seemingly irresistible sway of the principalities and powers that ignore and exploit poor people. Mark Gornik, reflecting on his experience in Baltimore, has observed that "the primary objective of the powers is to oppose all that supports, advances, and constitutes reconciliation."[24]

To oppose reconciliation is to attempt to block God's mission. The church's worship stands in opposition to rebellious powers. The church's worship is prophetic: it perceives, names, and repudiates the powers that the crucified and resurrected Christ has subdued. The church's worship is narrative: it tells a story that burns God's passion and project into the consciousness of the worshippers so that they know that God's mission is to reconcile all things. This vision of comprehensive shalom, which the church learns in worship, guides it and its members as they discern about inculturation. In what ways, for the sake of God's mission, will we put on the clothes of the culture? In what ways, equally for the sake of God's mission, will we critique the culture's clothing and throw it off? Above all, in every culture, how will we "clothe ourselves with Christ" (see Gal 3:27)?

What Christians Do in Worship
Christian worship traditions differ, and the churches' approaches differ from culture to culture. Andrew Walls and James White have reminded us that Christian worship practices have varied immensely across the centuries; and Charles Farhadian's *Christian Worship Worldwide* provides illustrations of the astonishing variety of Christian worship styles across the world today.[25] There are, of course, certain family resemblances. In Catholic and Pentecostal and Lutheran worship, worldwide patterns allow the worshipper to feel at home anywhere. But in these traditions there are also often forms of inculturation that indigenize the worship, giving local communities their distinctive flavors. Further sources of variety have to do with size and security. Some churches are tiny, meeting in houses; others are assemblies of thousands of people, meeting in auditoriums and basilicas or out of doors. In some places, churches have to be very cautious about welcoming outsiders; elsewhere they can

welcome anybody without worry. In some places, churches have to meet secretly; in other places they can safely employ highly visible advertising.

As the churches of the early centuries demonstrated, it is not necessary to be visible or to have outsiders present to be missional. Indeed, at times the church may grow most rapidly at times when its meetings are proscribed and outsiders cannot attend them. Such was the case in Ethiopia during the dictatorial rule of the Derg in the 1980s.[26] But in any case, the church does not worship for the sake of the outsiders; worship is what the believers offer to God. And true worship offered to God has a characteristic by-product: it results in a people who are distinctive because their lives are shaped by the One to whom they have ascribed worth. The people's worship attunes them to God's character, and it aligns them with God's purposes as participants in God's mission. The people who have worshipped God leave their assemblies with the following:

- *New sight*: They see the world and its struggles and systems in new ways, and they see God at work in the world beyond the church.
- *A focus on Jesus*: They have praised him, watched him and listened to him. He has demonstrated God's way to them, and they are learning to see the world through his eyes.
- *Different attitudes and characteristic affects*: joy, courage, gratitude, compassion.
- *The experience of distinctive Christian practices* that suggest intriguing secular analogues and new possibilities.
- *A sense of solidarity* with sisters and brothers locally and globally, whom they support in prayer and with material aid.
- *An expectation* that the Holy Spirit will enliven and empower daily lives.
- *The experience* that in worship they have touched, and been touched by, divine reality. They have "tasted and seen that the Lord is good" (Ps 34:8).
- *Buoyancy*: The worshippers have hope in the direction of history under the providential guidance of the One whose story they have told and become a part of.

As a result of all of this, the Christians who have gathered and now scattered will behave in ways that elicit questions. So will their church communities.

The worshippers come from faith communities of varying sizes, of course, and these communities differ in the security and insecurity of their situations. But all of them have a common task: to handle the "glorification-sanctification dialectic" so that their worship authentically praises God and opens them to the way that the God whom they worship equips them to be participants in God's mission.[27] Indeed, as we mature in our understanding of the *missio Dei*, we assess every aspect of our worship by this criterion: does it attune and align us with God's mission?

NINE

Worship Forms Mission II: Actions of Worship

L et us look at some of the actions of Christian worship.[1] How does a particular ritual, gesture, or song edify the Christian community? Does it equip the worshippers to be collaborators with God, whose mission is to reconcile all things in Christ and to bring all-embracing shalom (Col 1:20), or does it impede them? In this chapter we will explore a selection of actions of worship. We will leave many other actions—the offering, the sermon, the readings, the visual and dramatic arts, the benedictions, the prayers for healing—to others to address from a missional perspective.

What then do we do when we worship God?

We Gather

The primary act of Christian worship is meeting with other believers to ascribe worth to God. The very act of gathering—of doggedly, regularly showing up—is immensely important. It asserts, in an embodied way, that this God, and this God alone amid a plethora of other commitments and possibilities, is worthy of our undivided commitment and allegiance.[2] Further, the act of gathering is a statement that this people, rather than other social groupings, is our primary family. Its composition is diverse. Some of its members are very different from us; some of its members we may not like. But we have more reunions with this family than with any genetic family.

The act of gathering with these people has formative power. According to Philip Kenneson, the Christian gathering for worship is the primary environment in which "disciples of Jesus Christ are initiated into the comprehensive vision, the social imagination, that animates Christian life." As Christians spend time together, week by week, a countercultural, pilgrim community has opportunity to form. Individual Christians are apprenticed; they learn "the skills, convictions, and dispositions that animate [the community's] life in the world." And the entire community, which discusses issues and shares life experiences, forms a culture of mission. It learns how to participate in the *missio Dei*: it "learns how to make the prudential judgments necessary for living out the *ekklesia*'s mission in the world: to be an embodied sign and foretaste of God's continuing work of reconciliation and healing in the world."[3]

The Form of Gathering—A Catholic Microsociety
The church in Christendom was inclusive; its members were the local civic populace assembled for religious rites. In post-Christendom the church, in contrast, is voluntary in membership. It is a microsociety.[4] It often is an odd assortment of people, many of whom have little in common with each other except this: they confess that Jesus, crucified and risen, is Lord, and they believe that through him God is reconciling the world to himself and forming a new people who will bear embodied witness to what God has done and is doing. This is an improbable community. It is a universal community in miniature that is notable for the intensity of its members' local commitment—to each other and to their locality—as well as for the breadth of its members' sense of solidarity across space and time, ethnicity and social class. This catholicity is an important dimension of the church's pilgrim life.

Chronological Catholicity
The body that gathers is aware that it is a part of a movement that is two thousand years old and yet constantly being renewed. In the language of the Nairobi Statement on Worship and Culture, every Christian community is called to be *transcultural*; it will draw from its treasury "what is new and what is old" (Matt 13:52).[5] The community embodies a dialogue between living traditions that provides both classical spiritual resources and God's restless, pioneering work. The Holy Spirit does "new things" and discerns among traditions, at times emending and enriching them, at times setting them aside. This chronological catholicity also transcends the believers' age and stage of life. The church is unusual in that it recognizes that it needs the wisdom of older people as well as the energy and impatience of younger people. This catholicity requires

loving flexibility on the part of all—the young who are willing to accept continuity with classic expressions of the faith and the old who are constantly open to new questions and new idioms inspired by the Creator Spirit. This reciprocal deference must be genuine, and even in a time of rapid cultural change it is expressed and shaped in worship. The church catholic knows that it has a long time line.

Sociological Catholicity
The body that gathers is conscious of its need to be diverse in ethnicity and social class. This diversity is rooted in the church's origins, in which Jesus' followers confessed that evidence for his messiahship was the coming together of Jews and Gentiles (Eph 2:11ff.). Paul was moved by his experience, as a Jew, that "because of the death of Jesus, whom we confess as Messiah, outsiders have got in on our story."[6] The church, made up of former enemies, was an embodiment of God's reconciling wisdom, a demonstration to the world of the *missio Dei* (Eph 3:10). And Paul devoted a great deal of his writing and pastoral attention to enabling communities made up of both Jews and Gentiles to live together in unity and peace. As we have seen in chapter 6, Paul was concerned that both privileged and poor believers be equals in the life and worship of the one body. The church catholic has a solidarity that transcends economic and class divisions.

Worldwide Catholicity
The body that gathers has a strong sense of commitment to people in other cultures. It is indigenized locally, but its extraordinary solidarity with Christians in other parts of the world makes it pilgrim. In the language of the Nairobi Statement, the church is *cross-cultural*.[7] This cross-cultural affinity is not optional; it is essential to being Christian, and it is shaped by the church's worship. We will discuss this in greater detail in chapter 11, where we will study the ways that worship shapes the worldwide family of faith.

The Mission of God Requires Catholicity
Throughout the Christendom centuries, many churches—for example, Roman Catholics in County Clare, Ireland, or Southern Baptists in South Carolina in the United States—attempted to

express catholicity in their own geographic areas. These churches were often dominated by the rich and powerful; they were often ethnically monochrome; they generally had little sense of global solidarity; and young people, poor people, and women frequently felt excluded from the churches' leadership and decision making. So new churches emerged, and new denominations were formed that also, in their turn, took on predictable sociological configurations. These new churches have been useful in energizing disempowered people and enabling people of different ethnicities and generations to worship God in ways that they have found authentic. The house church movement in the United Kingdom in the 1970s and 1980s, the youth worship movement of the 1990s, and the current emergent church movement are all samples of this. At their best these gatherings for worship are liberating and have attracted new people to Christian discipleship that otherwise would have remained alienated. As Graham Cray has said of youth congregations: "[To] plant the church in an emerging cultural era has to begin with the young. Some of these experiments may pioneer ways of being church that will be multigenerational and the mainstream in a few decades time."[8]

God is working in history to bring about comprehensive reconciliation. So the splintering of Christians into monochrome worshipping communities—chronological or cultural—always prompts questions. Youth services are useful for a time, but how will they look ten years from now? Is the church to be divided up into quasi-denominations by decade or generation? Ethnic churches may be necessary responses to unwelcoming majority churches and may express genuine theological and pastoral differences. It is right to question the all-inclusive parish church model: Stuart Murray wonders whether "one-size-fits all churches [are] sustainable in post-Christendom."[9]

But there are good theological reasons to be uncomfortable with a church that is perpetually splitting. Is it right for churches to be divided, across generations, by ethnicity, sociology, and culture? There are obvious pastoral reasons why these separations are useful for a time. But since God's mission is comprehensive reconciliation, we hope that they will find ways of moving toward greater catholicity. And we wonder, Is it possible for worshipping communities to be flexible and adaptable, honoring the old but welcoming the new, allowing for reciprocal deference and creativity? A youth pastor has recently told us, "The importance of attending church and participating in the worship practices of the church can hardly be overstated when considering the Christian formation of youth. The same can be said of living daily in the company of loving Christian parents who are themselves committed to reenacting the story of God's reconciling love in their daily lives."[10]

When churches are sociologically constricted—as many churches are—they can take steps to enter into significant relationships that broaden their perspective. In the United States, members of predominantly white congregations have found new life when they have intentionally engaged in common programs with nearby African-American congregations. A table church can develop an intentional friendship with a nearby Pentecostal church or—by email and reciprocal visits— with a congregation in southern Argentina. In the United States and Colombia, Catholics and Mennonites have been meeting together to worship and build friendships, as a result of which they have been able to discuss their historical antagonisms and to collaborate on justice- and peacemaking projects.

The Impact of Gathering

Gathering is essential for the church's life. Without the disciplines of gathering, Christians are subjected to relentless assaults of the dominant culture's catechesis. For a time, believers who are hurt by the church—or disappointed with it or bored by it—can live by the odd story that is the source of their Christian identity without gathering regularly with other believers. But this is difficult, and across time it can rarely be maintained. A recent study of the decline in Christian observance in the North of England indicates that it is hard to exaggerate the importance of gathering for the survival of Christian belief.[11]

Gathering is essential to the individual members. Throughout the week we inhabit our everyday worlds of work and neighborhood, of family and causes, of hobbies and sports. But when we scatter, we embody the understandings, instincts, and reflexes that have been shaped by our worship. We go, not as individualists, but as people whose primary sense of identity is corporate and Christian. Our lives are newly aligned with the *missio Dei*. We know that we are scattered members of what the early Christians called a "new race"[12] with whom we have gathered in a disciplined way. And we know that we are part of something huge—the body of Christ whose solidarity extends across the millennia and across the globe. Disciplined gathering produces meaningful scattering.

We Praise God

Praise is the heart of the Christian life, and it is at the center of what Christians do when they gather for worship. Worshipping, as we have noted, is ascribing worth, and "we praise what we prize."[13] So when we gather in God's presence, we "enter his gates with thanksgiving, and his courts with praise" (Ps 100:4). The songs we sing, the Scriptures we hear, the liturgical texts we use as we gather are means of praising God. And why would we not begin in this way? For God's love is overflowing, extravagant, creative, and healing. And God in love invites us to respond with similar extravagance. As David Ford and Dan Hardy have written, "Praise of God is not necessary, it is an overflow, a generous extravagance of response."[14] This response of praise does not remain confined to the "praise section" at the beginning of the service; it floods through the worship service—through sermon and Eucharist (thanksgiving), the readings, testimonies, and prayers. Indeed praise becomes the leitmotif of the life of the worshipping Christian. Throughout the week as well as at worship, the Christian is a praising person.

Of course, like all wondrous things, praise can go awry. Some Christians, whom Ford and Hardy call the "stoics," are stifled by the thought of praise. They react against other believers whose praise seems effusive and shallow, cut off from the realities of life. Far better to cultivate a spirituality of endurance and resistance, to live lives of morality and neighbor love, and to have a prayer life that is intercessory. If apartheid ends or the Berlin Wall falls, our reflex will not be to praise God; instead, we will pray for the suffering people whose lives will be made precarious by the changes their countries are undergoing. Contrasting with this stoic approach—morality without doxology—is an approach of other Christians, which Walter Brueggemann calls "doxology without reason."[15] The worshippers may praise God at great length, but without specifically rooting their praise in the story of God's liberating acts and the vision of God's new creation. These Christians are not stoic; they are ahistorical. Their worship concentrates on God's attributes of majesty and glory but ignores God's actions that "brought down the powerful from their thrones, and lifted up the lowly" (Luke 1:52). Apartheid or the Berlin Wall are often off the radar screens of Christians who "just want to praise the Lord."

The antidote to these two deviations lies in the story that our congregations tell as they worship week by week. As we have noted in chapters 4 and 5, our communities are shaped by our narratives. We have noted that the Bible's narrative is odd in two ways: it assumes that God is active in history and in our world today and it has values that are upside down. The stoic Christians struggle with God's activity, and the ahistorical Christians—who are often captive to the dominant values of society—struggle with God's moral and social vision.

When we gather to worship God, we offer our praises out of the stories that have shaped us. Our songs of praise may state a reason for the praise; our biblical and liturgical texts and our prayers may give a rationale for our thanksgiving. But the whole reason will be spelled out by the entire life of the worshipping community as it seeks to follow Jesus in life and builds a fund of narrative that provides the grid by which its members interpret their world. The fund of narrative has a past: God has acted with overflowing love through Israel, Jesus Christ, and the church to bring salvation, healing, and hope to humanity. The church responds with praise. The fund of narrative has a present: in overflowing love, God is acting in the world now as God moves to reconcile all things in Christ. The church responds with praise. The fund of narrative has a future: God's mission is to move toward a new creation in which love will overflow and there will be right relations for all, in which all humans and all creation will praise God (Phil 2:10-11; Col 1:20; Rev 7:9). The church responds with praise.

The people who are most free in expressing praise are those who have experienced God's overflowing love in their own lives. We are most inclined to believe that God has acted generally in history and in the community's history if we know that *it has happened to us!* We who know that God has acted in our own lives and history— forgiving, surprising, reconciling, opening doors when all seemed blocked—are people who most freely offer praise to God and who participate most joyfully in God's mission. Nothing more powerfully motivates people to participate in the *missio Dei* than gratitude.[16] For worshipping communities who are gratefully and reflectively aware of the divine metanarrative and also of the personal histories of their members, gratitude becomes a dominant affection. And praise becomes "the church's mother tongue."[17]

We Confess that Jesus Is Lord

It is not just any collection of people who gathers, scatters, and praises. Christians are Jesus people. The earliest Christian hymn proclaims that "Jesus Christ is Lord, to the glory of God the Father" (Phil 2:11). The hymn anticipates the time when everyone will join in praise, worshipfully acknowledging Jesus' lordship. The community that gathers in worship looks forward to the time when God's mission will be fulfilled and all people—and all creation—will be reconciled in shalom.

"Jesus Christ is Lord" Clarifies What God's Mission Is About

In Jesus, the church confesses, the triune God took flesh and engaged in the ultimate self-disclosure of incarnation. If we want to know what God is like, we look at Jesus, the Word made flesh, dwelling in our midst. In this book we contend that the God whom we worship is a God of mission, a God whose project is to reconcile on this earth all things to himself, to bring comprehensive shalom. We have seen that God's preferred means is sending people. Jesus is the preeminent example of God's sending: as Paul put it, "when the fullness of time had come, God *sent* his Son" (Gal 4:4, our italics). Jesus, the *sent one*, God's missionary, shows us what God cares about and how God operates. Jesus' life shows him moving with God as he sees God at work among people—the Syrophoenician woman, the tax collectors, and the sinners—who were ethnically, ritually, and morally beyond the pale and whom his religiously observant contemporaries rejected. Jesus receives blessing from them, and he *eats* with them. "Never in Israel" had the astonished Jesus seen faith such as that of the Gentile occupation soldier who confessed faith in Jesus' capacity to heal his servant *in absentia*, which ignited in Jesus the vision of a meal—the great banquet (Matt 8:5-13). As Luke Bretherton has observed, "Through his hospitality, which has as its focal point actual feasting and table fellowship, Jesus turns the world around."[18]

Jesus' death shows the consequences of his mission, which unmasked the powers by eating with the wrong people, and the depths to which the loving God was willing to go in self-giving for human salvation. Jesus' resurrection shows that God vindicated his Son and that nothing that the powers can do will keep God from bringing the *missio Dei* to completion. Christians who ponder God's mission in light of Jesus' crucifixion and resurrection confess, "The zeal of the Lord of hosts will do this" (Isa 9:7). And to discover what this means to them—to the nature of God's mission and how they may participate in it—Christians gather in communities that tell the story of Jesus and carry on the story in the service that they do in his name. In other words, in their narrative worship, Christians watch God's sent One, Jesus, in action, and they give ultimate authority to his teachings, which illuminate his actions by carrying on his mission in their common life and their actions. For Jesus shows us the *missio Dei* made flesh.

"Jesus Christ Is Lord" Redefines Lordship
Christians are surrounded by conventional, hierarchical understandings of lordship. It is hard for Christians to resist these. According to the Gospel accounts, Jesus' disciples succumbed to these understandings, and Jesus confronted them strenuously: "You call me Teacher and Lord. . . . So if I, your Lord and Teacher, have washed your feet, you also ought to wash one another's feet." Jesus' humble, serving lordship determines the attitudes and behavior of his followers: "I have set you an example, that you also should do as I have done to you" (John 13:13-15). In Luke, Jesus differentiated himself from "those in authority," telling his disciples that "I am among you as one who serves" (Luke 22:25-27). When we gather for worship, we listen to the Lord Jesus as he speaks, we watch him in his actions, we learn his stories, and we observe what it meant for him to take up the cross. In obedience to his command, we burn into our hearts and reflexes his understandings of lordship as we play them liturgically—at the table and with the basin and towel. Christians who worship in this way experience deep dissonance whenever they encounter—in themselves or in others—conventional expressions of lordship.

"Jesus Christ Is Lord" Puts Other Lordships in Perspective
A church that worships and ponders Jesus has the capacity of spiritual perception. As Bob Goudzwaard has pointed out, it can name idols and their activities and be alert to "the role reversal characteristic of idol worship . . . what we ourselves have created ends up controlling us."[19] Jesus, the Lord in our midst, enables Christians to perceive the spiritual forces operating that keep creation groaning and people in their society from being gloriously free (Rom 8:21, 23).

Jesus the Lord in our midst also points unerringly to false allegiances. During World War II, "worshippers in Japanese Christian churches—before the beginning of the Sunday services—without hesitation would face the Imperial Palace and bow in deep respect in a patriotic ceremony." Only members of Holiness Churches and Plymouth Brethren assemblies and nonchurch Christians (*mukyokai*) resisted this, and they were "brutally suppressed." Fifty years after Japan's defeat, Japanese Christians from the Catholic Tokyo Archdiocese through the Japan Evangelical Association expressed repentance. They confessed that in their wartime attempts to avoid persecution they had broken the first commandment.[20] The Japanese imperial authorities were correct to note the implications of the lordship of Jesus Christ. As N. T. Wright observed, "Ultimately for the Roman point of view there was only one Lord of the world. According to Paul, he [the emperor] now had a rival."[21]

Christians in many Christendom and post-Christendom churches have been less alert to the lordship of violent nationalism than their Japanese brothers and sisters. The surges of patriotism after the attacks of September 11, 2001, are a sample. A tell-tale symbol of this refusal to choose between the lordships of Caesar and Christ are the flags displayed in many churches in the United States and the United Kingdom. Japanese Christians whom we know are deeply uncomfortable about these flags in Western churches. We share their discomfort. If there must be national flags in churches, let's have not just one but lots of them! We found an example of this in an Assemblies of God church in Michigan. It had many flags—we counted fifty—all of the same size, with the United States flag among them, and we recognized that these symbolized the many tribes and nations that will bow down to God and to the Lamb in eschatological worship.

"Jesus Christ Is Lord" Equips the Worshipping Body of Disciples to Be Obedient to Him

Jesus is *Lord*, but we must not forget that *Jesus* is Lord. And Jesus commanded his disciples, who he knew would worship him, to be obedient—to "hear these words of mine and act on them" (see Matt 7:24). Jesus wanted his disciples, for their own good, so their houses would not collapse, to ascribe worth to him, to worship him, not by saying "Lord, Lord" but by doing what he said (7:22-27). In light of this, it is astonishing how slight the impact of Jesus' words and teachings is on the worship of many Christian traditions. Many free-church Protestants go for weeks without reading the words of Jesus in their Sunday services; some rarely pray the Lord's Prayer. The liturgical traditions do better. In their Eucharists, the people stand when the Gospel is read, honoring Jesus by their attentive posture if not necessarily by their everyday lives. In Christendom, in which Jesus' teachings challenged many dominant values, this disconnect is understandable. In post-Christendom, when Christians are a "creative minority," the connection between the words of Jesus and the lives of the believers will reemerge.[22] Worship, Jesus said, must lead to obedience. As Dallas Willard has emphasized, worship produces disciples. The missional task of the church, he contends, is less one of outreach than that of *inreach* that produces "clear-headed and devoted apprentices of Jesus." Apprentices of Jesus will be produced by "example, teaching and ritual."[23] When we gather as a church to say "Lord, Lord" and are willing to do what Jesus says, we will scatter with Jesus' words and example imprinted on our inner selves. We will scatter purposefully, participating eagerly and creatively in God's mission.

We Tell the Big Story

When Christians gather to worship, they tell the big story. In chapter 4 we emphasized that a primary function of the worship services recorded in the Bible was storytelling. God's people have recounted the "historic signs," according to James McClendon, because they "make God's presence and power evident for redemptive purposes."[24] This is the story of God's mission, from creation to new creation. It is the story of God's passionate determination to reconcile people to the God from whom they are alienated, to reconcile people to their enemies, to reconcile people to the creation they exploit. The story of the missional God can course through all aspects of worship: Scripture reading, sermon, rites, testimonies, prayers, and blessings. All people are story-shaped, and we Christians especially need to be consciously shaped by our alternative story because it is an odd story, decisively different from the dominant stories of our time. In the biblical story God exalts the humble and humbles the mighty. In this story God saves the world by nonviolent means—through the election of a people and through incarnation, cross, and resurrection. In this story God acts through serendipity and miracle, climactically through God's vindication of Jesus and pouring out of the Holy Spirit. We must tell this story so that we know it deeply and indwell it and so that it serves as the lens through which we see—and evaluate—all other stories.

The big story of God requires a response. As Stanley Hauerwas has observed, "The story itself demands that only those who are willing to be the story are capable of following it. . . . What is crucial is not that Christians know the truth, but that they be the truth."[25] The story takes on life as its tellers live it and embody it. And so, in our jobs, in our families and neighborhoods, and in communities and nations across the globe, we attempt to collaborate with the God, whom we affirm is working among the humble and bringing justice and reconciliation in ways that, if we knew more, would astonish us. In our passion to see God's kingdom come and to participate in God's missional action, we orient ourselves and evaluate our actions by the big story. We ask ourselves, How does what I'm doing fit into the trajectory of God's big story? And as we look around us, where do we see folkways, habits, and initiatives that block God's mission—or promote it? These are always matters of dispute and discernment, and the issues will not always be clear-cut.

One mile from our church is the "Mega-Shredder," the largest reprocessor of dead cars in the world. The good news is that this provides jobs and recycles metal. The bad news is that it also pollutes the environment with vibrations, malodorous smells, noise, and explosions, blighting the lives of the poor people who live near it. Some of us have campaigned to have it closed down. Not all Christians agree that this campaign is an authentic expression of God's mission. But our singer-songwriter pastor has addressed it openly with his "Mega-Shredder Man," which he performs with prophetic passion. To him it is clear where the Shredder fits into God's Big Story.[26]

We Tell the "Little Stories"

When we Christians gather for worship, we also tell our own stories. So we do not only repeat the narratives of the historic signs. We also are attentive to the "providential signs" that, according to McClendon, are "instances of the distinctive guidance God gives to individual lives for designated kingdom tasks."[27] Christians believe that the missional God is at work, relentlessly if often reticently; and, as God adds new chapters to the story, we seek to be God's collaborators.

But what is God doing? When congregations gather, the members give "reports from the front." If their reports are to be helpful, they must be undergirded by a spirituality of listening prayer. According to Catholic missiologist Robert Schreiter, "What undergirds every successful process of reconciliation is a spirituality, a view of the world that recognizes and responds to God's reconciling action in the world."[28] One application of this insight is a spirituality for the whole day, encouraged in worship, which a local church might encourage.

Morning
As the day begins, we pray two prayers. We pray the Lord's Prayer: "Your kingdom come, your will be done." The Lord's Prayer is the kingdom prayer, and praying the kingdom is at the heart of our prayer lives. We also pray the missional prayer: "Lord, you will be at work today; help us notice where you are working, and show us how we can enter in." We listen, opening ourselves to the God who will give us niggles, impulses, about the day's activities. We contemplate. As we listen to what God is doing in the world, we realize that the story is alive. It is going on in smaller events that have the DNA of the bigger story and that carry the story on. So we go into the day expectantly, asking God to further God's mission of reconciliation and shalom—and that we may collaborate.

Midday
We stop, pray the kingdom prayer, and in silence engage in the spiritual act of "noticing."[29] Where have we seen God's reign

breaking into time, in ways small and big, and where have we seen God's mission frustrated?

Evening
At the day's end, in what spiritual writers call an examen of consciousness, we reflect on what we have noticed throughout the day. We offer prayers of thanks and lament.

Remembering
In an attempt not to be among those who "forget all God's benefits" (see Ps 103:2), we tell a friend or partner what we have seen or record what we have seen in a journal. When our faith community next meets, whether in a church building or at table, we bring our little stories—our testimonies. Testimonies are constantly adding to the communal fund of narrative. God's story goes on, and we find our little stories in God's story. As we become collaborators with God, our little stories are taken up into God's metanarrative—the story of God's mission.

We Perform Baptism, Eucharist, and Footwashing
Baptism
Baptism is the sacrament through which God incorporates people into God's family and the *missio Dei*. In the Christendom centuries, infants were customarily baptized soon after birth. In many places the laws required this; it was assumed that everyone in society would be incorporated in the Christian body and that baptism was the saving sacrament of entry. Baptism took place soon after birth, often privately; midwives frequently administered it. From the sixteenth century onward, some nonconformist churches dissented from the practice of infant baptism, sensing that it produced churches whose members often lacked deep personal commitment. After Christendom, both the pedobaptist and the believers baptism traditions continue. And one must note that, in some post-Christendom situations, both infant and believers baptism increasingly bear a similar theological significance. In some places in the West, the baptism of infants has become a countercultural act, and many people in the traditions that historically have baptized infants have begun to dedicate infants, not baptize them, with the prayer that, at an accountable age, they will make

a personal response to God's call and ask to be baptized. Today, around the world in many non-Christendom situations, baptism has taken on the significance that it had in the pre-Christendom church. Baptism is the watershed. It is not interest in Jesus or participation in a Bible study group that leads parents to disinherit their children and governments to persecute people. It is baptism. In whatever situation baptism is practiced, we note three things:

- *Baptism is entry into a different world.* The candidates die to their old solidarities; they repudiate the old order of "sin, death, and the devil"; they are raised into a new life and reborn into a new community. The community is voluntary, global, made up of dissimilar people. Its members now belong to a new, non-genetic, egalitarian family, whose miraculous "newness and togetherness explicitly relativize prior stratifications and classification."[30]
- *Baptism immerses people into God's mission.* Baptism initiates them into a community that lives under the lordship of Christ and therefore participates in his mission. To be baptized is to be ordained into a holy priesthood and commissioned into a life of obedience and suffering; the baptizands are baptized in water, the Spirit, and blood (1 John 5:8). The Holy Spirit enables the newly baptized believers to participate in this by pouring out *charismata*, which empower Christians to take part in the *missio Dei*. As Gibson Winter observed in the mid-twentieth century: "Until men and women are drawn into the missionary enterprise of the church, they do not discover the meaning of their baptism."[31]
- *The baptized must be catechized to live the life of God's mission.* Catechesis is necessary, either before their baptism (as in the early church and in traditions that practice believers baptism) or after their baptism (in pedobaptist traditions). In either tradition, ongoing catechesis is necessary. The baptized cannot participate in God's mission unless they know the big story; they cannot live missional lives unless they understand widely assumed myths such as the efficacy of redemptive violence, which subvert the story;[32] they cannot embody God's mission unless they are continually being trained in the practices of the Christians that make sense of the story. Baptismal candidates

learn these practices best by participating in them; they learn them more by doing—and watching master practitioners—than by thinking. In this continuing catechesis, they learn to evaluate their culture from the perspective of God's mission, with what Michael Budde calls "discernment and selectivity."[33] In this way, Christians learn the missional discipline of indigenization and develop the sensitivities necessary to be resident aliens; they learn when it is appropriate to "follow the customs of their country" and at what points they must "endure everything as foreigners."[34] Catechesis prepares people to live as Christians in inhospitable environments, as participants in God's reconciling mission. In the believers baptism tradition, the candidates' preparations culminate in a baptismal rite that is as imposing ritually as it is spiritually significant—which is very wet and is as messy and joyful as birth.[35]

Eucharist

In the Eucharist, the risen Christ meets his people and feeds them, shaping them into the forgiven and forgiving body of Christ. As they eat and drink, the people are filled with thanksgiving and go out with joy.

During the Christendom centuries, the joyful and communal dimensions were not always evident. Screens and fences separated priests from the people, and the priests spoke in a language that few people could understand. The liturgical movement of the twentieth century did much to restore to many churches the sense that the people participate fully in the mnemonic meal along with the presiding clerics; but many people continue to feel that the laity are bit-part players on the margins of the drama of the Lord's Supper. Nevertheless, at its heart the Eucharist remains a sacrament of God's mission.

- *The Eucharist tells the story of God.* It is the narrative sacrament par excellence. In it, the worshippers celebrate the coming together of past, present, and future; they recollect, they celebrate, and they longingly anticipate. By ritually playing this meal, the worshippers enter into it and become participants in the life, death, resurrection, and reign of Christ. By eating and drinking together and by making peace with one another, they also are re-membered as his body.[36]

- *The Eucharist commits the worshippers to participate in God's mission.* It is a renewal of the new covenant. In it, the believers, in the presence of Christ their host, renew their commitment to the "new covenant in his blood." As they do so, they enter into his mission and his politics. "The regular renewal of the covenant means that the people of God are constantly confirmed in and impelled to mission."[37] Through the Eucharist, Christ reconciles his disciples to God and makes them ministers of reconciliation to their neighbors and enemies. Anabaptist theologian Balthasar Hubmaier expressed this connection—which we have called "the motive clause"—at the conclusion of the communion service he wrote shortly before his martyrdom in 1528: "As Christ gave up his life for me, so I go forth to give up my life for others, for my sisters and brothers in faith, my neighbors, my enemies."[38] In the safer world of the 1960s, J. G. Davies also saw this connection. "Authentic worship," he wrote, "is . . . that in which the two dimensions are combined, viz. participation in Christ through communion and so participation in his mission to the world."[39]

- *In post-Christendom an increasing number of people long to celebrate the meal in ways that more explicitly express God's mission.* They want to have eucharistic meals in homes and in table churches as well as in large ecclesiastical buildings; they want to eat and drink together in ways that not only resemble meals but are meals.

The missional potential of eating together—both familial and sacramental—is indicated by the story of a young Mennonite pastor in Oregon who discovered that his youth group came alive as they became involved in what philosopher Albert Borgmann calls "focal practices."[40] Assisted by a potter, each young person made his or her own Communion cup and also one for someone as yet unknown who would join the group. Every week the group's members baked bread for the communal meal. And soon the group "moved from celebrating Communion in symbolic and ritual form only, to celebrating [it] as a fellowship [meal] that all wanted to participate in." The pastor reported that the young people participated in filling the cups they had made and in passing the elements as [they] told the Jesus story again each week. . . . When the ritual act of communion was complete [they] concluded the meeting by holding hands . . . for the closing blessing, "Just as Jesus rose from the dead after three days, I invite you to stand and walk in the resurrection of our Lord."

The young people testified to experiencing the presence of Jesus, and the group grew rapidly, necessitating the firing of new Communion cups. Within a year the group had quadrupled in number and attracted young people with no Christian background. This is a sample of the spontaneous variety of eucharistic celebration today, and to us it indicates that God can use the Eucharist to impel communities of faith to participate in God's mission.[41]

Footwashing
In comparison to baptism and the Eucharist, the rite of footwashing has been of marginal importance in Christian history. According to John's Gospel, Jesus gave a strong mandate to his disciples to practice footwashing. In John 13:14, after he had washed his disciples' feet, Jesus stated, "So if I, your Lord and Master, have washed your feet, you also ought to wash one another's feet." In verse 15 he repeated, "I have set you an example, that you also should do as I have done to you." In case his disciples still missed the point, in verse 17 he restated his mandate: "If you know these things, you will be blessed if you do them." And in verse 34 he reminded his disciples of the point of it all: "Love one another. Just as I have loved you."

Nevertheless, except for some Johannine communities, the Christians of the early centuries seem to have practiced footwashing rarely, generally as a part of the baptismal liturgies.[42] Throughout the post-Reformation Christendom centuries, it was primarily churches in the Anabaptist tradition—which found Christendom's practices to be oppressively hierarchical—that practiced footwashing. In the dominant traditions, footwashing played a minor role. Once a year, on Maundy Thursday, social and religious superiors washed the feet of their inferiors. In England, monarchs washed the feet of selected subjects until the late seventeenth century, when monarchs began the more sanitary current practice of "royal

Maundy"—giving specially minted coins to selected old-age pensioners. In the Roman Catholic tradition, the pope and other leading clerics washed the feet of less senior clergy. Missing in these
practices was the reciprocity Jesus had called for—the lesser clergy did not wash the pope's feet nor do pensioners give coins to the
Queen. Nevertheless, behind the Maundy practices of church and
state is a practice mandated and instituted by Jesus himself. This
practice, diminished and often forgotten in the Christendom centuries, in post-Christendom comes alive as a missional sacrament.

This does not happen easily. In the footwashing rite, disciples
take basins and towels and wash one another's feet, either in pairs
or in sequence around a circle, each one washing the feet of the
person next to them. After each washing, there is an embrace with
a word of blessing. Such behavior is not a normal part of the life
patterns of the well-shod people in post-Christendom Europe and
North America. For this reason, some people find the footwashing rite alien and unnatural; it is behavior that lacks ordinary analogues. To many, the footwashing rite elicits deep social discomfort; it seems an invasion of personal space, a "painfully intimate"
encroachment on another.[43] Some people are ready to have Christ
serve us with humble, menial service—from a safe distance, but
they recoil at the enactment of the rite he passed on to his disciples, which makes this service reciprocal, a lifestyle for the community that observes it. And do not all members need cleansing?
The rite dramatizes with shocking acuity the need of every member for God's cleansing, which comes through the work of Christ
and also at the hands of a brother or sister. So most Christians,
by their reluctance to practice this, seem to say, This action is too
countercultural to be a practice of a helpfully inculturated gospel.

Perhaps these objectors are right, and it might be advisable
to find a substitute that is less repugnant—handwashing, for
example. Handwashing can also be meaningful for people who,
for whatever reason, cannot physically kneel to wash the feet of
others. However, we think that the sheer discomfort that many
people feel at the thought of footwashing is a reason to take it
seriously. Arguably we should practice footwashing not because
it is attractive but because it is unattractive—an act of pilgrim
faithfulness in which the church's worship has a chance to shape
the church's mission in a distinctive way. What better way do we

have to learn to be a servant community in a society of comfort and consumerism? When a church practices footwashing in its worship, it says important things:

- *Jesus' words are authoritative for its life.* The church in mission listens to Jesus' teachings even when they do not fit neatly into our culture's conventions or mores. In the case of foot-washing, the church considers that Jesus must have had good reasons to tell his disciples three times to wash each other's feet as he had washed theirs. We as a community are willing to allow Jesus to persuade us.
- *The rite of footwashing is a gift Jesus gave us, a profound ritual with which we can play his own story.* The Bible's story is upside down and odd; it assumes that God is real; and it requires those who tell it to live in light of it.[44] The act of footwash-ing is like the Bible's story as a whole. According to Samuel Wells, "This act is socially subversive . . . in its playful turning of the world upside-down."[45] As we enact this story of Jesus, we find that the story is changing us. And, to our surprise, we experience the presence of Jesus: "I am among you as one who serves" (Luke 22:27).
- *The rite of footwashing is earthy and intimate, and the church is willing to recover the earthy and intimate in its worship services.* Christ's cleansing and humble service are the sources of its life, and the church is willing to accept these not only as ideas but as enacted realities. Our feet are earthy, with their idiosyncratic cal-luses and odors. Our feet also are intimate; they are private, *our* business. But, in the rite of footwashing, we vulnerably allow a fellow Christian to enter our space, our world of earth and inti-macy, to humble themselves as we reveal ourselves, to touch our feet, washing and drying them. And then we are willing to kneel before our sister or brother, to treat their earthiness with the same gentle service with which they have treated ours.
- *The rite of footwashing affects the rest of our life, shaping it to be a life of reciprocity and service.* Our Lord and Master makes us servants who give service and are also willing to receive service from others. In Jesus' mandate of footwashing to his disciples there is not a hint of hierarchy. He is the Master; we are his disciples and each other's siblings. He washes our feet to love

us and cleanse us, and further so that we will wash the feet of each other and of the needy outsider. Christians who participate in this rite are formed by it. So also are their churches. As Mark Thiessen Nation has observed, "Churches that practice footwashing are likely to be those that are committed to the components of footwashing in their daily lives and practices."[46] Footwashing makes us participants in Christ's mission, which we receive and pass on to the world in ways that make us distinctive. The churches of post-Christendom, we believe, will rediscover footwashing as a missional sacrament.[47]

The Impact of the Sacraments
All these sacraments—baptism, Eucharist, footwashing—spill out into life. They shape the character of the community that enacts them, and they change our character as Christians who, in our work and daily lives, will be egalitarian servants who have died to self and been raised up to live as servants of other people. The sacraments will profoundly shape us as a people who are a royal priesthood, who sacrificially and joyfully mediate God to the world. But this doesn't happen magically; the sacraments require a response. As Cyprian informed the catechumens of Carthage around 250: "It is of small account to be baptized and to receive the Eucharist, unless one profits by it both in deeds and works."[48] This shaping by the rites aligns us with God's mission of comprehensive reconciliation. It also is evangelistically interesting. In the words of Daniel Bell:

If Jesus is the justice of God, then going forth to do justice can only be about inviting others to be joined to Christ. Doing justice does not entail leaving the liturgy behind and taking up a secular theory, but is a matter of extending the liturgy so that all might be gathered in the communion of charity that is possible in Christ.[49]

We Make Peace and We Pray

When Christians gather to worship God, we make peace. We do so because of the nature of the God to whom we ascribe worth—God is "the God of peace" (Rom 15:33; 16:20; etc.). We celebrate the way that God in Christ has reconciled us to God (2 Cor 5:19); and we commit ourselves anew to God's mission, which is to bring about reconciliation for all. We can do this, however, only if we ourselves are children of God and hence "peacemakers" (Matt 5:9), and this peacemaking will permeate all aspects of our lives, especially our worship. In one of the New Testament's core worship texts, Matthew 5:23-24, Jesus instructs his disciples about priorities in worship. If they are approaching the altar to offer their gift and suddenly recall that their brother or sister has something against them, they must drop their gift and move, not toward the altar and but toward the offended sibling: "first be reconciled to your brother or sister, and then come and offer your gift." Peacemaking, according to Jesus, was a prerequisite for prayer and sacrifice. Many New Testament churches expressed this peacemaking in a ritual in their gatherings for worship: the "holy kiss" or the "kiss of love" (Rom 16:16; 1 Pet 5:14). Soon the early Christians were calling this the "kiss of peace" or simply the "peace."[50]

In the pre-Christendom centuries, many churches from the very early *Didache* onward took seriously Jesus' mandate of peacemaking before prayer.[51] We find this especially in two third-century writers, the North African Bishop Cyprian of Carthage and the Syrian author of the *Didascalia Apostolorum*. In his treatise on the Lord's Prayer, Cyprian notes that "God commands us to be peacemakers . . . and of one mind in his house." This was crucially important, Cyprian believed, because the integrity of the church's worship was at stake. As Jesus had stated, God does not hear the prayers of someone who is alienated from a sibling; God is only "appeased by the prayers of a peacemaker."[52] The author of the *Didascalia* agreed. True prayer was possible only where there was peace between Christian brothers and sisters. Like Cyprian he commented, citing Jesus' Matthew 5 instruction, "If then you keep any malice against your brother, or he against you, your prayer is not heard and your Eucharist is not accepted." To enable the church's prayers and Eucharists to be acceptable to God, the *Didascalia* prescribed a conflict resolution procedure that took place weekly in the church's services.[53] At the time of the "peace," the bishop would summon members whom he knew were at enmity and "appeal to them and make peace between them."[54] The importance of the peace to the believers was indicated by the way they practiced it not only when they were in worship but also when they were in the world; on a number of occasions the last thing Christians did before they were executed in the arena was to exchange the ritual kiss of peace that they had practiced weekly in worship.[55]

In the Christendom centuries, these peacemaking practices withered. The peace greeting became marginalized in the liturgies of the churches. And the peacemaking procedures that had been possible in small assemblies, where broken relationships were hard to hide, became almost impossible in throngs. In some places the peace provided an annual opportunity to bring about reconciliation between alienated parishioners,[56] but in general the peace was practiced rarely. And where the peace was practiced, it was done in stylized ways, largely by the clerics. At the same time, the prayers of the people were truncated and professionalized. Only since 1950—beginning with the Church of South India—has the peace greeting reentered and spread through the liturgies of the Western churches at the conclusion of the prayers and as a prelude to the Eucharist.[57] Indeed, the peace's emergence has coincided with the advent of post-Christendom, in which attendance at the churches has plummeted. Some parishioners, to be sure, hate the peace, which invades their privacy, but many now participate in the peace with warmth and commitment.

Post-Christendom is the time for the peace greeting, which has so helpfully come back to life, to regain the significance that it had in pre-Christendom. It is a time for Christians to reinstate Jesus' mandate to give priority to intracommunal peacemaking. Now the peace can be not only a friendly "nice to see you here" greeting or a blessing of the other in "the peace of Christ"; it can also be an opportunity to repent and restore relationships. As such, it can be a preparation for the community's prayers and an essential part of the celebration of the Lord's Supper.

If Jesus, Cyprian, and the *Didascalia* are right, how important peacemaking is to praying and how vital it is for praying people today to stand together in unsullied agreement about what they are saying to God. People who have been reconciled to one another through the disciplined practice of peacemaking can *agree* with one another (Matt 18:15-18, and especially 18:20) and can pray with collective passion. How urgent the task of prayer is for Christians today! How mammoth the challenges are that Christians are facing in a world that is in pain! In the early third century, Tertullian was graphic in his description of the prayer topics of the Carthaginian Christians:

Prayer washes away sins, repels temptations, extinguishes persecutions, consoles the discouraged, delights the generous, accompanies travelers, calms waves, paralyzes robbers, supports the poor, rules the rich, lifts up the fallen, upholds those who are falling, maintains those who are standing. Prayer is a wall of faith, our arms and weapons that protect us on every side against our enemy.[58]

Tertullian and his fellow Christians prayed standing, combating the powers and wrestling with God; he likened prayer to doing battle with God—"massing our forces to surround God" and "doing violence to God."[59] The challenges to praying today are even bigger. Congolese, Haitian, and Zimbabwean Christians who face desperate crises; Christians in the West who face inner-city gang wars, familial crises, and financial reverses; all of us who face ecological degradation, climate change, and nuclear proliferation—all of us know that we can survive only if God is real and intervenes to liberate us and others against powers that conspire to squash shalom. So the prayers of people who are united to intercede become not truncated but expansive and passionate—the "arms and weapons that protect us."[60] And when God answers in acts of deliverance, the prayers of the people turn to thanksgiving. Praise erupts and the people exult.

The Impact of Peacemaking Prayer
As we scatter, we have new faith as we enter into our troubled worlds and speak with new freedom about what we have seen and heard. We, who have known the disciplines of prayer and peacemaking in churches that are cultures of peace, go into our lives with new hope.[61] We who have learned to make peace in our worshipping communities bring special skills to our jobs, acute intuitions of what might be possible, and a deep conviction that what we are doing is an expression of the *missio Dei*. We enter the world as what Scott Appleby has called "the new breed of religious peacemakers."[62] People whom God forms in worship to make peace and pray can dismantle walls and reconcile enemies.

We Sing
When Christians talk about worship and mission, music often figures largely in the discussion. For good reason. Music, especially music that is sung, is profoundly important to humans in all cul-

tures. It is invisible, but it has power; it affects people's bodies and stirs their emotions. When people tell stories of ecstatic experiences that they have had, they often point to experiences of music.

Even though music is a vital part of every culture, the language of music is not universal. The texts, instrumentation, and use of the voice are not consistent across cultures. Music that moves the heart of an elderly Korean Presbyterian may leave a youthful worshipper in Seoul cold.

People who are concerned about worship and mission also talk about music because music's power often divides people into competing camps. Throughout church history, churches have often been seethingly at odds about music. "Music wars" are nothing new.[63] These conflicts are a shame, because churches that are emotionally polarized about something are unlikely to be instruments of God's reconciling mission in the world. What brief observations can we—music lovers that we are—make about this vital area?

Music Serves the Liturgy
We follow Nicholas Wolterstorff's lead in asserting that worship calls for music; worship is enhanced by music. But music is not a vehicle for performance—individual, group, or instrumental—within a worship service. Music needs to be "fitting" to the specific liturgical action.[64]

Music Glorifies God and Edifies the Believing Community
The primary question about music in worship does not have to do with music's impact on the outsiders who visit us; it has to do with the way the music glorifies God and edifies the believing community. God is glorified when the community tells the story of God truly and praises God wholeheartedly. Narratival worship builds the community's identity; the community's praise energizes it for action as God's story continues.

Musical Worship that Reflects the Story Builds Up a Catholic Peoplehood
All too often our preoccupation is not with this big dimension. Discussion about worship music often centers on questions of personal preference or style. A better way to choose is to consider, first of all, the music's "fittingness."[65] How does a particular musical setting enhance a particular worship movement—confession,

lament, praise? Of course, musical style does matter. Church musicians must be sensitive to the emotional content and to the ease, by skill and comfort, with which the people can appropriate a particular musical setting in their worship.[66] Because worship music can build a catholic peoplehood, the music that the people sing and hear in worship has the potential to be intriguingly varied. Of course, there are times when it is appropriate for one style to predominate—for example, in a Taizé service, a youth service, a charismatic prayer meeting, a service in a retirement center, or a house church meeting. But for the ordinary congregation, which is catholic and multigenerational, the usual pattern will be to draw on a variety of musical idioms. A church will have a future when its music is not musically monochrome.

So the church's music must be catholic across time: it must include the classics that the Holy Spirit has inspired in the past as well as the music that composers and songwriters, similarly inspired, are writing now. Older music may be the "heart music" of older Christians, and this should make it precious to all members who love their elders. But the older Christians should recall that every generation will at times re-express older music in the idioms of the present. We can imagine how shocked Lutheran Christians were in the early eighteenth century when Bach reharmonized the old chorale tunes. Further, younger Christians will seek to write and perform new music or play with the old, crossing it over with the new, in ways that reflect their idioms and cultures. A few of these new creations will become their "heart music" and make new contributions to the church's worshipping life. And the older Christians will find these songs precious because they love the young Christians and know that the church, led by the Holy Spirit, will always be changing.

Christians Sing Their Deepest Beliefs
Adam Tice, Mennonite pastor and hymn writer, has rephrased Jesus' words like this: "Who do you sing that I am?"[67] And so we ask, Who is the Jesus that we sing about? Who is the God to whom our songs pay homage?

What we sing is especially important because sung beliefs are the resources that are most available to people when they are under pressure, in danger, or in the process of dying. So it is

crucial for Christians throughout their lives to develop a repertoire of classics to which they and their churches are constantly
adding. If Christians wish to have something strong to draw on
when they are being oppressed or persecuted or as their brains
are failing them, the songs of the faith must be stored in their
memories. How can this happen if their churches perform only
music written in the past decade?

Many song texts that come out of the heart of Christendom
present theological problems. It is imperative that the theology of
the church's songs is robust, humble, and true. Theologian George
Hendry has stated that one of the functions that he shares with
his theological colleagues is to "keep a critical eye on the songs we
sing."[68]

Theologians and writers of text and music should befriend each
other and engage in candid conversation. Do the songs we sing
declare the truth about God's character and purpose? Do they tell
the story of God's liberating metanarrative? Do they root the story
in the local terrain and climate—for example, in Australia bearing reference to "the wide land, Christmas carols about summer
and Easter songs about autumn"?[69] Do they offer praise for God's
reconciling mission in the world? Do they enable the worshippers
to lament as well as praise? Do they give as much attention to
God's justice-making, new-creation-bringing actions as they do to
God's attributes? Do they tell God's story in such a way that what
we have called in chapter 3 the "motive clause" is evident? One
simple, old refrain does just this: "Freely, freely you have received;
freely, freely give!"

We observe that though Philippians 2:6-11 has inspired
many hymn writers, practically none include the idea in verse 5:
"Let the same mind be in you that was in Christ Jesus." That is,
because God has acted in Christ by emptying himself to identify
with humans and to become their slave to the point of death,
God also calls for the singers to empty themselves and become
the slaves of others. When we celebrate that God in Christ has
laid down his life for us, do we also praise God for calling us "to
lay down our lives for one another" and to devote our worldly
goods to help "a brother or sister in need" (1 John 3:16-17)? Let's
search out the hymns and songs that do this and write new ones.
The church that sings the motive clause will participate in God's

mission by behaving toward others as God has toward us (Rom 15:7).

Everyone Participates in Song

Everyone participates in song. Thomas Troeger has expressed this well: singing in worship means people "setting our own throat, mouth, ears, and head vibrating with the sound of God's praise."[70] If the expertise of musical leaders silences the congregational voice or if the sheer volume of an organ or an amplified praise band deafens the worshippers so they cannot hear their own voices, the church's music has gone off course. It fails Paul's criterion—it does not edify the body of Christ.

Sung Prayer Unifies the Body of Christ

In a unique way, music can serve the prayer of the church locally and, as we shall see in chapter 11, globally. Michael Hawn has put it well: "Raising our voices in sung prayer with the song of Christians around the world creates a parable of oneness in Christ."[71]

The Impact of Song

The church's music has the opportunity to bring everything together. There are some churches in which worship equals singing. We think of the worship of the Taizé community, in which meditative singing lasts much longer than the short Bible readings, and we think of the worship of many charismatic churches, in which "the time of worship," which is half of the service, is made up almost entirely of music. As this chapter has indicated, this form of worship has its place; music is the servant of worship. But music is not big enough to carry the full worship life of a congregation involved in God's mission. And not everyone is able to sing or finds singing a way of expressing their heart's worship. There must be equal room for members with poetic, dramatic, and visual sensibilities to exercise their gifts.

But how precious music is! It unites the ecstatic with the call to action; it etches the story in our memory; it lives in our lives throughout the week. Sung words are irrepressible; they spring up, almost unbidden, as we are doing other things. The church's song at its best carries the message of God's mission and opens us to be its instruments.

Transformations

As we Christians gather and engage in these communal acts of worship, we are transformed. We are transformed personally: each member discovers that we have something to contribute to the church's worship and common life. And we are transformed in our inner beings. Having experienced God's holiness, we are equipped to participate in the danger and challenge that the *missio Dei* will open up to us.

We Find Our Voice

As we Christians gather in communities that are practicing multivoiced worship, we discover that we have a voice. The priest, pastor, or community leader has insight and a special role in behalf of the common good, but other people become accustomed to the reality that, through their life experiences and the work of the Holy Spirit, all of us have things to say. Everyone has a potential voice, a contribution to make. After studying the churches of the early centuries, Robin Lane Fox observed that they "made the least-expected social groups articulate."[72] Multivoiced worship, which was present in the Pauline house churches, apparently lasted on as communities grew in size. Many people took part, not just the communities' hosts or designated spiritual leaders. In the worship of the pre-Christendom Christians, the body of Christ offered its worship through words that were increasingly being prescribed in the nascent liturgies, in songs, and in responses that the members said with sizzle. As Justin reported in Rome, at the conclusion of the president's eucharistic prayer, the people "sing out their assent by saying 'Amen.'"[73] But the members also contributed in their own words—in prayers, in testimony, and in words of lament, admonition, and prophecy. This was multivoiced worship, and it developed a participatory people who possessed corporate as well as individual articulacy.

In the Christendom centuries, clericalism came to dominate. The words and gestures of priests mattered in worship, and a rapt gaze and appropriately timed physical gestures were all that were required of the laity. A clericalist approach will not flourish in post-Christendom environments. The great Dominican scholar Yves Congar kept pointing the church toward "baptismal ordination," beckoning the church to move from the presbyterial priesthood to the baptismal priesthood.[74]

The recovery of testimony is central in this. When the faith community meets—on Sunday or at some other time during the week—we go to the gathering for worship, expecting to hear the word of God spoken by any member. We go bearing the experiences of the week, very possibly equipped with testimony. "I have told the glad news of deliverance in the great congregation; see, I have not restrained my lips" (Ps 40:9). We express God's faithfulness and invite others to join us in praise (Luke 15:6, 9). Or we cry out that God has been silent and not quelled the injustice that is choking our people, and we ask others to join us in lament and intercession. The great story that the Christian church tells enables us to pray that God will act. "Your kingdom come" is the heart of our prayer life as well as the center of the Sermon on the Mount, and we look for signs of God's action.[75] Our worship encourages us and enables us to see signs of God at work in our neighborhoods and lives and world. The God of the reconciliatory mission is at work! To see this—and to give voice to it and to exult in it—increases our faith; it enables us to build up each other's faith. This worship, which gives voice to the voiceless, points the way forward for Christians of many traditions in post-Christendom.

The Impact of Multivoiced Worship
We Christians, who discover in worship that we have something to contribute, find that we also have a voice in a staff meeting at work or in a neighborhood association or in a parent-teacher meeting. When the city council is meeting, we can ask for the floor, tell of our experiences, and give voice to our insights. The multivoiced *ekklesia* functions as a political reality, and we who are trained in it learn to function articulately in other assemblies as well.[76] The culture of the church makes a difference. It influences the cultures of work and extended families, of civic organizations and political debate. It enables the voiceless—children, the disabled, and the inarticulate— to find their voice. When God through worship empowers all the believers to speak (Num 11:29), not simply the professionals who were trained in seminaries, anything can happen.

We Experience the Holy
In worship we meet God. We not only think that we meet God. In an uncanny way, we sense that God is truly present, that we are

encountering, touching, and being touched by the Holy One. We encounter God in words, but not just in words; in ideas, but not only in ideas; in music and the visual arts, but not only in music and art; in ritual acts, but not only in ritual acts; in brothers and sisters, but not only in the Christian family. God is enthroned in the praises of God's people, and the Holy Spirit moves when God's people pray: "*Veni, sancte Spiritus!*" "Come, Holy Spirit!" A divine-human encounter takes place. When we emerge to go home, we sense that we have encountered the Holy One, whose presence elicits both fascination and fear, both attraction and terror. We have had to take off our shoes, to "worship and bow down," for we have been on holy ground.

Where in the worship service does this happen for us? Classically, for Christians in the liturgical churches, this has happened in the Eucharist: "O taste and see that the Lord is good" (Ps 34:8). Christians in the Pentecostal and holiness traditions similarly appeal to tasting, but also speak of God's immediacy and action: "[We] have tasted the goodness of the word of God and the powers of the age to come" (Heb 6:4). This "tasting" often occurs at the "altar," at which people gather for prayer and healing. In many Protestant traditions, the sermon is the primary sacrament; in one church, on the Sunday after September 11, 2001, worshippers found that God spoke powerfully through the sermon, "reorienting people to God's Reign."[77] In some North American Mennonite churches, members sense that they meet God in brothers and sisters; they spend extensive time talking with others before and after the service; they also place value on sharing time, which, at its best, is a means of encountering God. Paul reports that it was in the contribution of many members that visitors to the Corinthian congregation sensed that God is "really present" (see 1 Cor 14:25). In any or all of these, week after week Christians encounter the Holy One.

Before we gather as the church, on Sunday or during the week, we pray that the worship service will glorify God and that God's power and presence will be manifested; we pray that the gifts of the Holy Spirit will be evident; we pray that we and the other members, newly envisioned and empowered by their experience of God, will emerge to participate in God's mission.

The Impact of Experiencing the Holy

So we depart from the worship service knowing that the Holy One who touched us goes with us. In Christendom years, the experience of God was often associated with grand and glorious sounds, sights, and spaces. As a teenager, the young French composer Olivier Messiaen had a life-changing experience of God's holiness while viewing the exquisite stained glass of the gothic Sainte Chapelle in Paris, and more recently Christian worship bands in many parts of the world have attempted to lead worshippers into an experience of God's holiness with sounds as overwhelming as those of the great pipe organ of La Trinité that Messiaen loved so much. In post-Christendom, we can rediscover something that the early Christians knew: God's holiness can be experienced in meetings of face-to-face communities in domestic settings. As John Koenig has reminded us, drawing on evidence in 1 Corinthians 11–14, "The mysteries of God's charismata were most regularly experienced during worship at table."[78]

Whether our services are grand or intimate, we pray en route to the assembly that God will meet us in worship. And we leave giving thanks to God for meeting us and for allowing us, in our unworthiness, to experience the "beauty of holiness" (Ps 96:9 KJV). We will realize how essential this experience is to us, especially if we are involved in the struggles that always accompany the inbreaking of God's mission. We may join the early fourth-century Donatists in knowing that "we cannot go without the Lord's Supper"[79]—or we may know that we cannot survive without the church's songs of praise or common prayer. We approach the worshipping assembly expectantly, anticipating that the God whose presence and power have encountered us will be lurking, working, and subverting the world toward comprehensive reconciliation. And we pray that God will use our humble efforts in God's mission. Orthodox theologian Ion Bria speaks of this as "the liturgy after the liturgy."[80] Elder Harris, a Pentecostal pastor from Baltimore, puts it more colloquially: "And now, church begins after we leave here."[81]

TEN

Worship Forms Mission III: Worshipping Christians in the World

We who have gathered to worship God scatter into our daily life. We go into our many worlds, seeking to ascribe worth to God in all we do, aware that the lesser gods will be parading their seductive wares. In many places in the post-Christendom West, we will encounter boredom with Christianity or antagonism to it; we also meet a curious amalgam of ignorance about Christianity and fear of it. We are likely to meet an interest in "spirituality" that may be an inarticulate way of talking about a hunger for God. And we meet many people whose preoccupations are keeping their jobs and feeding their families.

In 2008, the British Humanist Association, followed by its counterpart in the United States, placed posters on buses in various cities that read, "There's probably no God. Now stop worrying and enjoy your life." These adverts elicited some controversy, which gave the articulate atheist apologist Richard Dawkins yet another occasion to speak:

> Religious organizations have an automatic tax-free charitable status. Bishops sit in the House of Lords, automatically. Religious leaders get preferential treatment on all sorts of commissions. This campaign to put alternative slogans on London buses will make people think—and thinking is anathema to religion.[1]

Of course there is some truth in what Dawkins says. He points to the advantages that Christendom has given Christianity, which are somewhat reduced but still real. As Christianity increasingly emerges as a voluntary, nonestablished faith, many of its institutionalized supports will rightly wither. But it is unlikely that this will lead, as he implies, to Christianity's demise. As never before, Christianity is flourishing worldwide, especially where it does not have state support. And we find Dawkins's statement that "thinking is anathema to religion" to be somewhat unhumble.

How should Christians respond to Dawkins—or to other critics? Some Christians respond to the humanist challenge on the level of philosophical apologetics, proving that Christians *can* think and refute the irrefutable. But the fuller Christian response will come on other levels: witness and being.

Witness

Christians should not seek to win every argument with their conversation partners who are humanists or adherents of other religions. Christians know that we are ultimately dealing with matters that human prowess cannot decisively prove. Indeed, human prowess can get in the way. As John Howard Yoder has contended, debates about "truth claims" can be counterproductive because they revert to the level "of theocratic compulsion or of pretensions to infallibility." Instead, he proposes, "let us use the more biblical phrases 'witness' and 'proclamation' as naming forms of communication which do not coerce the hearer."[2] We don't want to use the weapons of Christendom to attempt to crush the critics of Christianity. Let us rather converse with others, listening to their experiences of Christianity (which may be horrendous) and speaking in terms of what we have heard and seen and looked at and touched (1 John 1:1). At all points, let us speak winsomely, nonviolently, allowing God to work in the hearts and heads of our friends.

Being

Christians speak to others well aware that our witness is only convincing when our words are backed up by embodiment: the embodied truth of Christians who are Christlike, living the teachings of Jesus with joyful freedom and the embodied truth of Christian communities whose common life provides evidence of God's shalom. In the apologetic writings of the pre-Christendom Christians, the authors gladly debated ideas. But what is so surprising in contrast to today's apologetics is the lengthy, detailed passages that the early apologists devoted to the Christians' ways of being: to the attitudes that irradiated their lives and to the behavioral patterns that were reflexive in the Christian communities. The early Christian apologists especially referred to the Christians' obedience to Jesus' command to love their enemies.[3] They were confident in doing this, because they knew that this was how the Christians lived and because they believed that the Christians' behavior was attractive and intriguing. Christian attitudes and actions were noncoercive but potent evidences of the gospel to which the Christians gave witness, and they invited a response. Similarly, the Anabaptists of the Reformation era saw the Christian communities as sacramental, living the distinctive life of love of neighbor and enemy, and being an embodiment of God's presence and self-revelation in the world.[4]

As we have argued in this book, the worship of God's people glorifies God and changes the worshippers in the areas of attitude and behavior. Methodist liturgical theologian Don Saliers has played an important historical role in emphasizing the connection between liturgy and ethics. Communal prayer and ritual action form people and communities who embody "affections and virtues."[5]

As Christians gather to worship God, God shapes the Christians and their communities. Saliers sees this formation in areas of "affections and virtues"; we instead will concentrate on the formation of affections (motivating emotions) and actions (behavior). Formed by worship, Christians witness by what they are and do.

Affections

Christians participate in God's mission because their churches shape their affections—the disposition of their hearts. Christians' missional participation is noticeable because they are people filled with hope, living in a world—especially in the post-Christendom West—whose people have an apprehensive disposition. Social scientist Frank Furedi has described the contemporary Western worldview as a "culture of fear": "[Western culture is] deeply pessimistic about prospects for the future. The pessimism is paralleled by an unprecedented mood of misanthropy."[6]

Many Christians share this pessimism and fearful distaste of others. We are surrounded by what Scott Bader-Saye has called "the ethic of safety." In train stations and airports, disembodied recorded voices warn us of unattended bags and packages, suspicious actions by suspicious-looking people—threats that lurk around us. The media remind us of the shakiness of investments and the instability of governmental institutions. Authority figures tempt us to be terrified. Fear can shackle us. As Bader-Saye puts it, "Fear tempts us to make safety and self-preservation our highest goals, and when we do so our moral focus becomes the protection of our lives and health."[7]

But as we gather to ascribe worth to God, God changes us. God in worship edifies us. God challenges our fear and our ethic of safety and transforms our affections. The worship of our churches or communities determines what these affections will be, and they will take on the distinctive character that our denominational traditions have schooled us to expect and experience. Steven Land contends that the worship of Pentecostal communities not only informs people, it also liberates people, especially in their "religious affections" of gratitude, compassion, and courage. These affections grow out of the worshippers' sense that "God not only has acted generally in history, but has done so in their history."[8] These affections "are not passing feelings or sensate episodes. [They] are abiding dispositions which dispose the person toward God and the neighbor in ways appropriate to their source and goal in God."[9] Gratitude, compassion, and courage—these have been the mainspring of the phenomenal worldwide growth of Pentecostal Christianity in the past century. Philip Kenneson uses a different image to deal with a similar reality. Instead of affections, he speaks of "good posture" which Christians learn in worship. "Worship," he writes, "cultivates a posture of dependence"—and also postures of humility, trust, and hope.[10]

In our contemporary culture of fear, hope is a countercultural affection. We noted in chapter 5 that communities that worship the God of the cosmic drama "remember the future" with expectancy. We Christians do not have an expectant orientation toward the future because we gloss over the injustices and violence of the present; in worship we perceive these acutely, lament them, and pray against them. But in our worship we also "behold what is to come. . . . [The church's] assemblies must be unabashedly events of shared apocalyptic vision. 'Going to church' must be a journey to the place where we will behold our destiny."[11]

The biblical metanarrative enables us to behold our destiny. So also does the church that acknowledges the irruptions of the future in the present—in our communities' countercultural lives and in the reportage we receive of God's work in the world. An example of this was in our own congregation's sharing time. In reports scattered over several months, members reported, "The neighborhood was going to decline; the school building was going to be destroyed. But God worked through residents and organizers and pastors to save the building. The city council gave in, and the building has been renovated. It now acts as an anchor of our community's life, a place of community services and affordable housing. A city councilor has moved in with his family!" The church erupts in praise. And its members step out in hope.

This vision of the *eschaton*, coupled with realized anticipations of a utopian future, revolutionizes Christians' affections.[12] Worship of this sort casts out fear; it ignites hope. It empowers us today to "take first steps, small beginning acts of undistorted justice and unperverted love in the midst of powerful ideologies."[13] We whose affections have been made hopeful by worship, and by experiences of God at work in the world that are reflected in worship, will be willing to try new things and to take risks. We will be missional, ready to incarnate our faith in ways that collaborate with God in God's mission. Affections lead to actions.

Actions

Christians participate in God's mission as an active expression of who they are. Christians' affections, formed in worship, provide the emotional, affective resource to sustain alternative ways of living and acting. Christian communities, whose virtues are formed by their worship, develop distinctive corporate lifestyles. And individual Christians will manifest unusual approaches to common problems in their workplaces that the Holy Spirit will have triggered in their minds as they have worshipped.

In post-Christendom, some Christians may engage in intellectual wrestling with spokespeople for other religions or no religion, but they will recognize that the debate will not be won or lost on the level of the intellect. Nor will it be won or lost on the level of advertising—who has the most attention-grabbing posters on the side of a bus?—or even on the level of who has the most attractive form of worship. The contest ultimately will be proved on the level of incarnation. The question we all will face is this: What does the way that we live our lives demonstrate about what is true, loving, good, and "working with the grain of the universe"?[14]

Pre-Christendom Christians embodied the gospel. They knew that it was crucial to their witness. As the third-century North African theologian Tertullian put it, the Christians win disciples because they "teach by deeds."[15] The Christian communities taught by deeds that addressed major issues of their time: they provided free burial for all members; they fed poor people, including non-Christians; in a society in which people "exposed" unwanted babies on the dumps to die of the elements and rodents, Christians rescued and raised them as their own children; in a society marked by pestilences that cut huge swathes through society, Christians at personal risk provided nursing care for Christians and non-Christians who were suffering from the plague.[16] People observed the Christians' behavior and, although they were not always attracted by their ideas, they took them seriously because of their embodied virtue. People asked questions, "Why do you. . . ?" And the Christian answer, stated by Bishop Cyprian during the great plague of 251, was that the Christians were doing in life what they have learned in worship.[17]

What might it mean for us in post-Christendom to live lives that creatively address painful, divisive issues in our societies because of what we have experienced as we have worshipped God? What might this mean for us as we realize that God is forming a people who are "an embodied witness and living invitation to God's peaceable reign in the world"?[18] What practical things, interesting things, things "more interesting" than those that occur to the conventional self-protective Westerner, might the Christian communities do to express in life what they have experienced in worship?[19] Here are some "more interesting" things that people have done:

- *Forgiving enemies*: Amish Christians in Pennsylvania, five of whose children were shot by a gunman, forgave the gunman's family, astonishing the watching world. They responded as they did because they pray the Lord's Prayer eight times a day.[20]
- *Carbon-consciousness*: Some Christians are making lifestyle decisions based on care for the earth rooted in "liturgical

asceticism," including imposing on themselves a "voluntary gas tax," the proceeds of which they pay to organizations that promote a cleaner environment and alternative modes of transportation.[21]

- *Localism*: Moving to a neighborhood and staying there—worshipping, praying, and sharing everyday life, building trust and friendships, and especially learning to know the local children.
- *Sponsoring* a member to go on a Christian Peacemaker Teams delegation to an international crisis spot.
- *Paying delinquent utility bills*: On Easter Sunday 2003, the utility companies in Freemantle, Australia, wrote to debtors informing them that, thanks to the generosity of the city's churches, their utilities had been reconnected and their debts cancelled.[22]
- *Christmas*: Letting the biblical story shape the festival, which affects spending, giving, and attention to the marginalized.[23]
- *Eating with the neighborhood*: The Missio Dei community in Minneapolis eats together twice a week—one meal indoors for community members and the other meal outdoors for passersby or neighbors, who often come from many nationalities. Both meals consist of wholesome food served on crockery dinnerware with metal cutlery. The strategy of using nondisposable crockery is intentional; it slows the meal down and leads to extended conversations. In 2008 this meal for people of many nations, within walking distance of the Republican National Convention, appeared suspicious to Homeland Security officials, who came, asked many questions, and discussed theology as they ate dinner with the community's members.[24]
- *Hospitality*: A middle-aged Christian couple invites a homeless mother and her three children to live with them, sharing their kitchen and bathroom.
- *A radical donation*: A new pastor discovers that he shares a rare blood type with a seriously ill church member and gives her one of his kidneys.[25]
- *Christians on the street*—an explicit Christian pastoral or peacemaking endeavor. "Street Pastors" in English cities or Mennonites in a Colorado university city served as a calm-

ing "third presence" when the community was threatened by riots.[26]

- *Involvement with local tasks*: Feeding hungry people, teaching English to immigrants, working in community development. Christians, concerned for the shalom of the city (Jer 29:7), volunteer, working alongside people of any background. These programs may be sponsored by a church, or they may be sponsored by a secular organization; in either case, Christians and non-Christians work side by side, sharing a common sense of belonging.
- *A single-issue campaign, local or global*: Christians get involved along with people of many backgrounds. The issues are vital, and Christians know that their involvement grows out of the vision of God's shalom-making work, which they celebrate in worship.

These forms of involvement are "more interesting" in themselves—they are unanticipated and surprising. They meet needs and build new relationships. They often involve Christians *going* onto the turf of people of other faiths or no faith, eating their food, and receiving hospitality from them. At times these forms of "more interesting" behavior can result in explicit witness. A radical English socialist, intrigued by the persistent witness of Christian peace campaigners, asked them, "What does God have to do with it?" and really wanted to know. "More interesting" behavior is important in itself because it is doing work that fits in with God's mission of all-embracing shalom-making. It also builds friendship, enables trusting conversations, and involves Christians going onto the turf—and at times into the homes—of others.

All these forms of "more interesting" behavior manifest one thing—hope. Hope is the "the most important currency a congregation has to spend."[27] Christians in worship are renewed in hope—by the big story, the little stories, and their encounter with God in sacraments, words, and brothers and sisters. The New Testament does not urge Christians to evangelize other people; it commands Christians to "give account of the hope that is within them" (1 Pet 3:15; see also Col 4:5-6). The Christians' main task is not so much faith sharing as "hope sharing."[28]

Deviance: Individual and Corporate

Worship, which Christians offer to God, transforms the affections of Christians but also their actions. It turns Christian communities into bodies of people whose common life interprets the gospel. As David Bosch put it, the church is "challenged to be God's experimental garden on earth, a fragment of the reign of God."[29] The common life of these Christians is marked by fruit-bearing, hope-filled, question-posing inventiveness. An American emerging church testified, "People become interested in God because of how we live together."[30]

Inherited churches as well as emerging churches can be question posing. When most people are scared and cynical, how can you live with such buoyancy and hope? Is it true that your church gives a tenth of its building funds to churches in Africa? Why do your members spend two evenings per week teaching English to immigrants? Why are so many of your members involved in nonprofit social organizations? Why do your members seem to be unafraid of dying? Why do so many of your church members walk or cycle to work and to the store? Why does your church have a prayer request box by its front door? Why are your denomination's leaders having conversations with the leaders of countries that our country views as enemies?

Churches of whom people ask these questions are not necessarily going to grow. As John Witvliet has commented, "Missional Christianity lives in a constant, question-asking, liminal, restless state—a kind of holy restlessness that comes from loving people and loving the gospel at the same time."[31] The liminality is expressed in a complex dialectic between going and staying. The members are constantly going onto the turf of other people—working together, being involved in common projects, eating their food, listening to their concerns.[32] Friendships often develop slowly. And it may take years before a member will sense it appropriate to invite people to come into their church's worship, which can be life-giving and formative for the Christian, but often seems strange and off-putting to the outsider.

Some Christians will choose, for Christ's sake, to stay in their local area, to nurture the relationships, to get involved in the neighborhood's concerns, and to work for its shalom. Over the years they will learn what American writer Wendell Berry calls "the difficulty and discipline of locality"—or what sixth-century monastic founder Benedict of Nursia called "stability."[33] In an age marked by restlessness and mobility, this behavior will be strange. Local people may take their odd Christian neighbors for granted.

On the other hand, as time passes, relationships with neighbors grow. Friendships develop. And the neighbors who are becoming friends ask for each other's help, offer drinks and meals, and talk about what matters. They and we share convictions and questions. And our answers flow from words and actions. We explain: we do what we do because of Jesus. Our friends may change the subject. But at times they will ask, "And what does that mean?"

Through the conversations that friendship and stability enable, some people may commit their lives to Christ and share in the Christian hope. Rather more will be cautious, suspicious of the church and fearful of the consequences of commitments. We will continue to be friends. In the words of Benedictine theologian Jeremy Hall, we will be "sacraments—an outward and visible sign to others—of desire for God, for God's reign, for the nurturing and extension of God's life and love in the world."[34] And the time may come when it is right to invite these people—new believers and curious but wary unbelievers—to the worshipping communities, inherited or emergent, in which we find life.

What will they find? When the "outsider and unbeliever" comes to our church, will they want to come again? Will they want to join in God's odd, upside-down story as we embody it? We will deal with these questions in chapters 12 and 13.

ELEVEN

Missional Worship in the Worldwide Church

When we worship God, God changes us. The God whom we worship is the God whose mission is comprehensive reconciliation. As we worship God, God's reconciling mission forms us. It gives us a sense of what our lives are for—to participate in that part of the *missio Dei* that is God's call to us. It also gives us our primary identity. To be sure, we have many identities—family, ethnic, national. But more important than any of these is our identity as members of God's family. This family is worldwide; the catholic composition of its membership anticipates the completion of God's mission. And its task grows out of its identity and its worship. Since God is God of all nations and since God's mission is reconciliation, the church and its members exist to be instruments of God's reconciliation between very different people and cultures. The God whom we worship draws us into the *missio Dei*.

The worldwide identity of Christians has always been their birthright. But now that Christians in the West are becoming marginal, that identity is clearer than it was when Western Christianity was dominant. It is clearer in post-Christendom than it was in Christendom. Our identity is immensely important; indeed, it changes everything. As the rest of this chapter will demonstrate, our worldwide identity affects the way we view ourselves and relate to others. It alters the way we worship and participate in God's mission. It transforms our political perspectives and challenges the way we watch the news and spend our money.

Civil authorities may perceive the globalization of the church as subversive. The nation-state attempts to constrict the freedom of affinity groups that come between the individual citizen and the nation, especially if they are intrinsically transnational. This is what the church of pre-Christendom was and the church of post-Christendom is. William Cavanaugh rightly notes, "Christianity produces divisions within the state body precisely because it pretends to be a body which transcends state boundaries."[1] We Christians have a prior loyalty, and a larger loyalty, than the nation-state.

Of course, as Christians we are inculturated. As we saw in chapter 6, to be inculturated means to be indigenized—for example, we may be authentically American or Canadian. But inculturation also requires that we be pilgrim, and an essential part of our being pilgrim is being cross-cultural, a part of a global family. We who are American or Canadian in so many ways, like the early Christians will "follow the customs of the country" in many ways; we will eat American food, dress like Canadians, and so on. But we are countercultural in our loyalties because we are cross-cultural, members of a "new people" who span the globe.[2]

We Worship the God of All the Nations

Christian worship glorifies God and sanctifies worshippers. We know that not all worship is true worship. The God of the Bible's story whose self-disclosure is perfect in Jesus Christ is not a territorial or tribal deity. Yahweh is God of the whole earth. Yahweh is Israel's God and God of "all the nations" (Ps 86:9). When we gather to worship God, we worship the God who does not love one part of the earth more than other parts or one people more than other peoples. We worship the God who passionately and compassionately embraces all people and all of creation.

The God we worship has a mission that Jesus embodied and was constantly alert to. In his people's enemy, a Roman centurion, Jesus could with astonishment and joy anticipate the great banquet that completes God's mission: "Many will come from east and west and will eat with Abraham and Isaac and Jacob in the kingdom of heaven" (Matt 8:11). Jesus knew that the destiny of history, in God's missional providence, is cosmic reconciliation, and his life, struggle, death, and resurrection are the decisive breakthrough toward that healing destiny. When we gather to worship God and bow before Jesus, we are ascribing worth to the God of this reconciling mission. Through our attentive, awe-filled retelling of this story, God sanctifies us.

The Worldwide Vision of the New Testament

From the earliest days of the church onward—from the resurrected Jesus in the upper room with his disciples, from the Holy Spirit's igniting them on Pentecost—there was a colossal vista and a centrifugal vision. Jesus was preparing his Jewish disciples, and the Holy Spirit was enabling them, to be his instruments in creating a cross-cultural people that embodies and agitates for God's reconciled new order.

According to the book of Acts (11:19-26), it happened spontaneously in Antioch. And the Antioch congregation, inspired in worship by the words of prophets, laid hands on Paul to make the formation of a cross-cultural people his life work (13:1-3). God, Paul announced, was "in Christ . . . reconciling the world to himself" (2 Cor 5:19). In Christ, God had broken down the wall that divided people—Jews from Gentiles, pure from impure, insiders from outsiders—and had brought into being a "new humanity" (Eph 2:14-16). This had staggering implications for systematic theology, but that was not Paul's main concern. His concern was mission. He devoted his life to providing guidance and inspiration for this cross-cultural people. In visits and letters he helped it cope with the perplexing cultural problems of being a people both diverse and united, enemies who were now siblings. Paul never ceased to be astonished at God's grace, which had brought uncircumcised and circumcised together in "new creation" (Gal 6:15). Paul's passion was to see all of humanity reconciled in the worship of Christ (Phil 2:11). He longed to see everything and everybody—in heaven and on earth—gathered up in Christ (Eph 1:10). This, Paul believed, was the goal of history, and the believers in his expanding circle celebrated it in worship.

But it was not simply a matter of worship. The communities that gathered to worship were shaped, mysteriously, into the body of Christ. Diverse though they were—Jews and Gentiles, slaves and free, male and female—they were baptized into one body, and the Holy Spirit enabled them to live as one body. In this one body they all had gifts to share. They all were incomplete, so they needed each other; and they were bound together by a common empathy. All members experienced the suffering, the joy, or the honor of the other members (1 Cor 12:7, 13, 26).

Pakisa Tshimika and Tim Lind, Mennonites from Congo and the United States, have seen this at work globally and state it with deep insight: "It is the dynamic and mutual interplay of gifts and needs that make it possible for many members to be one body."[3] Paul devoted his life to stitching this body together. The scattered communities of believers were marginal; in terms of Greco-Roman religions, the Christians were statistically insignificant. But Paul visited them with joyful commitment. He worked alongside their members to support himself financially; he talked with them late into the night, interacting with their questions and keeping them clear-sighted about their significance in God's mission (Acts 20:11). From his perspective, these tiny communities—and not the imperial court, senate, or legions—were where the action was.

Paul's best teaching device was the "collection." The churches that he had founded collected money for him to deliver to the church in Jerusalem that had many needy members. The collection gave practical expression to a radical vision of reciprocity within the body. Paul gave more attention to the collection than to any other project; it keeps recurring in his epistles (Rom 15:25-28; 1 Cor 16:1-4; 2 Cor 8–9). His vision was rooted in the "grace of our Lord Jesus Christ" (2 Cor 8:9); its aim was equality (8:13-15); and it involved both giving and receiving. Christians in Jerusalem had shared spiritual riches with believers elsewhere; they now had material needs. As each part gave generously, there was blessing and a mutual sharing of gifts. Paul implemented what Tshimika and Lind have called a "Global Gift Sharing Program," which Paul said would lead to a "harvest of . . . righteousness," to mutual enrichment, and to a body united by longing and prayer (2 Cor 9:11, 14).[4]

Other early Christian writers shared this catholic vision. Their sense of oneness despite geographic distances is amazing. Many early Christians traveled long distances; Peter wrote his first epistle from Rome to believers a thousand miles away in northern Asia Minor (1 Pet 1:1). In their travels and letters, the Christians acted in anticipation of the cosmic worship at the end of history when "a great multitude that no one could count, from every nation, from all tribes and peoples and languages, standing before the throne and before the Lamb . . . cried out in a loud voice, saying: 'Salvation belongs to our God who is seated on the throne, and to the Lamb!'" (Rev 7:9).

The multiethnic composition of many congregations prefigured this eschatological worship. The worshippers must have sensed that the new heaven and new earth, toward which they were living, were already breaking into their history (Rev 21:1).[5]

Pre-Christendom: A Worldwide Vision

Throughout the pre-Christendom centuries, many Christians held this catholic vision. Wherever they were, Christians were members one of another, which expressed itself in travel, hospitality, and long-distance letter writing. The Christians needed to stay in touch with each other! The Christian commitment to pray for the worldwide church is exemplified by Polycarp, the aged bishop of Smyrna. In 157, just before he was martyred, Polycarp briefly went into hiding, where—according to the community's account—"Day and night he did little else but pray for everyone and for all the churches scattered throughout the world."[6] When the Christians in Lyons were subjected to a pogrom in 177, their reaction was to send a long letter recounting their ordeal as "resident aliens" in Gaul to their "brothers" in Asia Minor "who have the same faith and hope in the redemption."[7] Christians were a tiny minority, but they had the sense of belonging to a universal movement that had a glorious destination.

Christendom: The Vision Narrows

As Christendom took shape in the fourth to sixth centuries, this sense of worldwide solidarity curiously changed. In a way, the Christians' sense of solidarity became broader—everyone in the local society was a Christian. But it also became narrower. If everyone was a Christian, as law and social convention now required, one's primary sense of identity was determined—not by one's faith—but by one's local affinities. Localism triumphed, and tribes and territory became the primary determinants of identity, even for Christians. A significant indicator of triumphant localism, on the part of Catholic Christians, is the ninth-century collection of Romano-German prayers dedicating swords and blessing armies and military flags. The prayers, for example, asked God that the flag "may excite terror in all enemies of the Christian people." Of course, the enemies of Christian people were often Christian people of another territory.[8] Church leaders not only wrote prayers in behalf of local interests, they also brought the just war theory to the service of localism. LeRoy Walters has studied four conflicts between Christian principalities dating from 1350 to 1650; he has concluded that "all of the theorists used just war categories to argue that their own countries had a just cause for war."[9] Local affinities—tribal, territorial—triumphed over universal membership in the body of Christ.

The Reformation made things worse. According to John Howard Yoder, the formation of churches identified with the nation constituted "the real sectarianism, in the biblical sense of unchristian divisiveness."[10] On top of this, as William Cavanaugh has argued, the advent of the secular state, as rationalized by Hobbes, Locke, and Rousseau, took things further, privatizing Christian commitment and fashioning a religion that is specifically civil—not universal—as a glue that holds together the nation state.[11]

The localizing tendencies were present long before the Enlightenment; they were embedded in the Catholic Church as well as in Protestant national churches, impeding them from being what the church is called to be—an authentically catholic, cross-cultural, transnational witness to the universal lordship of Christ. They were the product of Christendom, and their effect is nowhere more poignantly expressed than in America's second use of the atomic bomb in 1945. American pilots, given spiritual sustenance by Roman Catholic padres, flew the plane that carried "Fat Man." Since the primary target, Kokura, was cloud-covered, the Catholic airmen dropped the bomb on their secondary target, Nagasaki, whose epicenter was the Urakami cathedral, the largest cathedral in East Asia and venerable center of Japanese Catholic life, killing thousands of people, including many Catholics. "If one member suffers, all suffer together with it" (1 Cor 12:26). Why did the Catholic American airmen not share a primary, familial identity with the two orders of Catholic Japanese nuns whom they were incinerating? Because the thought never crossed their minds. Their primary body, the church catholic, was deformed, in part by the modern state of Hobbes, Locke, and Rousseau, but also by the localistic primacy of tribe and territory that was characteristic of Christendom.

Christianity Becomes Worldwide Again

In the decades that separate us from the nuclear bombings of 1945 the Christian world has changed enormously. In the 1920s, Hilaire Belloc's "The Faith is Europe and Europe is the faith" still made sense to many English people;[12] in 1945 the American airmen were probably comfortable viewing the United States as a "Christian country." Since then, as we have noted in chapter 3, things have changed dramatically. Christendom institutions and assumptions have broken down in the West, and a global church of unprecedented size and dynamism has come into being. Our missional God, using the missionary movement and the subsequent spontaneous explosion of Christianity in many countries, has transformed global Christianity. There is now a worldwide Christian movement, which is growing rapidly. According to one scholar, its statistical center is Timbuktu in Mali.[13] Some Christians who in the West are aware that Christendom is crumbling are tempted to idealize Christians in the majority world. We should resist this temptation. Christians globally are facing colossal problems, theological as well as political, and we must not glamorize them.[14]

But, for Christians throughout the world, now is the time to participate in God's mission. God calls some Christians in every society to become missionaries in the classical sense, moving out omnidirectionally, from everywhere to everywhere, in response to the requests of local Christians. But God calls all Christians to become missional, to invest their lives in the *missio Dei*, in two ways. First, God calls all Christians to work locally; everywhere there is need for the freedom and forgiveness that Jesus brings, for justice in relationships, and for the healing of bodies and the ecosystem. Second, God calls all Christians to work to realize a vision of worldwide Christian interdependence. They will rediscover what the pre-Christendom Christians knew—that to be a Christian is to participate in a family that spans miles and cultures. Andrew Walls calls this a "global church of mutual sharing."[15] In it, each Christian community brings its gifts and its needs. Each, as it meets Christians from other countries, discovers that it is meeting sisters and brothers to whom it has primary loyalty—a loyalty based on a reality more fundamental than tribe or territory.

Post-Christendom: Worldwide Interdependence
What difference does it make to belong to a worldwide church? What difference does it make to individual Christians? What difference does it make to our faith communities and their worship and mission? The differences start with relationships.

Relationships

Beyond Donor-Recipient

Since the modern missionary movement began in late Christendom, the churches of the West have often positioned themselves as donors toward the churches of the South and East. Christendom's heartland was in the industrialized West, where Christianity's numerical strength and economic wealth were concentrated. From this heartland, Christians brought the gospel to many places, bringing varied gifts—the gospel, the Bible, liturgies, education, financial subventions. New Christians have received these gifts, at times with gratitude and profound appropriation of the gifts, at times with discomfort and sullen resistance, and at times with a longing for a relationship of reciprocity and equality, not of donor-recipient. As Congolese church leader Pakisa Tshimika commented, reflecting on his childhood relationship with Western missionaries, "I learned that there were two categories of people—those who gave and those who received."[16]

It has been difficult to breach the dividing wall between donor and recipient. Disparities of many sorts have separated Western Christians from their brothers and sisters in the global South. There is the disparity of wealth. Money has always been divisive in the worldwide church.[17] A 2006 study of our own denomination—the communion of Anabaptist Christians associated with the Mennonite World Conference—revealed that 43 percent of the worldwide membership was African, but that the Africans represented less than 1 percent of the Mennonite World Conference membership's estimated wealth.[18] Our denomination is not untypical in this; other denominations tell a similar story.

Further, there is the disparity of power. The headquarters of many world communions and denominations are in the West. Churches in the West often have well-funded educational institutions; especially in North America, church buildings have elaborate educational wings and luxurious restrooms. It is not surprising that Christians in the North see churches in Africa, Asia, and Latin America as "needy," while they, perhaps with some discomfort, see themselves as "wealthy" people who ought to give more. Of course, Christians in Europe and North America are often happy to respond to appeals from the needy churches. The Westerners are comfortable in the role of having the money and being the givers; the Christians of the global South have the need and are the recipients. The relationship, according to one observer, is infantilizing.[19] It is far from the biblical vision of an interdependent worldwide body of Christ in which all members are gifted, the sharing of gifts is reciprocal, and God's mission flows in all directions.[20]

A Needy Church: North and South

In recent years, church attendance has plummeted in many parts of the North and even in the United States is sparser and less committed than conventional wisdom has assumed.[21] Furthermore, as Walls has observed, syncretism—the unquestioning interweaving of Christianity with local assumptions and lifestyle—is widespread and debilitating in the Western churches.[22] At the same time, Western Christians hear about the rapid numerical growth of Christianity in Africa. Some of us have met African Christians of radiant faith and transparent Christlikeness who have given us insight and hope. Inspired by such people and mesmerized by the statistics of church growth in the South, Westerners are tempted to engage in "an uncritical, mythological hallowing of the churches overseas."[23] It is worth recalling that, according to Ugandan theologian Emmanuel Katongole, syncretism is not a problem only in the West. In parts of Africa as well the "uncritical quest for inculturation" has contributed to a superficial cultural Christianity that ratifies rather than challenges ethnic and tribal divisions.[24]

A Gifted Church: North and South

The reality, as Paul would remind us, is more hopeful than this. In all places, by God's grace, the church is gifted as well as needy; in all places it has resources to share with Christians in other places. The needs may be greater in the North than in the South;[25] we Christians in the North are oppressed by syncretism, wealth, rationalism, and the heritage of Christian dominance that was at the heart of Christendom. But because of the way the body of Christ is formed and functions, neither the North nor the South can flourish as instruments of God's mission without the gifts offered by the other. As with the congregations that contributed to Paul's collection, Christians today have the opportunity to minister reciprocally from strengths to needs. Darrell Guder has observed, "This is perhaps the most profound reason for ecumenical exchange: the continuing mutual conversion of Christian communities in diverse cultures. Every particular culture's translation of the gospel contributes a witness that corrects, expands, and challenges all other forms of witness in the worldwide church."[26]

What is necessary is interdependence that involves a "global gift sharing."[27] The process of gift sharing and the gifts that flow back and forth can transform Christians everywhere. Our focus here—because this book deals with the West after Christendom—will be on ways that the gifts of the global church can speak to Western Christians.

Gift Sharing: Friendship

The global gift exchange is profound. It can deeply impact our worship and our mission, but it is far more than learning new songs or acquiring novel evangelistic techniques. The global gift exchange is primarily a matter of relationships. Christians who listen to each other, Christians who love each other, Christians who across many miles and cultures become friends—relationships are the soil out of which global gift sharing grows. As Tshimika and Lind so eloquently put it:

> We believe it is essential that the global church family develops a true sense of interrelatedness among the different parts of the family—parts that are separated by geography, history, culture, language, race, and many other factors. We need to become more real, more connected, to each other, not simply so we can have warm family feelings toward each other, but so we can empower our respective gifts to further God's purpose, God's vision for the world. It is through the sharing of gifts that relationships can be built, nurtured, and strengthened.[28]

How do we live toward this vision? By becoming friends who share gifts, including the gift of attentive listening. And as this happens, our worship changes.

A few suggestions indicate how this can begin.

- *Locally*: Let us learn to know Christians in churches in our own neighborhood that have a different ethnic composition from our own. In London, on Sunday there are more Christians of color than white Christians in worship services.[29] In smaller cities in England, there are vigorous black and Asian congregations. In the neighborhood where we live in a middle-sized city in Indiana, there is a plethora of African-American and Hispanic congregations, some of them pulsating with life. Even in rural parts of the United States in which industries have sprung up there are gatherings of, for example, Laotian or Ethiopian Christians. Let us learn to know them, welcome them, shop at their businesses, eat at their restaurants. Let us invite their leaders into local ministers groups. Let us listen to their stories and needs. What's life like for them? What are their concerns, their joys? Let's attend their services, enjoy their hospitality, eat their food, receive their blessings. Out of gift exchange comes friendship—locally.

- *When traveling*: Let us visit Christians and worship with them. On vacation, even if you don't know the local language, go to church. In Egypt, worship with the Copts (or other Christian churches) as well as photograph the pyramids. A friend of ours was in Texas on Sunday and attended the nearest church, which happened to be a Hispanic church. The members were celebrating Communion. Our friend reported, "I didn't understand a word, but I haven't been so moved in worship in years."

- *Attending an international denominational or interdenominational gathering*: Let us attend an assembly of the Mennonite World Conference or the Lutheran World Federation. Or let us participate in an international gathering at Taizé, of a renewal movement such as Focolare or YWAM. Or let us visit believers of another Christian tradition to learn from them. In 1997 the Syrian Orthodox Church invited leaders of the North American Mennonites to visit Syria to join in their celebration of Easter and to grow in friendship. The Mennonite visitors encountered things that were new to them: elaborate processions and vestments; people standing through lengthy services; continuous chanting; icons, bells, candles, incense; powerful no-notes preaching, the bishop holding the cross in one hand and the staff in the other; benedictions that the people drank in as blessings. Reflecting on their experiences afterward, the Mennonites knew that they would not import Syrian practices wholesale. But they were deeply impressed and challenged to imagine ways of learning from what they had seen and heard. The posture, gestures, and use of color and movement of the Syrian worshippers had taught them much. Above all, the power of the Eucharist had changed them and would affect the worship of their home congregations.[30]

- *Volunteering for an assignment*, rebuilding houses and churches after a hurricane and so on.
- *Being informed*: There are innumerable sources of information—denominations and mission societies have publications and websites. Christian papers, periodicals, and websites add much more. Congregations can appoint a "connector" whose task is to be alert to global concerns and to report these for congregational prayers. If worshippers hear Zimbabwe mentioned week after week, they will take notice—and will be changed.
- *Being hospitable*: The New Testament abounds in admonitions to offer hospitality—to receive guests, who may to our surprise be angels (Heb 13:2)—and also to accept hospitality, to be received as guests. Christine Pohl has observed that hospitality is "a potent force of social witness and resistance."[31] Let us host international students in our homes for coffee or a meal, for a Bible study group, or to spend the Christmas holidays. Opportunities for this occur especially in cities where there are universities and colleges. Visitors of other cultures are involved in business and industry across Canada and the United States; hospitable gestures to non-Christians—to "the stranger who is our neighbor"—have led to conversions and to remarkable breakthroughs for the global Christian movement.[32]
- *Listening to our international visitors*: Let's ask them questions. What are their concerns? How do they pray? How do they worship? If they are Christians, what problems are their churches facing? Where have they seen God at work? Let's give them the platform—the opportunity to share their stories with the entire congregation. Tanzanian theologian Laurenti Magesa has observed that hospitality— "open hearted sharing"—is at the ethical heart of traditional African religion. "The purpose of hospitality is to enhance life in all its dimensions."[33]

All these steps strengthen relationships. Even if some of these can remain superficial, they can also energize deep affinities and friendships that result in the exchange of emails, presents, and visits. The congregations of people involved in these exchanges may not be large, but their members have a huge vision in the tradition of Polycarp and the pre-Christendom Christians. How puny by comparison is the vision of many Western churches—some of them highly "successful"—whose outlooks are tribal and territorial.

Gift Sharing: Structures
Global Organizations
The global structures of Christian traditions vary markedly. Some great world communions have assemblies in which only clerics participate; lay people may assemble for meetings of specialist groupings such as International Fellowship of Evangelical Students or Pax Christi. But there are many worldwide families whose meetings are attended by ordinary Christians as well as specialists, by lay people as well as clergy. It is important for churches to devote administrative structure and staffing to foster the development of relationships between churches of differing countries. It is important for members to make financial sacrifices to attend these meetings and to enable other Christians, who have less wealth, to attend as well. The heart of global gift sharing is relational; it grows out of eating and praying together, listening to each other's experiences and concerns—simply being together. With deepening relationships comes a sense of solidarity and accountability. Structures that facilitate gift sharing culminate in friendship.

Partnerships
Since the 1960s, a great deal of thought and effort has gone into the development of partnerships between Christians in various parts of the world. Some of these are sponsored by denominations. Others have sprung up spontaneously, as a result of the relationships and friendships that we have already mentioned. Some of the partnerships link a diocese in the West with a diocese in the global South, or clusters of congregations North and South. Occasionally, there are partnerships between sister congregations. And at times, a Western congregation commits itself to a particular ministry in another culture. We will provide four stories, all of which illustrate

global gift sharing's potential to pose questions, convert lives, and change worship patterns for post-Christendom Christians. We recognize that these are testimonies of Westerners; the stories as told by Southern Christians might well have very different accents.

Support of a Ministry: Pennsylvania–Uganda: Scott Bader-Saye has reflected on the experience of his Episcopal church's relationship with a ministry to pygmies in Uganda. The pygmies' lives have been uprooted by economic development, and they have become refugees who are economically impoverished and, in the view of other Ugandans, are the "least of the least." According to Bader-Saye,

> What is most remarkable to those of us who assist in this ministry is the deep joy displayed by the Ugandans with whom we have contact. Despite living in a region that suffers from high mortality rates and the ever present danger of disease, starvation, and civil unrest, these Ugandans could not be rightly described as living in fear. One evening, as a group of us from the church reflected on the remarkable peacefulness and good-naturedness of our Ugandan friends, we began to wonder whether their expectations of life were so much lower that they were not anxious about what might happen to them next. But we decided it was truer to say that they simply refused to have expectations about what life owed them. . . . They are somehow able to be grateful for every offering without being offended or angry that there is not more. Everything that comes their way is a gift from God; they are not burdened by a sense of entitlement. God does not owe them something, and even in the midst of devastating circumstances, they find reason to give God thanks.[34]

This encounter, between Christians from Pennsylvania and their Ugandan friends led the Americans to ask profound questions that may, by God's grace, change their lives and give them those nonquantifiable commodities that are so scarce in the United States: contentment, thanksgiving, and joy.

Reciprocal Friendship Between Congregations: United Kingdom–Congo: Alison Phelps, a pastoral worker in a medium-sized Baptist church in Chapeltown, an inner-city part of Leeds, England, reports:

Harehills Lane Baptist Church in Leeds has been enriched, some-times reluctantly, by a gradually growing cultural diversity since the 1950s. The testimony of one 14-year-old asylum seeker from Uvira, eastern Democratic Republic of Congo, galvanized the congregation to a deeper level of gift sharing involvement. At the beginning of the 1998 war, which resulted in over five million deaths, rebel soldiers had shot Wilondja's father, a Baptist pastor, along with most of his family. The church building was also destroyed. The Leeds congrega-tion was so moved by this story, and by Wilondja's confidence and joy in praying and solo singing in morning worship that there was a real warmth about wanting to make a practical response as part of developing friendship.

Enough money was raised in a year to pay for the materials for reconstructing the church building, and then the Leeds fellowship was invited to visit Uvira to celebrate the completion. The welcome and hospitality was overwhelming and the team returned with pro-found respect for the Uviran church's faith in the power of prayer and for the creative energy of their choirs, as well as bubbling with ideas about continuing this covenant partnership.

Three leaders from Uvira visited Leeds the following year, preached and prayed, observed and learnt that material wealth does not necessarily bring happiness and that the independence of our elderly can lead to loneliness. The next trip to Uvira was threatened by news of further fighting in the Congo, but was life-changing for the three who went. Listening to the experiences of war, witness-ing the power of education, sharing in generous worship, hearing the longings of brothers and sisters and exchanging presents were pivotal events.

Only after four years of relationship did the Leeds church learn that the dying pastor had prophesied that God would not abandon his people in Uvira and that the latter glory would exceed the for-mer. This put a different perspective on all the robust discussions in Leeds about our partnership concerning trust, paternalism, mis-understanding, and compassion fatigue. Ongoing debate includes discerning best ways to continue the relationship in the light of global warming and preparing young people in both cultures for the future of the church.[35]

Reciprocal Friendship Between Congregations: Oregon–Colombia: Connections between churches in the North and South can also transform the missional involvements of Christians in the North. Rod Stafford, pastor of the two-hundred-plus member Portland Mennonite Church, on the Pacific Coast, reflects on the impact of the church's partnership with a congregation in Colombia:

The inevitable tendency in all of us is to narrow our vision down to what is right in front of us—kids to soccer and dinner to fix, bills to pay, the project due at work. Very quickly we lose sight of the breadth and width of Christ's world-changing gospel.

In 2002, Portland Mennonite Church (PMC) was invited by the Mennonite Church in Colombia to form a sister-church relationship. The purpose was fraternal (visiting, praying, and supporting each other). It was also, frankly, strategic and political. Colombian Christians recognize that the United States, through Plan Colombia, exerts enormous influence in their country. They have little say in American policy, but their brothers and sisters in the north have the capacity to participate in the political system. Sister-churches agree to respond together to "the wounds, fear and brokenness that injustice and conflict engender."

Since 2003, PMC has partnered with a congregation in the small farming community of Anolaima. Pastors of the congregations have exchanged visits, letters are written monthly, and prayer concerns are shared in worship. At the request of the Anolaima church, a PMC member has spent two years there teaching English as a second language. PMC has also become much more politically active in response to news and concerns shared by the Colombian church. The church has hosted speakers, written politicians and legislators in both the U.S. and Colombia, and participated in the "Days of Prayer and Action." When word came that a leader of Justapaz, a Christian human rights organization that we were involved in, was in danger of being arrested, members of the congregation prayed for him and sent large numbers of emails to Colombian government agencies as well as to the U.S. State Department. Our Colombian brother was not arrested!

This relationship has widened our vision and shaped our worship. Through news shared and prayers offered, our congregation is directly connected to the church of Christ that transcends national borders. Through political action and personal service, our worship is connected to God's work of shalom-building in the world.

We are sister-churches. We don't look alike, act alike, or sound alike, but we are being made one by the power of Christ's reconciling Spirit. Thanks be to God![36]

Reciprocity Between a Congregation and a College: Indiana–Benin: A moderate-sized Mennonite church in Indiana has established a partnership with Benin Bible Institute, which trains men and women for ministry in West African countries. We heard that this relationship had led to reciprocal visits that had profoundly changed the life of the Indiana congregation. We interviewed its two pastors and an interested member, and the following story emerged.

For some time, the lead pastor sensed that "we needed a global connection." So the Indiana congregation built on relationships already present in the church; some of its members had done short- and long-term assignments in Benin. Of course, distance, costs, and language were barriers, but over the past five years they have managed annual alternating exchange visits lasting from ten to twenty-eight days. Hosting in homes, talking long over shared meals, exploring local neighborhoods in both countries—these have enabled deep friendships to grow.

How has this partnership affected the American church? As the African guests taught their hosts new songs, gave testimonies, served Communion, blessed their children, and led strong prayers, the worshipping church realized they had embarked on an exciting journey. The excitement was intensified when the Americans visited the Beninese congregations. They commented to each other, "The African worship is so social! Why do they all pray at once? Why do their preachers shout?" They noticed how, persistent in prayer, the Africans believed they would see God act in specific ways. Long services, multiple sermons, dancing, praising, offering—sometimes it all seemed over the top. What could the Americans learn from all this?

They told us that, after several years of the exchange, many members of the congregation had taken some steps: "We are taking the risk to ask hard questions, to expect God will change us, to seek a greater fervor in our faith, to devote more time to prayer and praise, to be more generous in giving. Studying the Bible together, we have discovered how differently Americans and Africans can understand a particular Gospel story or passage, and the way it might affect our worship and life together. This is both provocative and humbling. We are learning joy in worship, giving more time and energy to praising and thanking God."

The Americans have seen that in their worship they are being changed. They are more alert to God's character and concerns. God is engaged in something much bigger than their local program. The Africans have challenged them: "Why do you Christians chit-chat so much and not speak more openly about spiritual matters? Why do you not engage more directly with your neighbors about the gospel?" Checkbooks have opened as global economic inequities have taken on relational dimensions. As the Beninese have exposed the Americans to an African worldview, in which God confronts and overcomes evil, they have challenged the Americans to pray more fervently and persistently. Americans, used to being in control, see that in cross-cultural engagement they must become like children: they have to ask questions; they don't know the "rules"; they're not in control of things. God is the one who can do what needs to be done.

The Africans, according to our interviewees, reported that they have grown too. They have grown in their understanding of the American Christians' quieter spirituality, which they can see is necessary in the pressurized North American culture. They particularly value the American church's peace tradition and have wanted to ponder, talk about, and dwell on the practical implications of the centrality of peace to the gospel. There is inquisitiveness and hunger for this perspective, which seems to have immediate relevance to their situation.

Common threads also emerged. According to an American church member, both groups see the need to "differentiate between practices growing out of culture and those inspired by faith," the vital role of personal experience, and the importance of listening to each other. And Africans and Americans expressed gratitude for the partnership, which was deepening and changing them all in mutuality and friendship.[37]

All these partnerships have been transformative. We do not know how the relationship with the Ugandan Christians changed the worship of their friends in Pennsylvania. We do know some ways in which the Congolese, Colombians, and Beninese have changed their partners in England, Oregon, and Indiana. But in all cases, whatever changes take place in worship are not cherry-picking; they are not adding a new song or two that are "kinda cool"; nor are they making changes that, in typical imperialist fashion, are a new import of exotica. No, changes are the product of friendship that is deeply mutual—and that allows for direct talk and hard questions. What are your struggles? Where do you find spiritual resources? How do you build community? How do you follow Jesus in your culture?

In all four places—Pennsylvania, England, Oregon, and Indiana—the main challenge is inculturating the gospel faithfully. Canadian Mennonite pastor Harold Hildebrand Schlegel has likened it to riding a bicycle that functions well as long as it is in balance and moving forward. But if it tilts too much toward indigenization on the one hand or an unflexible pilgrim approach on the other, or if it stops moving, it gets in trouble. It's so easy in our church's life and worship to fall off the bicycle.[38] This is the issue everywhere, How does the church develop "practices that can make possible the kind of discriminating judgments about the church's relation to the social orders in which it finds itself"?[39] To a much greater degree than we have realized in the West—whether in Christendom or in post-Christendom—the answer may be the worldwide church. As Andrew Kirk has observed, after long experience in many countries: "If different regional churches can listen to one another, there is much more chance of preventing either the domestication (too local) or the abstraction (too general) of the gospel."[40]

A relationship of global gift exchange enables this kind of interchange to take place. Together we are a world communion. As we receive and give, we are built up. Surprising things can happen. Tshimika and Lind "see a consultant from Congo advising a congregation's building committee in the US."[41] We in the West may need the input of the worldwide church more than we realize. Students of church history have often commented that renewal of the church tends to come not from the center but from the margins. But, in post-Christendom, the question is, Where are the margins? Perhaps in a church that is under pressure in many places—in the West from consumerism and spiritual asphyxiation, in parts of the South from civil war and uncritical inculturation[42]—many of us are on the margins, and God can use us to renew each other, including each other's worship life.

Changes in Worship and Mission

As we become a global family of faith, we become accustomed to taking part in an interdependent church in which there is global

gift giving. All parties will change. Not completely, of course. Canadian churches will remain recognizably Canadian; authentic inculturation in Canada requires this. But churches in every place will
be affected by their relationships with Christians elsewhere. The
result will be a globe-spanning pattern of Christian worship and
witness that is infinitely varied and always shifting. Congregations
will differ, not only because of their denominational traditions,
but also on the basis of their socioeconomic and cultural settings.
Some churches will move more rapidly than others to appropriate
insights from their global partners. The results will be diverse, in
every country.

Paul Bradshaw has argued that the worship of the pre-Christendom churches was marked by variety, not uniformity. With the advent
of Christendom, a process of "homogenization" set in, in which the
ecclesiastical authorities (in collaboration with imperial authorities)
squashed local variations in liturgical practice. Bradshaw has advocated "a much greater increase in variety of liturgical practice . . . a
valuing of a deep diversity and pluriformity in liturgical theology and
practice."[43] This is exciting. Thanks to the globalization of Christianity
and the advent of the Pentecostal movement, what C. Michael Hawn
has called "liturgical plurality" is now a reality. There is no single right
way to worship; but in every place there must be a dialogue between
the local cultures and the cross-cultural dimensions of the faith that
will lead to various forms of synthesis. The syntheses are significant,
for worship that reflects only one culture misses the opportunity to
prefigure the cosmic reconciliation that is the goal of God's mission;
it makes it hard for the worshippers to glimpse heavenly worship in
which people from every tribe and territory are worshipping God and
the Lamb.[44]

Of course every church that receives worship materials and practices as gifts from their global partners must engage in discernment.
Hawn proposes criteria. We find these helpful because he is alert to
two dangers: some gifts might not have "cross-cultural potential"
and might never be at home in the West, and some Westerners may
appropriate the gifts thoughtlessly, stereotyping and denigrating
the sending culture.[45] When Christians are sensitive to these issues,
we believe that an interdependent worldwide church opens wonderful opportunities for the worship and mission of Christians in the
post-Christendom West. It could be that, as Christians engage in a

global gift exchange, Christian worship will be richer in the twenty-first century than it has been at any point in the church's history.

Gifts for Worship

Worldwide Christianity is phenomenally varied. A selection of areas in which worldwide Christians can offer gifts to the worship of the post-Christendom West includes:

Prayer

Christians in the global South offer new possibilities for how we pray. Some of them tell stories of praying fervently in times of crisis: after the attacks on New York and Washington on September 11, 2001, Congolese Mennonites engaged in all-night prayer vigils. Christians in Indonesia whom we know gather every morning at 5:30 for prayer. Many Christians also pray expectantly in preparation for their weekly worship services; inspired by them, on Sundays we could get up earlier to pray instead of sleeping in. As we walk or drive to church, we can pray that our worship will glorify God and that God's Spirit will move to sanctify us as disciples of Jesus. Our global siblings can remind us, backed by endless anecdotal evidence, that expectancy in prayer transforms worship and the worshippers. Worldwide, Christians offer us a range of prayer practices: strict adherence to a prayer book; fervent prayer through singing; free, simultaneous, vocalized prayer. Some of these practices may strike us as disorderly, but in the revivalist and Pentecostal traditions in the West, they are not strange.

In the Anabaptist tradition there is an interesting analogue. In 1576 several ministers of the established (Lutheran) church in Strasbourg furtively infiltrated a secretive Anabaptist gathering in a forest near the city. One of the ministers, Elias Schad, left an account of the Anabaptist's worship. He did not like what he found, especially the Anabaptists' way of praying:

> Thereupon they scattered, all knelt, each usually before an oak tree as if he were worshipping it. The prayer lasted at least a good fifteen minutes, perhaps closer to thirty. There was a great audible murmuring as if a nest of hornets were swarming; they waved their arms and beat their breasts almost like priests when they read the mass. And although I managed to get close to some of them and

listened intently beside or behind them, I was unable to make out a single word, much less a sentence; for they never raised their heads and they sighed and groaned and moaned like a tired old horse pulling a cart or wagon.[46]

Schad's account is hostile. But he uncovered—on the extralegal margins of Christendom—a prayer practice that is similar to practices of Christians today in many parts of the global South. Of course, there are questions of inculturation here; modes of prayer must to some extent reflect the underlying cultures of their societies. But could it also be that Christians who cannot control their lives, whose economic conditions are dire, whose lives are endangered by illness or war or persecution will find that orderly, reverential, prescribed prayers are not enough? The gifts of global Christians may enable us to pray with new passion, "Out of the depths I *cry* to you" (Ps 130:1, our italics).

Music
Musical gift exchange has been going on for a long time. Western Christians, visiting a church in, say, Taiwan or India, are often startled to find themselves surrounded by fervent singing of "My Jesus, I Love Thee" or one of any number of nineteenth-century hymns—the legacy of the Western missionary movement. By now such hymns and songs are deeply embedded in the piety of Christians in many cultures. Westerners cannot say, "Those are our songs. You shouldn't be singing Western hymns." Many old hymns have come to belong to all of us, globally.

But transferring worship music from one culture to another calls for careful thought and sensitivity. When the mission department of a church in the Netherlands sent a musician to Zambia to collect hymns used by churches in Africa, they said, "We felt it would be a good way to introduce more liveliness and diversity into our worship." Searching for liveliness and diversity is not a valid reason to import worship songs cross-culturally.

Hawn has suggested a better principle: learning and incorporating a worship song cross-culturally makes visible and present those who have otherwise been invisible, ignored, or forgotten.[47] An example comes to mind. When two Zimbabwean Christians visited our church in Indiana, they were asked to bring a testimony or a message. They brought us a song that captured for them the character of their church back home: *"Som'landela, som'landel'u-Jesu"* ("We Will Follow, We Will Follow Jesus"). We learned the song on the spot, and it has become precious to us.[48] As we use this Zulu song in our own worship, we remember our two Zimbabwean brothers and the churches they represent, and we too pledge ourselves to follow Jesus anew.

Cross-cultural borrowing can increase empathy. In 1930 Dietrich Bonhoeffer worshipped with African Americans in New York City and was deeply impressed with the marginalization and pain of their slave history. Five years later, back in Germany, he taught the spirituals to the young seminarians of the Confessing Church at Finkenwalde. As they sang those haunting cries of oppressed blacks in America, the seminarians' eyes were opened to the plight of the Jewish people in their own country, who were experiencing horrific exclusion and persecution heading toward the Holocaust. The seminarians were energized to pray and to take risks to help their Jewish neighbors.[49]

Learning and borrowing music across cultures can be immensely enriching. But it requires dealing with an important question: How do we evaluate when borrowing is valuable or when it might be inappropriate or even an act of theft? Six church musicians help us to answer this question.

John Bell, hymnwriter of the Iona Community in Scotland, has been a pioneer in promoting global music and teaching Westerners how to appropriate it. An early example of his sensitivity is the 1991 selection of songs *Sent by the Lord: Songs of the World Church*.[50] Many are from Central and South America. Published on the five-hundredth anniversary of Christopher Columbus's "discovery" of the Americas, these songs "may be used as an antidote to the triumphalism which western countries may be tempted to associate with the centenary."[51] These are songs of ordinary Christian people, and they speak directly to the experience of Christians across many cultures. These are appropriate for worship. Common song creates bonding.

Ross Langmead, an Australian Baptist missiologist, has not only thought carefully about appropriating songs of other cultures; he has also written inculturated Australian songs. He argues that "music in worship is actually just one example of the challenge of multiculturalism." This is important because it reflects "the growing sense that we are different but fundamentally united in Jesus Christ."[52]

Michael Hawn, an American Baptist theologian of music in worship, has been particularly aware of the vitality and unity that come to Christians when they sing together across cultural boundaries. He uses the metaphor of polyrhythm, which "suggests an energy of competing rhythms that come together in an aural mosaic . . . [in which] uniqueness is valued and the energy of each perspective contributes to the wholeness of the entire community."[53] The point is not to synthesize these artificially, but to allow dissimilar contributions from the worldwide church to stand side by side as they make an integrated whole. His seven criteria to evaluate whether authentic "liturgical plurality" is happening are worth pondering.[54]

Mary Oyer, a Mennonite church musician and ethnomusicologist, has had extensive experience in Africa and Asia. From her perspective, the most urgent consideration when we consider borrowing a song from another culture is that the borrowed song's function is not to be "novel, exciting or entertaining." Rather it is to be appropriate in serving the particular point in the worship. "Its function must be clear. That is very important."[55]

John Witvliet, a Reformed worship theologian, observes that American contemporary worship music is washing over churches in other cultures.[56] And he wonders whether the wide adoption of this Western music truly unifies the body of Christ, or is it simply another Western takeover? To Witvliet, this doesn't look like inculturation; it looks more like old-fashioned imperialism. The principles of sensitivity and functionality somehow get lost. Global music gift sharing should produce as much music coming from the South and the East as music going the other way. It is good if a church is aware of its global connections and wants to expand its musical repertoire. But it is critical how a church uses the global songs. Instead of plugging them in as "special music," worship leaders do better to incorporate them as short, musical responses.[57]

In summary, incorporating global song cross-culturally should not be an act of imperialism, plunder, or theft. It should create genuine enrichment in a mutually interdependent body of Christ.[58] Global song-sharing helps to anticipate the great song around God's throne (Rev 7:9-10) when all tribes and peoples and tongues will cry out, "Salvation belongs to our God . . . and to the Lamb!"

Visuals

The Salvadoran folk art of painted crosses has become widely familiar. The designs are simple with bright colors and include pictures of rural life. Many were painted during a wartime of great poverty and pain. Some crosses picture the face of Christ with community scenes revealing hope and resurrection in the face of suffering. These crosses have become part of the fabric of worship, revealing the themes of God and Christ involved in the lives and struggles of the people.

Western Christians have imported Salvadoran crosses for use in their churches and chapels. The John Bunyan Baptist Church in Cowley, on the edge of Oxford, England, has done something more interesting. Its members painted a large Salvadoran-type cross of their own, depicting local scenes and figures, factories, parks, shops, and their own church building. Their Salvadoran-Cowley cross hangs prominently in the church. This, a sample of the "gift giving" from Salvador to Oxford, reminds the people of their history and encourages them to hope.

Hunger cloths or hunger veils are curtains that churches in the West have used since the tenth century to veil altars during Lent. Painted or embroidered on the cloths are depictions of a cycle of stories, usually taken from the Gospels. These large cloth banners obscured the bare Lenten altar and taught people the Lenten Gospel stories. Some churches today have revived this form of liturgical art and employ the cloths as guides for teaching, raising consciousness, and praying. Wonderful examples have forged links between Western and majority world Christians.[59]

Other forms of visual gift sharing include art works in which Christian artists from many countries depict Jesus in the skin tones, clothing, and settings of their own cultures. A recent book containing paintings by artists from five Asian countries reminds Western Christians that Jesus' incarnation transcends tribe and territory, as does his body, the church.[60] Jesus is Lord of all. At times we return to the paintings of the seventeenth-century Dutch painter, Rembrandt, which so movingly emphasize that Jesus was a Jew. And from the Orthodox tradition come icons, which bring us all a vision of Christ's glory and victory that is timeless, almost supracultural, and therefore universally helpful in prayer.

Offering
In many parts of the world, the people offer their gifts to God with joy and dancing. This is true of financial gifts; it is also true of the Communion elements, which some churches dance forward, holding the gifts high. A similar mood of joyful giving is present in the offerings of some African-American Christians in the United States, who bring their offerings forward to the beat of exuberant music and who receive an anointing with oil from their ministers. These practices can come as gifts to Anglo-Western Christians whose financial offerings are usually private and too often accompanied by funereal music. But then, in wealthy cultures it is sad to part with money!

Affections
Christians in many parts of the world are poor—and joyful. As an Australian friend of ours who worshipped regularly with an Anglican parish in Alexandra Township, South Africa, reported to us, "I learned what joy really was—from them." The response of Westerners can be to spend more time giving God thanks and praise, and discovering that the by-product of thanks and praise is joy.

Gifts for Mission
The non-Western church can offer gifts to Western Christians who are stymied in the area of mission. These gifts include the following:

Articulacy
Many African Christians model a form of discourse in which it is not artificial and cripplingly embarrassing to refer to God. Their gift to us is their example, but also their questions, "Why do you find it so difficult to talk about God? What inhibits you?" They remind us that a thankful spirit often elicits explicit grateful references to God, and vice versa.

Languages
Christians in many societies—especially African Christians—speak many languages. They know that the gospel must be incarnated, but it must also be spoken in the language native to the hearer. In the West, many of us have lived in monolingual settings. We can live our entire life without speaking another language until

we suddenly discover that we have neighbors—either new arrivals or neighbors who have been there for many years—who speak and pray in another language. A gift to us Westerners from worldwide Christians can be the reminder that it is important to learn another language and to incorporate words of another language in our services. Some years ago, Anglican whites in New Zealand (Pakehas) began using Maori in their Eucharists, beginning with the Lord's Prayer. A New Zealand Prayer Book, with its parallel columns in the two languages, is the result, as well as congregations that are no longer monocultural.[61] In the United States, Christians in many areas are discovering that it is important to learn Spanish. In the United States, as in New Zealand, the Lord's Prayer leads the way.

Local Mission
Christian brothers and sisters from the majority world often astonish us by their expectation that they will find ways to be involved in God's mission locally. They are surprised when we, no doubt reflecting a Christendom heritage, assume that mission will happen somewhere else, performed by specialists. Their gift to Westerners can be to ask us, Why do we not look for God's action near at hand? If we're not seeing God's work in our surroundings, is it because we are not praying to see it? Do we conceive of our jobs in light of God's multidimensional reconciling mission? Further, how do we view our localities? Within a mile radius of the homes of many Westerners there is a wide diversity of people and multilayered need. If we listen for God's call, we can become involved in mission locally. We can get involved in common causes with others. We can accept invitations to their clubs or homes. After all, as Andrew Walls reminds us, the "fundamental missionary experience is to live on terms set by others."[62]

Receiving Missionaries from the South
Missionaries are increasingly coming to the North, either as economic migrants who are habitual evangelists or as emissaries specifically sent by churches in the global South. They can be a gift to us. The additional fragmentation that their churches may bring is a small price to pay for the encouragement they provide in post-Christendom situations in which many people view practicing Christians as eccentrics or fanatics. To the new missionaries from the South, our invitation should be, Welcome, be our neighbors,

and join in the work of God's mission.[63] If the missionaries from the South want to be effective evangelists among the people of the post-Christendom West, they will do what all missionaries must do—inculturate themselves in the cultures of their neighbors, listen to their concerns, and eat their food. They may also need to stifle triumphalistic Christendom assumptions they learned from their Western missionary teachers.

Gift Sharing

Our brothers and sisters in the worldwide church have much to give us. As Andrew Kirk has commented, "How hard it is for us to receive."[64] And yet a gift that the worldwide Christian family can give us is an invitation to come to them—as short-term visitors to share life with them; as people who bring a special competence in psychology or youth work or the theology and practice of peacemaking. There will continue to be need for some Westerners—like Don and Dorothy, whom we met in chapter 2—to go as long-term missional partners in other societies, at times taking on the citizenship of those societies. Whatever form this reciprocal visiting may take, it will be easier for Westerners to listen to our brothers and sisters if we sit in their homes, eat their food, and enter into their worship. Gift sharing must go both ways.

Worldwide Christianity: A Transcultural Community

The challenges of becoming a worldwide church will never be fully met, but working to meet them can be intensely rewarding. Learning to see the history of the church as a global story; studying the Bible together as Christians of many cultures in which a "reading from the South" is prominent; and engaging in collaborative writing projects dealing with global Christian issues—all these lead to liberating breakthroughs for the global Christian movement. The most difficult task may be for the theologians in the West to take seriously the theologies emanating from African and Asian theologians. Thirty years ago, Kenyan theologian John Mbiti despairingly wrote of Western theologians and theological educators:

> It is utterly scandalous for so many Christian scholars in older Christendom to know so much about heretical movements in the second and third centuries, when so few of them know anything

about Christian movements in areas of the younger churches. We feel deeply affronted and wonder whether it is more meaningful theologically to have academic fellowship with heretics long dead than with the living brethren of the Church today in the so-called Third World.[65]

Theological educators are important, for they train Western pastors who become vision setters and gatekeepers for their congregations. Ancient heresies are perennial and need to be addressed. But seminaries benefit everybody when their teachers address the modern heresies, dominant in the West, of rationalism, relativism, and the marginalization of Jesus. Theological educators serve the church when they broaden their "ecclesiastical cartography," when they explore the theological insights that come from non-Western theologians, and when they and their students read the Bible "through the eyes of another."[66] In post-Christendom, theological educators must prepare their students to be pilgrim people whose calling it is to equip their congregations to live as resident aliens. A decisive dimension of the Christians' pilgrim distinctiveness is their cross-cultural identity rooted in the "wall-breaching" work of Jesus Christ (Eph 2:14).

Increasingly, Western theologians will open their own eyes—and the eyes of their students—to the riches of the writings of non-Western theologians. As a result, we will see things differently. Lamin Sanneh has commented, "The mental habits of Christendom predisposed us to look for one essence of the faith . . . whereas world Christianity challenges us to pay attention to the dynamic power of the gospel and to the open-ended character of communities of faith."[67] In post-Christendom, change is coming. It is coming as change usually does—from the edges, from the bottom up. It is coming as a result of friendships and partnerships in which ordinary Christians, South and North, listen to each other and bear testimony about what they have seen God do in their lives and their communities. It is coming as a result of our encounter with Christians whose worship and mission bear fascinating similarities to the worship and mission of pre-Christendom Christians. These encounters at times may be unsettling and painful and will require good listening and mutual forbearance.

But how important it is for brothers and sisters from many lands to exchange gifts. This global gift exchange will change us. Our worldwide friendships will make us more interesting. In the post-Christendom West, we may attract "outsiders" and "unbelievers" to faith in Jesus Christ (1 Cor 14:24), not because we are strong, but because, in our marginality, we are living lives that are hope filled and question posing. As a result, as we shall see in our final chapters, the outsiders may want to come to our churches' worship to check it out. Might they find that worship is the source of the Christians' hope and love?

TWELVE

Outsiders Come to Worship I: What the Outsiders Experience

"Outsiders or unbelievers enter." These words of Paul (1 Cor 14:23) do not state the primary reason why Christians gathered to worship in Corinth. As we have seen, the Christians gathered to worship God and, in all aspects of worship, to be "edified" (14:26)—to be built up as the body of Christ. But outsiders came, and Paul viewed this as normal. He also wanted the Corinthian Christians to take the outsiders' presence seriously— not as a limitation but as an opportunity.

There are good reasons why Paul was concerned for the outsiders. After all, God loves the outsider as much as the insider. And the outsiders are important. They represent the future of healthy congregations, which cannot propagate themselves by genetic means but must grow by means of attraction and conversion. Negatively put, without outsiders who become insiders, a congregation has no future. Positively put, the outsiders represent the trajectory of history. When God's mission is complete, outsiders and insiders together will worship Jesus Christ as Lord in a reconciled cosmos (Phil 2:11; Col 1:20).

Worship and Outsiders in Christian History

So how do the outsiders join the people of God? And how does the worship of the church relate to this mission of reconciliation and incorporation? Broadly speaking, across the two thousand years of Christianity, the church's worship has related to its mission according to four patterns.

Christendom—Worship in a World Without Outsiders
By social convention as well as law, in Christendom there technically were no outsiders. Everyone in society was a church member and was expected to attend the church's services.[1] Those who attempted to be outsiders, avoiding the church's worship, could be accused of the crime of "heresy" before church courts.

Pre-Christendom—Worship Without Outsiders, for Reasons of Security
In the years after AD 64, when persecution began under Emperor Nero, until Emperor Constantine ended persecution in the early fourth century, Christian churches excluded outsiders from their worship. The churches admitted the catechumens (those who were being catechized) to the first part of the service—the service of the word; but to the Eucharist that followed they admitted only those who had been baptized. The churches nevertheless grew rapidly. Their members' lives, shaped by worship, were attractive and per-suaded outsiders to undergo a lengthy catechesis leading to baptism and the dangerous life of extralegal Christianity.

Early Christendom and Late Christendom—Worship to Attract Outsiders
From 312, when Constantine legalized Christianity, until 529, when Justinian I made it compulsory, church leaders used worship services to motivate people who persisted in being outsiders to stop hesitating and be baptized. They choreographed awesome liturgies, preached spine-tingling sermons, and commissioned exquisite buildings laden with works of art that told the Christian story with mosaics, gold, and jewels. In early Christendom, worship was evangelistic. Worship was also often evangelistic in late Christendom, from the eighteenth century onward, when Christianity was losing its power to compel. The challenge now came from "back-sliders," nonobservant Christians whose smoldering, somnolent faith the church leaders sought to "revive" or "awaken." In this they drew on sermons that excited nostalgia or terror, heart-rending music, and rituals that enabled the outsiders to express symbolically their act of "coming home."

The New Testament Church and Post-Christendom—Worship in the Presence of Outsiders
In the church's earliest days, before the AD sixties, worship and mission were integrally related. As we have observed it in the house

church in Corinth to which Paul was writing, worship was primarily for the Christians, but their worship, especially at meals and the conversations which followed, was a setting in which the Christians hospitably received interested outsiders. The outsiders could observe the worship, hear the gospel, and experience the gifts of the Spirit. It was in domestic worship services that the outsiders were converted and became insiders. In post-Christendom—because of crusades and inquisitions and well-reported instances of clerical abuse—it is more difficult for outsiders and unbelievers to view Christianity as something exciting and hope-giving than it was in Paul's day. Nevertheless, once again in our time outsiders are coming to Christian worship services. They are coming freely, often as a countercultural act, in their search for God. Their arrival confronts the church with a privilege and a responsibility: How should Christians worship God in light of the watching, freely present outsider?

Why Outsiders Come

Christian communities should not worship God primarily to address the needs or attract the allegiances of the "outsiders and unbelievers." There are times when it is right for congregations to sponsor special services to address the concerns of the outsiders and to call them to faith in Christ (we shall look at some of these later). But as a rule the worship of the churches is not instrumental, a means of accomplishing goals. Instead, the churches' worship is devoted to glorifying God with the by-product of sanctifying the worshipper, in the belief that by worshipping God the Christians will be seized by the vision of God's mission and will participate in it. And the outsiders are a significant part of God's mission. Either they have entered the churches already to scout them out or they are watching Christians dubiously from a distance, considering whether there is anything in Christianity that could possibly persuade them to look at the inside of a Christian meeting.

What is it that draws outsiders to move toward churches, gatherings, or whatever one wants to call meetings in which Christians worship?[2]

Christians, Active or Nonpracticing
Some outsiders come to our churches for what we may consider ordinary Christian reasons. One group of these are the mobile

Christians, whose studies or jobs move them to a new area, where they hunt for a Christian congregation or community with whom they can worship God and find a common life in the body of Christ. Another group of outsiders, increasingly common in late or post-Christendom, are Christians who have had a bad experience in one church but who are still willing to try another. Then there are the nonpracticing Christians. Often these people believe in God and know that the spiritual dimension of life is important. But years ago they stopped going to church. They may have been exhausted by earlier experiences in the church or hurt by them, or they may have serious questions about some aspect of Christian teaching or practice. Nevertheless, for example because of the birth of a child or the ongoing nurture of children, they are willing to give Christianity another try. Often these people have found churches unappealing but still find Jesus attractive.

Needy People
Other outsiders come to the church because of intense need. Some people are comfortable economically but inwardly desperate. They may have failed professionally, or serious illness or bereavement may have brought them to a crisis in which they are willing to try anything. So they are willing to explore Christianity, or various forms of therapy, and come as outsiders to a Christian meeting. Other people are in deep trouble. They may have lost jobs or may have excessive debt. One partner may be in prison, or their children may be involved in drugs or gangs. They may be poorly fed, lonely, or fearful, and they approach Christians as people who can perhaps feed them and bring them help. And some people are hungry for God. They do not want ideas about God; they do not want schemes of social engineering; they do not want campaigns for change or a cause to rally around. They want God, and are drawn to the church or a Christian community because of the rumor that God is there.

The Intrigued
Some people are drawn toward Christianity by friends, neighbors, or colleagues who seem appealingly unusual. These people are attracted by Christians who have been formed by their worship to be alert to God's mission and involved in it. That is why these Christian friends see new possibilities at work and why they have inner vitality and

hope. As we have seen earlier in this book, Christians and Christian communities for the sake of God's mission do unusual, creative things. Outsiders are intrigued by the Christians' distinctive ways of behaving, including the ways they deal with conflict and violence, and by their creative and hopeful approaches to seemingly insoluble problems. Today, as in pre-Christendom, the Christians' lifestyle, which is intriguing and question posing, is the outsiders' main magnet drawing them toward the Christian faith.[3] John V. Taylor noted of the earliest church: "The primary effect of the pentecostal experience was to fuse the individuals of that company into a fellowship which in the same moment was caught up in the life of the risen Lord. In a new awareness of him and of one another they burst into praise, and the world came running for an explanation."[4]

When a community behaves in interesting ways; when it prays with disciplined expectancy; when lives begin to change and conditions in a neighborhood start to improve; when Christians work together for social change, living at odds with dominant values—people notice. If "the world" doesn't come running for an explanation, some creative misfits who long for a synthesis of social action and committed prayer will come, at least to explore. Jesus knew that the religious people who were well adjusted and prosperous found him unappealing, so he called marginal people, people on the move, people whose relationship to the status quo was dissonant, to be his followers in seeking God's kingdom and his justice.[5] People who long for change, but who sense that they cannot bring it about unless the change is rooted in worship and prayer, are often drawn to new expressions of church.

Friends
Friendship is the most basic reason outsiders come into the gravitational field of Christian churches and communities. Outsiders watch the Christians, often for many years. They have learned to trust the Christians and to enjoy them. They have sensed themselves safe with the Christians, able to share reciprocally questions and concerns, pleasures and passionate commitments. They have eaten together. The quality of life of wives or girlfriends is especially important in attracting men toward the Christian faith. Friendship alone cannot draw outsiders toward worshipping communities, but studies have indicated that friendship is the most important single force behind

people becoming Christian.[6] The purpose of friendship is never the conversion of the other; like worship, friendship cannot be instrumental. And yet the sensitive Christian will know the right moment to invite the friend to come close to Christians as they worship God.

What the Outsiders See: Paul's Concerns

In his first letter to the church in Corinth, Paul assumed that there would be "outsiders and unbelievers" in their worship services. He was concerned that the church would worship aware of the outsiders among them, for to Paul, as an ambassador for Christ and a practitioner of God's mission (2 Cor 5:20; Eph 6:20), hospitality was a cardinal virtue. He urged his friends to "extend hospitality to strangers" and to welcome one another as God in Christ had welcomed them (Rom 12:13; 15:7).

So Paul was happy for the church in Corinth to inculturate its worship, indigenizing its meetings within the structure of a recognizable social institution—the Greco-Roman banquet. For the sake of the community's members as well as the outsiders who were their guests, it was right for the church to be at home in the *polis*. But then Paul urged his Corinthians friends to remember that inculturation also required the pilgrim dimension, which is always ill at ease within the *polis*. The Corinthian leaders were failing to critique the banquet by criteria of God's reconciling mission. Was the worship at table just? Did it edify the entire community, treating the poor in the same way that it treated the powerful, telling and enacting God's odd story? Or did it capitulate to conventional stories in which the prosperous believers set their own rules and did not discern the body of Christ? In both 1 Corinthians 11 and 14, Paul encouraged worship that edified the body of Christ, building it into a unity in which all members were empowered by God's Spirit.

In Paul's vision, the outsiders were also important. Paul was acutely aware that as the Corinthian Christians worshipped in their house churches, nonmembers, often unbelievers, were there, watching. Paul wanted the church's life and worship, which the outsiders saw and experienced, to attract them. So he asked questions, dealing with four areas:

- *Comprehensibility*: Was the worship comprehensible (14:9)? It was important for the outsiders to "know what is being said." Christians, Paul asserted, did not want to "be speaking into the air." In fact, it was important for the worship to build up and instruct the outsiders (14:17, 19).
- *Participation*: Were the outsiders able to understand well enough that they could take part in the responses, saying the "Amen" (14:16)?
- *Resemblance to non-Christian worship*: Was the worship of the Christians so much like that of ecstatic pagan cults that outsiders could reasonably conclude that the Christians, like the pagans, were "out of their minds" (see 14:23)?
- *Exegeting the character of God*: Was the Christian worship so chaotic that outsiders could infer that God is a God of disorder, not of peace (14:33)?

Paul's conviction was that when outsiders participated in a community that was worshipping comprehensibly, distinctively, and with wide participation, the lives of the outsiders could be transformed. The outsiders, he knew, had arrived at the Christian meeting with hearts that contained a variety of "secrets"; but in the worship they had the opportunity to discover that God graciously knew them and loved them. And, when the "secrets of their hearts" had been addressed, they would bow down and join in the worship, exclaiming "God is really among you" (14:25). The outsiders had taken the first step to being insiders, collaborators in God's mission.

Where the Outsiders Meet Christians: A Liminal Space

What do the outsiders see when they come to a Christian gathering today? Some enthusiastic Christians invite the outsiders immediately to a Saturday evening Mass in their parish or to a Sunday morning church service with a twenty-five-minute sermon. But often the Christians first meet and spend time with the outsider in a liminal space.

The liminal space is an in-between place, a threshold of transition and insecurity.[7] To enter into liminality the Christians must leave their buildings and structures and enter a space where they are not in control and where surprise and new discovery can happen. A liminal space can be a nonchurchy project that Christians understand to be an expression of God's mission—"a divine activity that invites human collaboration."[8] So Christians may respond to their friends' invitation to work together on local concerns—cleaning up an environmental area or painting over gang graffiti that have appeared on houses. Or Christians may invite their friends to work with them, surveying the assets and needs in a neighborhood, building a house with Habitat for Humanity, feeding hungry people or joining in a demonstration against a war.

Franciscan retreat giver Richard Rohr has helped Christians today to understand the assumption that undergirded the early Christians' catechetical approach: "Christians do not think their way into a new life; they live their way into a new kind of thinking."[9] Social psychologists underscore this learning. "One of social psychology's premier lessons is that we are as likely to act ourselves into a way of thinking as to think ourselves into action."[10] As they work together in the liminal space of a common project, both the outsiders and the Christians change and learn. When the outsiders see Christians leaving their positions of strength and doing interesting things, and when they themselves become collaborators in the missional action, change begins. Solidarity develops. People who have worked together in the liminal space of the common project now gather in another unthreatening space—a backyard, where there is a barbecue, or a coffee shop, or a home—where they eat and drink together and become friends. At some point, they may reflect about what they have done. "We've done this work together. Why? What was our motivation? Social obligation? Feel-good? Compensation for guilt feelings? Imitating someone I admire? Religious motivation?"

For some middle-class people, the home is a possible liminal space. Christians and their outsider friends may have been eating together for years in restaurants but also in each other's homes. So it may be natural to gather there after a common project. And many outsiders find it easier to cross the threshold to a home church, where Jesus' presence is acknowledged in a meal, or to a Wednesday evening house fellowship, than it is to enter a church building for a gathering of a Christian congregation. Robert Webber observed that a normal progression functions as follows: Christians learn to know their friends over time; then they invite them to "neighborhood community fellowship" where there is eating, socializing, and a discussion of spiritual issues; finally, when the time seems right, the friends can move on to the congregation where the gospel is "embodied in community and rehearsed in worship."[11]

The Outsiders in Christian Worship: Inculturation

Before the outsider enters the church building, however, let us reflect a bit on inculturation. In chapter 3 we saw that when Christianity takes root in culture, it must be both indigenized and pilgrim. In the words of Rowan Williams, the Jesus of the New Testament, a Jewish artisan, was "both a native and a stranger." In the practice of mission, Christians keep discovering that "[Jesus] is both native and stranger in all human contexts, addressing fundamental searchings in the life of human communities, so that what he offers is recognizable, against all probability, in vastly diverse settings, and never simply being absorbed into any human context or system in such a way that he cannot speak beyond it."[12]

Indigenized

Jesus the native was indigenized in first-century Jewish culture; and as God's mission has spread to new cultures, Jesus has repeatedly been discovered there, indigenized, as a Saxon tribesman or an Inuit hunter-fisherman. So when Christians follow Jesus, they discover that they do not need to discard their own culture, for Jesus is already in their midst. All cultures to some extent express the grace and goodness of God, and all the nations bring their gifts to God, who accepts these gifts (Isa 60:5; Rev 21:24-26). Andrew Walls has served us well by reminding us that Christianity has always been indigenized and needs to be indigenized in every society. "All churches are culture churches—including our own."[13] So Christians must constantly be asking, How can the Christian faith be translated into the languages and cultures of our own nation? And the Christians must expect to find, in every nation, signs of God's work that the church can appropriate and that will give every church its unique character.

The great Japanese Christian Uchimura Kanzo put it like this: "A Japanese by becoming a Christian does not cease to be Japanese. On the contrary, he becomes more Japanese by becoming a Christian."[14] So in the first century, Paul expected to find God already at work in the cities to which he went, and he was able to adopt the Greco-Roman banquet as a suitable vehicle for worshipping the indigenized Savior. Today we Christians in the post-Christendom West are challenged to discern where the missional God is graciously at work in our societies. What aspects of contemporary Canadian or American culture are hospitable to the gospel? What cultural forms are gifts that Christians should not resist but receive? Can we imagine saying, with Uchimura, "An American by becoming a Christian does not cease to be American. On the contrary she becomes more American by becoming a Christian"? What in American culture is "graced," a gift of God to all and something congruent with the gospel? A spirit of energy and openness to the new? Love of the great outdoors? Friendliness? Baseball? Rhythm and blues? Electronic communication with visual images? The Simpsons?[15]

When Christians do not respond to their changing local cultures with alertness and respect, the result is alienation and decline. George Hunter III is a passionate advocate of indigenized worship. He is convinced that mainline Christians in America distance themselves from the surrounding community by a "culture barrier," behind which they barricade themselves within their own traditions, jargon, and "antiquated, or even foreign, tastes in music, art and architecture." The way forward for the churches is to "exegete" the surrounding cultures and indigenize the church's language, music, and style to communicate the gospel to the church's neighbors in their own idioms.[16] In his writing, Hunter parallels the thinking of Roman Catholic writers such as Anscar Chupungco, who since Vatican II have advocated "liturgical inculturation."[17] And Catholics in many countries, such as Cardinal Pio Taofinu'u of Samoa, have sought to express the Catholic Mass in forms that embrace local cultures. In Samoa, the Mass includes dancing in processions and when the Gospel is read, and blessing a roasted pig that will be consumed in the feast afterward. Cardinal Pio comments: "The future of the church in Samoa and possibly the world depends on an evangelization that speaks the language and culture of the people."[18] Lamin Sanneh speaks of this process, which is going on in countless countries worldwide, as "the vernacularization of the Gospel in the idioms of the folk, the people of the world."[19]

The question it poses for us in the contemporary, consumerist West is how Christians should respond to its post-Christendom surroundings in light of its Christendom traditions. Darrell Guder suggests that our worship services should take the risk of translation. No culture is normative. So "the language we use, the forms

of communication we adopt, the music and symbolism, the liturgies—all of this can and must be translated for the sake of the witness we are to be and to do."[20] J. G. Davies pointedly says, "Participation in the *missio Dei* puts repeatedly to all liturgical forms the
question: why?"[21]

Pilgrim
On the other hand, Jesus the stranger was often ill at ease in first-
century Jewish culture. He critiqued his culture, and his culture's
leaders crucified him. As bearers of God's mission encounter people
in new cultures, they will find Jesus there, as a pilgrim as well as a
native. So Davies's question, "Why?" is a good one. It does not compel Christians to repudiate everything in their worship that is different from local cultures. But it pushes Christians to have good reasons—reasons rooted in God's mission—if they are to be different.

In his conversations with young churches, Paul was concerned
to form them as Christian cultures.[22] He was helping the churches
that he founded to develop their own culture. In Corinth, for example, the church worshipped in the context of the Greco-Roman
meal—its worship life was indigenized. But the church's worship
was also pilgrim. Its meals were to be different from those of the
typical banquet; they were to be occasions of justice, sharing, and
empowering the weak. After the meals, multivoiced, spirited worship took place; but it was unlike the worship of the ecstatic cults—
the *orgia*. The church that met in the home was local, but it also
was a cross-cultural body that was constantly in correspondence
and hospitable connection with Christians in many countries. To
enter into a Pauline house church was to enter into something that
looked familiar; but it also was to enter into a larger world that
had a story that was expansive, history encompassing, and goal
directed. By bringing together Jews and Gentiles, people of many
backgrounds, into a new unity, the tiny house church was a part
of God's huge mission of reconciling all people and all creation to
God in Christ. In this project, the outsiders are essential, and Paul
in 1 Corinthians 14 gives a mandate to take them seriously. The
outsiders must understand the words; they must be able to say the
responses; they must be able to contribute their gifts. Pauline worship was an expression of Hunter's concern: it exegeted the contemporary culture—its cultural forms and the particular ways in

which it experienced alienation and pain. But Pauline worship also exegeted the character of God, the God of peace whose aim was cosmic—the reconciliation of all things in Christ.

And so today, the church is to be a culture, living in the midst of cultures in which it expects God to be working already. It seeks to express its treasure in languages and cultural forms that the local culture can understand. But the church's culture has a pilgrim character. Because it follows Jesus the stranger, it is countercultural. It is part of a movement across two thousand years—it is transcultural. It also has a sense of worldwide belonging today—it is cross-cultural.[23] The churches in post-Christendom cultivate this bigger picture. They meet in places, use language, and sing songs that reflect the local culture, but they also meet, speak, and sing in ways that challenge the local culture by expressing God's mission to reconcile all things in Christ.

Because churches as Christian cultures seek to follow Jesus, who was both native and stranger—both indigenized and pilgrim—their worship is both familiar and odd; it is both culturally attuned and culturally dissonant. It expresses itself in this culturally ambivalent way because it worships the God who expresses himself in every culture but who has a mission that is different from the current norm of any culture. The people who worship God are sanctified—they are being transformed into his likeness—and because of that are alive and question posing. People do not come to Christian gatherings because they find the Christians' worship instantly comprehensible. Rather, they come to Christian gatherings because the Christians whom they have learned to know are vital and intriguing. And the outsiders might be curious. Are the Christians distinctive because of their worship? Do you think we could find life here as well?

Five Models of Church: Domestic, Megachurch, Cathedral, Congregation, Outsider-Directed

What kind of churches will outsiders come to? Some of these, variously called "new ways of being church," "emerging church," or "fresh expressions," are springing up in many parts of the world.[24] Often they meet in homes, where people not only eat meals and have lively conversation but also worship God, pray, and mutually discern the way forward. Home churches, often called table churches, are a contemporary analogue to the house churches of the New Testament.

Patterns of life and worship that Paul describes in 1 Corinthians were culturally appropriate in pre-Christendom, and they are once again emerging as Christendom wanes.[25]

There are real advantages to the domestic, table church. Far more than a traditional congregation, the domestic church is a liminal space. It is a potentially unthreatening environment into which to invite the outsider. And the kind of worship that is possible in it—meal plus conversation—is similar to what Paul assumed to be normal. The home church may not simply be a secondary option, an inferior state en route to the more perfect worship in a purpose-built church building. Various contemporary observers predict that worship in houses, as in the early church, will be the normal experience of a growing number of Christians after Christendom.[26] And the home church has missional advantages. Michael Hawn observed, "It is possible to create places of worship that invite outsiders and integrate the body of Christ with each other rather than exclude some and stifle the interactions of the assembly."[27] These places may vary: if not in homes, in other settings with a home-like character—an outdoor patio, the upper room of a local shop, a side room of a restaurant, under a tree, by a river (Lydia and friends, Acts 16:13ff.). In these gatherings with a domestic ethos, the worshippers eat together: the meal is central to meetings of the table church. The worshippers share about their lives and give "reports from the front"; there is wide participation as they sing and contribute spiritual gifts and pray for each other. And the participants listen, expecting that, through all this, God will speak to them. The visibility of the church will not be the church's buildings but their common life, their service to their neighbors, and their collaboration in the *missio Dei*. And the outsiders and unbelievers, whom the members invite into this setting, observe the worship as participants.

But home churches are not to everyone's taste. In the United States, as in many other countries, there is also the recent phenomenon of the megachurch—"the full service church." These large, bustling congregations have accomplished worship bands, gripping teaching, well-equipped Sunday schools and childcare, coffee bars, gymnasiums, Bible studies, and weekday social events of many kinds. At times they provide substantial help to poor people. And these churches can be hospitable, for some outsiders feel safe attending a large church where they, as anonymous onlookers, can experience a kind of liminality.

Today there are also examples of the classic forms of church life in the Christendom centuries. Cathedrals in England and large congregations in the United States are flourishing, providing devoted, well-crafted worship services in glorious settings, and many people are attracted to attend. Worshipping communities of intermediate size—parish churches and congregations—have loyal attendees and show every sign of surviving.[28] Post-Christendom does not necessarily mean small.

Some Christian worship today is specifically directed toward the outsider. In the United States, many churches—following the lead of Willow Creek Community Church in Illinois—have developed their main Sunday service, not as an occasion to edify the believing community, but as a "seeker service" to communicate the ideas of the gospel to the outsider. Many churches throughout the English-speaking world have sought to adapt the "seeker sensitive" model, at least for some of their services.[29] On the European continent there is an alternative approach, the Thomas Mass, which seeks to communicate the gospel through liturgy to people alienated from Christianity. Radiating out from Finland, the Thomas Mass sponsors services, often in the evenings, in which doubters are confronted, not with talks, but with worship. People alienated from the church confess their sins to another person, light candles, write intercessions on sheets of paper, participate in the Eucharist, and engage in a serendipitous event marked by what its original founder calls "holy chaos."[30]

The transformation of the Taizé community is a powerful and influential parallel example of this. Founded in the years immediately after World War II, Taizé was a monastic renewal that attracted Reformed as well as Catholic Christians to a common life, based in a rule, centered in disciplined worship. To the brothers' astonishment, the youth of Europe discovered Taizé and came there in rapidly increasing numbers because it was rumored that God was there. The effects of the outsiders on the ordered monastic life were disruptive, which led the leaders of Taizé to reconsider their calling. The result was a reordering of the community's life to serve the outsiders. The drastic simplification of worship that this entailed—shorter readings, much longer singing—led to a crisis of communal vision in which some brothers, true to their early vocation, left the community. But Taizé's contemplative worship has been a setting in which thousands of outsiders have found a way into a living faith.

When outsiders comes to a worship service in these churches—home church, megachurch, cathedral, congregation, or outsider-directed—what do they see? Will they want to come back? Does the common life and worship they encounter enable them to detect the ferment of God's mission—"the fascination of a world that is changed"?[31]

What they see is immensely important, for the church of whatever size or sociological form is meant to be a demonstration of God's mission in action. Chris Wright has pointed to the importance of the outsiders in God's purposes: "God always acts among his own people with an eye on the watching nations. The nations are not just part of the incidental scenery of the narrative. They are the intended witnesses of the action. These things happen 'before their eyes.'"[32]

What the Outsiders See: Actions of Christian Worship

So when the watching nations—the outsiders—enter the building and observe the Christians at worship, what do they see? Unfortunately, in many congregations in Britain and the United States, they can see worship that is decayed and de-spirited, out of tune with God's mission. This is disastrous, and the outsiders are sure to detect the bad smell. But in other churches of every size and many sorts, the outsiders can encounter worship that is alive and attuned to the character and purposes of God. Such worship is embodied, enacted evidence that "the world can and does look different."[33]

We present here an overview of some Christian actions of worship in a body of any size—domestic church, megachurch, cathedral, congregation—that is alive and healthy. When outsiders visit such a community, they will see the Christians

- *Engage in praise.* The outsiders note that the words and the ambience of the Christian worshippers are thankful. The dominant character is not one of unexpressed weariness, complaint, or cynicism, but one of praise to God.
- *Declare that Jesus is Lord.* The outsiders are astonished by the amount of attention the Christians in worship give to Jesus. The Christians listen to Jesus and memorize his sayings; he is their rabbi! But there is more. The Christians seem to believe that in Jesus God shows them himself in human form, demonstrating for them what it means to be fully alive. So the worshippers work at making sense of Jesus,

and in their sermons or talks—and their testimonies—they show signs of their struggle to give him ultimate authority in their lives. They ponder his parables and his actions, his eating with sinners, and his love for his enemies. Especially they tell and retell the story of his passion and his resurrection that they believe is the center and climax of history. Their worship shows that they desire to become a Jesus people.

- *Tell a big story.* The outsiders may be surprised by a group that, in a postmodern age, has the audacity to tell a huge story. The metanarrative that the Christians tell in worship is Jewish but it is also global; it is as old as creation, but it blazes a trail into the future. Since it is God's story, it is an odd story—a holy story. Telling it turns the lives of the tellers upside down; it makes them expectant that they will meet the God of the story in their lives; and it gives them hope. The outsiders will note that, because of this story, the worshippers are part of a huge peoplehood—all kinds of people mingle in this church, and it has connections with many parts of the world. Greetings, news, and prayer requests flow back and forth within the "transcultural, global 'network' of local communities."[34] The outsiders are amazed as they sense that to become a Christian is to enter a bigger room.

- *Tell the "little stories."* The outsiders listen closely as the worshippers claim that God is at work in the present. God's big story has changed them. God's love and liberation have touched them. And in gratitude they open themselves to being people whose priorities, values, and reflexes are becoming loving and liberating. In worship they tell little stories, describing with awe and gratitude where they have seen God's grace and love at work in them and in others. For these worshippers, the big story has become their personal story and the story of their congregation. With amazement the outsiders observe that for the worshippers history is not dead; history is invading their lives.[35]

- *Perform rituals.* The outsiders are not strangers to rituals; the media, the fashion industry, work, and free-time activities are all filled with symbolic systems. So the outsiders are not surprised when they encounter rituals in Christian gatherings. What they would find difficult in Christian worship would be a lack of rituals, or rituals that seem impoverished or shallow.[36] But in Christian worship, the outsiders can observe Christian communities performing rituals that are rich. The outsiders on occasion can watch baptism, in which people respond to Jesus' grace and make promises in response to his call, "Follow me." They hear the seriousness of the promises; they grasp the drama of a journey through water; they sense the joy of the community that welcomes new members. Only later might they grasp that this is a matter of death and life, in which the Spirit descends and the baptized die to old allegiances and are reborn into new life shaped by Jesus Christ their Lord. The outsiders, whether seated at a meal table or in a large building, observe—and possibly participate in—a meal that the Christians call Communion or Eucharist, in which the community reenacts the story of Christ's life, death, and resurrection. Those who take part are nourished by the gift of Christ's presence as they eat and drink, and all are called to drink the cup of costly discipleship (Matt 20:22) and to walk in his way. In some churches, outsiders watch Christians engage in a ritual that is even more unusual culturally: washing each other's feet, praising God that Christ has washed their feet, and ritually expressing their commitment to wash the feet of each other and the world. As the worshippers perform any of these rituals, outsiders may detect that something is "happening," that the Christians are adoring God and being directed "away from self-preoccupation, anxiety, and defensiveness."[37]

- *Make peace and pray.* The outsiders observe that the worshipping community has a particular concern for reconciliation. They may not initially understand that this grows out of the worshippers' understanding of God's mission, which is to reconcile all things and all people in and to God in Christ. But they note the worshippers' concern for peace in the world; peace permeates their prayers. They also observe that the worshippers are concerned that, in a world at war, it is vital for them to be at peace with each other; the peace greeting symbolizes this concern in an embodied, wholehearted way. The prayers of the community are wide ranging and passionate. They bring the broken world, with its wars, hunger, injustice, and persecution, before God with trusting concentration; and they cry out to God that God will bring his kingdom of justice, peace, and joy. The worshippers view prayer as something that matters intensely, that is customary but not routine, and the outsiders may find this challenging or baffling.

- *Sing.* The outsiders may be drawn in or put off by the music that Christians use in worship. Some of the music is performed, and the worshippers listen. But much of it involves the worshippers singing. What astonishes the outsider is the range of music that the Christians sing. The outsiders may notice the historical breadth of the texts, and may reflect that this shows a deep tradition but also an openness to try new things. The outsider will hear the Christians sing hymns of Bernard of Clairvaux and Isaac Watts; but they will also sing hymns of Delores Dufner and Graham Kendrick, chants from Taizé, and songs from the worldwide church. The congregation's band accompanies contemporary songs, at times with driving rhythms and high decibel levels. The outsiders may not like some of the songs and not be sure how to join in. But what amazes them is the range of the church's music and the commitment, on the part of worshippers of all ages, to sing in different idioms.

- *Be multivoiced.* The outsiders encountering Christian worship enter into a communal event. They note that the worshippers sing and say their responses with intensity; they observe that many worshippers take part—in readings, in prayers, in bringing testimony. The worship forces them to consider the worshippers' explanation that the community is the body of Christ and that God is at work today. It does not surprise them that the worshippers, who are able to speak in the worship services, discover that they are also articulate in other settings: they can talk to others about their faith; they can speak up—in the press and to politicians—on behalf of the oppressed and in support of peace and reconciliation.[38] Those who have experienced God empowering them in their worship also expect to see God at work throughout the week and in the world, and they learn to anticipate God's empowerment as they collaborate in God's reconciling mission in the world.

What the Outsiders Intuit: The Church's Ethos

The actions of the worshipping church are important, but to the outsider its ethos is decisive. Ethos is a complex reality, a "mixture of style, values, priority and mood."[39] It is often not something that church leaders consciously create, but is the product of illuminating intangibles that reflect the reality of the community's inner life. It is important, of course, that we pay attention to everything our congregations do and say in worship, but it is also important that we are sensitive to the feeling, tone, and atmosphere of our congregational life, for this is what the outsiders will pick up. Stuart Murray has contended, "A church's shape may deter or attract some potential joiners; but its ethos is more significant."[40]

The outsiders are usually not anthropologists or journalists, but people on a personal journey. So what illuminating intangibles might they note that would attract them further?

- *People who are at home*: Do the worshippers seem relaxed or tense? Do they seem to feel at home with each other? Is there room for spontaneity? Are they physically at ease?
- *Humility*: Does the church seem to be a place where people can agree and disagree safely without wounding each other or breaking fellowship? Do they express disdain for the people with whom they disagree—inside or outside the church? In prayers, testimonies, or over coffee, do members dismiss other Christians, gays, soldiers, poor people, rich people, Muslims, the United States, prominent politicians? Do the members reveal narratives that implicitly diminish others: "I used to be an evangelical/liberal"?
- *Questions and answers*: Is there room, in this community, to accommodate people at different stages of faith and to allow for the vigorous questioning that is appropriate in postmodernity and post-Christendom? Some outsiders whose lives are in disarray may want firm guidance; others may want to know that it is safe to express their doubts and struggles without someone immediately setting them right.
- *Grace*: Does the church seem to be a culture of grace? Does the church's common life and worship convey that because of God's love and forgiveness there is room for failure as well as success; for people whose lives are messed up or

who don't speak well or dress properly? Is it possible for the
church's members to be less than perfect? If someone mis-
speaks or makes a loud musical error, does it matter?

• *Risk*: Do the members seem to be addicted to security, or do
they expect that God will intervene to show them new ways
forward? Are they trying to hold on to the familiar, or are they
willing to take risks and to sacrifice convenience and comfort?
Is the new a joy, not a burden; an opportunity, not a threat?

• *Transparency*: Can the members talk truthfully about their
lives, with praise and struggle? Or about prayer, God, and
God's work or silence in their experience? Is there room for
testimony?

• *Emotions*: Do people seem free, or are they buttoned up? Is
there openness for the members' emotional expression—
anger, lament, grief, joy, celebration?

• *Conflict*: Do their worship services give any indication how
the members deal with differences within the congregation?

• *Power*: Does one person or clique seem to dominate? Who
exercises power, and how does the community make decisions? If leadership is unclear, outsiders may feel uncomfortable. But outsiders will also notice how many voices are heard
and whether there is room for the voices of women, children,
the elderly, and the disabled.

• *Ritual and icon*: Do the worship services provide room for mediated imagery as well as the spoken word? Does the community
value symbols, ritual gestures, and works of visual art?[41]

• *Beauty*: Do these people care about the aesthetic setting? Do
they pay attention to the senses—to color, light, space, sound,
the acoustic environment? Is there evidence of creativity and
sensitivity to beauty?

• *Meals*: Does sharing food seem important to the church members? Is their approach to Communion joyful and expectant?
Are they aware of God's presence as they celebrate the feast?
Do they make a connection between their Eucharists and other
shared meals and potlucks? Are they involved in feeding hungry
people? Are they a community of many tables, eating in members' hospitable homes?[42] When the members profoundly realize that eating is primal and that it is central in building relationships and forming community, outsiders are fascinated.

What the Outsiders Intuit: About God

Who Is God?

The outsiders' antennae will be sensitized to the God a community worships. Paul reminded the Corinthians that their acts of worship exegeted God's character (1 Cor 14:33), and our worship today does the same to the observant outsiders who come into our worship. Many outsiders have been alienated from Christianity by the view that God is a demanding, hostile judge ("Uncle George," in the language of spiritual guide Gerard Hughes[43]). Other outsiders have found it difficult to worship God because they, constricted by Newtonian physics, have viewed God as a mechanistic deity who cannot be involved in the lives of members and who cannot answer prayer.

In chapter 9 we noted the action in our worship that declares that Jesus is Lord. Jesus, whom we worship and follow, shapes our view of God. Jesus' view, the outsiders will observe, is neither the angry judge nor the distant establisher of natural law. Instead, the God whom Jesus reveals is "Abba," the loving parent. The worshippers have a proper fear of God. God, according to Jesus, will judge our indifference to the hungry and homeless people in whom Christ is present (Matt 25:42-43), and God will have most difficulty with us when we, like the pious Pharisee, view ourselves as superior to other people (Luke 18:9-14).

What Is God Doing?

The church in worship seeks to deepen its relationship with the God who is at work. The outsiders may sense this and get glimpses of God's action. Worshippers may reveal—in many ways—that God is at work in their lives, protecting them in danger, providing for their needs, guiding them through confusion, loving them intimately, and forgiving their massive debts (Matt 18:27). Outsiders may also observe that in worship Christians reaffirm their faith in the God whose kingdom of justice, peace, and joy Jesus proclaimed and which, they believe, God is actively bringing in difficult situations today, often using improbable people. The outsiders may even sense God working in their lives, addressing them personally. In 1928 Bakht Singh, an Indian studying at the University of Manitoba, was traveling to Canada on a British ship. Out of curiosity he attended an Anglican service, during which he suddenly found himself violently shaking and blurting out the words, "Lord Jesus, blessed be thy name!" The following year Singh converted to Christianity and became one of the outstanding evangelists in twentieth-century India.[44] God, in the midst of a worship service, because of the words of the service or despite the words of the service, can call outsiders to become insiders. In post-Christendom, we must remember that some people who are exploring church cautiously after years of absence may need to be reassured that the God whom the community worships is not oppressive.

Is God Present?
This God, Christians believe, is really present as they worship. The outsiders may be intrigued by the behavior of Christians, but they are drawn to the God who is the source of that behavior. God's holiness frightens humans as well as attracts them, but attraction wins out. As a result, people are willing to travel thousands of miles to Taizé because God is reputed to be there; people rush to experience God's healing presence in a Pentecostal service; people gravitate toward the "real presence" of Christ in the Catholic Mass; and people are drawn to the real presence evident in congregations that practice multi-voiced worship with spiritual discernment ("God is really among you," 1 Cor 14:25). The sense of the attractive power of the divine presence in worship has been especially well developed in the Orthodox traditions. The birth of Russian Orthodoxy came in the 980s with a visit of Russian delegates to Constantinople. After experiencing the beauty of the liturgy in the Hagia Sophia, they testified, "We knew not whether we were in heaven or on earth. . . . We know that God dwells there among men."[45] To Orthodox theologian M. V. George, this experience is normal: "We confess Christ today to the non-Christians who attend the Liturgy casually at first. Conversions still take place through the magnetic attraction of the Eucharistic service."[46] The presence of God addresses people in a materialist culture in which God-hunger is acute, and postmodernity gives people freedom to express their hunger.

Does God Make a Difference in the Lives of the Worshippers?
When a Christian community believes that God is real, at work, and bringing to birth a new creation, outsiders take notice. They sense that these people are worshipping God not just out of habit but because they expect God to break into their world and do new things. The God they worship gives these people a bigger vision than that of the newspaper columnists or politicians.

The outsider especially notices whether the community's worship seems to make a discernable difference in the worshippers' attitudes and priorities. From their prayers and testimonies, the outsider will detect whether the worshippers live lives that are distinctive, different from other Americans or Canadians. If they are different, the outsider will wonder where the difference comes from. Are they different because of what the outsider has observed in worship? Is it because, as a community of praise would seem to indicate, God's generosity to them has motivated them to treat others in the same way? Are the Christians' lives imaginative and question posing, not because they are driven by rules or dominated by the superego, but because they are grateful?[47] Is this why there is a lightness of tone in Christian worship, which spreads through the Christians' entire life? Is this what Jesus calls abundance of life (see John 10:10)?

Abundance of life—if this is what the outsiders who have come to worship have observed and intuited, the outsiders may wonder, Can I have this too? Can I be at home with these people? Do I want to be like them? Do I trust these people? Would they want me, accept me, and welcome me? Can I imagine these people being my people?

THIRTEEN

Outsiders Come to Worship II: Hospitality and Wholeness

I n post-Christendom there are lots of outsiders. How different
from Christendom, in which for centuries there were by definition no outsiders. Since in society there was "no place where
Christ was denied,"[1] all people belonged to the Church—Catholic
or Orthodox—or to the state-related churches established after
the Reformation in various European principalities. The society-
encompassing churches have gradually broken down, and today
across the post-Christendom West the religious scene is kaleido-
scopic. There are numerous competing Christian traditions. New
churches, many with origins in Africa or Asia, spring up every year,
and old traditions, alas, experience divisions. There are of course
also millions of people who adhere to non-Christian religions, who
militantly adhere to no religion, or who find the whole subject of
religion tedious and irrelevant. Today in the post-Christendom
West, even in the United States, there is a myriad of religious
options. And one's religious commitments are not the product of
decisions of parliaments, tribal elders, and tradition; they are the
product of individual decisions.

Attending Church by Choice

Already in the 1970s, the great Jesuit theologian Karl Rahner
appreciated the magnitude of the shift that was taking place.

> [We have moved from the] *Volkskirche* (the church of all the people),
> corresponding to the former homogeneous, secular society and cul-

ture, to a church as that community of believers who critically disas-
sociate themselves, in virtue of free personal decision in every case,
from the current opinions and feelings of their social environment
. . . [and] to a church made up of those who have struggled against
their environment in order to reach a personally clearly and explicitly
responsible decision of faith. This will be the Church or there will be
no Church at all. . . . The Church of the future must grow in its reality
quite differently from the past, from below, from groups of those who
have come to believe as a result of their own free, personal decision.[2]

The Christendom church relied on the devotion and consent of
the people, but ultimately it was based on compulsion. With the
disappearance of social inducement and the enforced baptism of
all children, the churches have waned. Now, as in pre-Christendom,
churches cannot compel. And, as Rahner argues, without compulsion the churches will have to survive and grow as a result of free,
personal decisions. They will flourish if they embody God's presence and promote God's purposes in such an attractive, life-giving
way that members want to remain believers and are committed
to passing on their living faith to their children; outsiders choose
to join the churches because of the vitality and life that they find
there; and all of them get caught up in the worship and mission of
God. After Christendom, the churches will not survive because of
duty; they will survive because they edify the insider and attract
and welcome the outsider.

Hospitality: A Task for All Christians
In post-Christendom, welcome becomes critical to the church's future.
Hospitality—love of the stranger and outsider in which there is a giving and receiving of gifts—is a constant theme in the Gospel accounts
of Jesus. In the New Testament, Jesus was continually a guest of
others. And hospitality became a characteristic of faithful Christian
discipleship. Jesus informed his disciples that he was present in the
outsider: "I was a stranger and you welcomed me" (Matt 25:35). It is
so important, in post-Christendom, that we follow Jesus by being in
the position of the stranger, as guests receiving the generosity of others. At the same time we also follow Jesus by being hosts. The author
of the book of Hebrews declared that Christians who take in strangers could "entertain angels unawares" (see Heb 13:2). Paul urged

Christians to "practice hospitality" (Rom 12:13 NIV). An important qualification for a church leader was being hospitable (1 Tim 3:2). The tradition of hospitality became deeply engrained in the life of the pre-Christendom Christian communities.

With the establishment of Christianity in the fourth and fifth centuries, the Christian commitment to hospitality continued, but in more specialized form. Christian churches established programs to feed poor people; Christian leaders founded hospices for the sick and needy; monastic communities excelled in receiving the outsider. But hospitality moved from being a general task of all Christians to a specialized task of Christian institutions. And indeed, in a society in which all members were Christians, there were travelers—but few genuine outsiders—to receive.

In post-Christendom, hospitality has once again become a general task of all Christians and of all worshipping communities/ churches. In a world in which Christianity is marginal and lacks the capacity to twist arms, Christianity's survival depends on its openness to outsiders. Whether in their neighborhoods and workplaces or at church, Christians welcome outsiders; they listen to them; they exchange gifts with them. Especially, they eat with them.[3] And as Christians do this, they rediscover their essence. Rooted in grace, hospitable Christians embody the "motive clause" by welcoming others "as Christ has welcomed you" (Rom 15:7).

The Christians' hospitality to the outsider grows out of the Christian culture that has shaped them, in which they have welcomed each other. As they experience "edification" as the body of Christ, they discover resources for receiving the outsider. As Christine Pohl has commented, "churches that have not nurtured a common life among members will find hospitality to strangers quite difficult."[4] Conversation by conversation, invitation by invitation, churches develop a culture of hospitality. Gradually they develop the reflexes of being hospitable, first of all among themselves, but especially to the outsiders, talking to them instead of staying in cliques, opening themselves to the outsiders and inviting them to their hearts and homes. In these relationships they discover the presence of God, which "is embodied in the stranger and in Christian hospitality to the stranger."[5]

Hospitality in Worship

Churches that have members whose lives are hospitable, who are not self-absorbed or focused on their own interests, find that outsiders come to their worship services. As we have noted, the outsiders come for many reasons. And the outsiders are tremendously important. They are, as Paul noted in 1 Corinthians 14, observers who have the opportunity to be participants. The worship service does not take place with them primarily in mind; Christians gather to worship God and to be edified as Christian disciples. But the outsiders must always be in the minds of those who lead worship and indeed of all the worshippers. Paul asks, Can the outsiders understand the words of the service? Can the outsiders "say the 'Amen' to your thanksgiving" (1 Cor 14:11, 16)? Does the service give the outsiders a true impression of the Christian faith and an accurate exegesis of God's character (vv. 23, 33)? And does the service provide freedom for the Holy Spirit to use all the actions of worship to address the secrets of the outsiders' hearts? If so—when these elements work together properly—the worship that for years has been forming the character of the members begins to form the character of the outsiders. And the outsiders, convinced that "God is really among you," want to come back.

In what ways do the community and its worship leaders receive the outsiders? The members are hospitable, alert to the outsiders' concerns.[6] The liturgical leaders simultaneously give the outsiders welcome and space to be anonymous. They are careful to explain what is going on in the service, telling the outsiders what books to use, where to find songs and readings. The speakers do not use acronyms or "in" information. The leaders seek to be aware of the literary limitations or musical cultures that the outsiders represent and, as John Witvliet puts it, to "practice vital improvisatory ministry, faithful to ancient patterns, alert to life-giving innovations, aware of the Holy Spirit's work in each."[7] Well-practiced rituals may be especially hospitable to the outsiders, providing a social cover that gives the outsiders safety and enables them to enter into the action or simply to watch.[8]

The homilies and sermons, teachings and testimonies of a community can be especially important in speaking to the hearts of the outsiders. Of course, the talks or homilies will be primarily directed to glorifying God and edifying the community's members. But no sermon will be abstract or impersonal; all will be directed to the people. And the people, as Walter Brueggemann has pointed out, are at various places in their journeys. Some are young people—beloved children who have not yet become "believe-ful adults." The sermons must address the questions and concerns of these outsider-insiders so they will want to affirm their faith and to identify with the faith community. Others in the congregation are adults who have accommodated themselves to the dominant culture, compromised with its values, and become dependent on its systems of security. For these insiders who inwardly have become outsiders, the sermons seek to "'re-tent' . . . [the members] into the passionate vision of risk and vulnerability that is decisive for the community." There are also, of course, the newly arrived outsiders whom the speaker calls to fullness of life as insiders in the covenanted community.[9]

With all these people in mind—insiders and various kinds of outsiders—the preachers speak God's word. They are not in Christendom, so they do not assume that their hearers have faith. Instead, they preach in ways that call people to commit their lives to Jesus as Savior and Lord, and to God's mission, which he proclaimed and embodied. For example, some African-American churches in our neighborhood have an "altar call" every Sunday; in other places preachers provide occasional opportunities in a variety of ways— when the Spirit moves—to enable outsiders to commit themselves and insiders to recommit themselves. We note that, in certain parts of Germany, Catholic leaders have sensed the necessity of having occasional celebrations of covenant renewal, which have grown out of the program of "the self-evangelization of the baptized."[10] Evangelism is not something restricted to Christians who accost people on the street or talk to them at work. Rather, it is a normal part of the Christians' worshipping life, which assumes that insiders need to be reevangelized and that outsiders who are present need to come in. As Mark Gornik has commented, "Evangelization is . . . a *universal* invitation to all women and men to become a part of the pilgrim people of God in the march toward the new order of life that is the Kingdom of God"[11] (our italics). The evangelistic sermon, as a universal invitation, is an act of hospitality.

If the outsiders choose to respond to the invitation to faith, what happens next? Patterns vary. Some churches follow the model of late Christendom. In these the outsiders say a simple prayer, confess their faith in Christ as Savior and Lord, are baptized (if they were not baptized as infants), and become members of the church. A period of teaching—catechesis—may or may not follow their baptism; if it does not, the new believers are unlikely to be effective participants in the *missio Dei*. Other churches follow the primary model of the pre-Christendom church. In these, the outsiders journeying toward faith experience an extended period of pre-baptismal catechesis in which they are formed as Christians by practice as well as instruction.

In post-Christendom there is a rediscovery of catechesis.[12] In the Christendom centuries, people learned the Christian story and rudimentary Christian ethics by a process of osmosis, from parents and the wider culture as well as from the church. But in post-Christendom these sources of learning have largely dried up. Today people are catechized by the global culture industries and by advertisers who prey without ceasing on our susceptibilities. If outsiders are to become followers of Jesus in post-Christendom, they need to engage in a process of deconstructing old assumptions and learning new ways of thinking and behaving. If they are to learn the elements of God's mission—love of God in Christ; love of the neighbor; love of God's reconciling work (including love of the enemy); and love of creation—they will need the support of the wider Christian family and of companions on the road.[13] Lee Camp has perceptively likened groups of apprentice Christians to twelve-step groups: "Addicts do not come to know sobriety apart from the fellowship of a recovery group. In the same way, disciples do not come to know transformation apart from communion with fellow pilgrims on the way."[14]

When the catechumens have come to a place where, according to their mentors, they have made considerable progress in living the faith and in understanding it, they will be recommended for baptism (or confirmation).

Outsiders and the Table: Three Approaches

What is the place of the Eucharist in churches in which outsiders are present? Should Christians welcome outsiders to their Communion meals and services? These are important questions, for within the past hundred years the Eucharist has become significantly more important in the lives of Western Christians than it was throughout the Christendom centuries. The twentieth-century liturgical movement, whose influence in many Western traditions has been immense, sought to reclaim the celebration of the Eucharist as a communal event. The people no longer simply watch the unfolding action, taking Communion rarely; now they participate actively in the service, receiving the elements weekly. Even in nonconformist traditions relatively untouched by the liturgical movement, there is a new openness to the enriching potential of more frequent Communion.[15] And many "emerging" churches today have developed new ways of observing Communion; often these take place weekly. If we were to describe the ways that the churches worldwide celebrate Communion, the picture would become even richer and more complex.

In the West, there have been three models of eucharistic practice, each of which treats the outsiders in a distinctive fashion.

Domestic Churches' Approach: Outsiders at the Table

As we noted in chapters 6 and 7, the early house churches met weekly for worship that often included a meal followed by a time of free worship. Paul, in 1 Corinthians 14, makes it clear that inquirers—nonbaptized outsiders—were present for the free worship, and it is likely that they were present for the meal that preceded it.[16] Did they eat the food? If there were special blessings and rituals for "eucharistic" parts of the meal, did the outsiders partake of these? We cannot know. In the late first century, the author of the *Didache* ordered leaders of Christian communities to allow to "eat and drink of your Eucharist . . . [only] those baptized in the Lord's name," which implies that the unbaptized were at the eucharistic meals and had probably been partaking the consecrated elements (wrongly, in the view of the Didachist).[17] In the middle of the second century in Rome, the church of Justin Martyr probably still met in a home, but it now served the eucharistic food only to people who met three criteria: who believed Christian truth, who had been baptized, and who "lived as Christ handed down to us."[18] The first two criteria to which Justin referred—Communion only for those who believed correctly and were baptized—had probably become standard Roman practice; they certainly became central to the tradition of Western Christendom. But at some point the third criterion, that the communicant should live as Christ taught, withered.

Nevertheless, today some Christians in table churches—in the freedom offered by post-Christendom and postmodernity—are playing with the ambiguities of Pauline house church practice. The meal has come to be central, and participants eat bread and drink wine as acts of worship of Christ; but the table liturgies are not classic. Many do not contain the ceremonial "words of institution" that Christians since the fourth century have seen as constitutive of the Eucharist. And many assume that outsiders and inquirers belong in the table services and that it would be inhospitable, indeed contrary to God's mission, to exclude them from fully taking part in the whole event.

We expect that domestic, relational churches will proliferate in the post-Christendom West. In them the worshippers can feel at home; they share a real meal, which can be profoundly bonding; and they are participants in a homely rite in which they can be real, testimonies of joy and lament can happen naturally, and the gifts of the Spirit can flourish. Domestic churches can also be a natural, unthreatening place to welcome outsiders. But domestic churches face questions that require serious thought. How will they resist insularity and combat heresy? How will they develop communities that relate to the wider Christian tradition across time and geography? How, in the domestic setting, will they invite the outsiders to conversion? How will they catechize people and ignite in them the longing to be baptized? How will they pass on the church's faith and practices to the next generation?

The Classic Approach: Outsiders Are Excluded

As we have seen, pre-Christendom churches as early as the one addressed in the *Didache* forbade unbaptized outsiders to take part in the Eucharist. And from the second century, only the baptized could be present at the Eucharist. So it has continued as Christendom developed in the fourth century and across the history of Christianity both Western and Eastern: baptism has been a prerequisite for participation in Communion—unbaptized outsiders have often been excluded from observing it.

This tradition has had great strengths. It has rooted its practice in the assumption that Jesus participated in two sorts of meals: meals of radical openness with all sorts of people, including "tax collectors and sinners," and meals of radical intentionality with Jesus' inner circle (of which the Last Supper is paradigmatic), in which his disciples express willingness to join Jesus in "drinking the cup" (Mark

10:38; Luke 22:17). For the church, baptism in which one dies to an old life has come to be the necessary precondition for participation in the meals of Jesus' kingdom life; for the kingdom meals empower Jesus' disciples to live the life of sacrificial self-giving that expresses itself in radical hospitality.

Some people today view boundaries as unwelcoming, but adherents of this position observe that welcome is genuine only when it is welcome to a community that unabashedly stands for something and whose members have sacrificed in order to join it. Boundaries can be hospitable. Furthermore, boundaried communities can be missionally alert; they can issue a genuine invitation, not just to casual participation, but to covenant in baptism, which leads to the feast of the new covenant. Until the outsiders are catechized and baptized, they will engage in the countercultural discipline of longing, which, at the right moment, will be joyously satisfied at the eucharistic table.

This boundaried approach has been dominant in the West. In this, members of the Anabaptist tradition have agreed with Christians in the great Christendom traditions—outsiders should not be served at the Communion table.[19] We believe that, where this tradition is functioning at its best, it can be missional and attract outsiders in post-Christendom. Baptism is the pathway to the Eucharist.

However, we offer four cautions to churches that maintain this classic, "bounded set" approach. First, these churches must emphasize the significance of baptism. Their Eucharists are open only to those who have submitted themselves to the way and cup of Jesus in baptism; so for many Christian traditions, the "bounded set" position requires baptismal renewal—the baptism of catechized believers, or at least the baptism of children of parents who commit themselves to raising their children as disciples of Jesus who, at the right time, will be intensively catechized. Second, "bounded set" churches must bless the outsiders. In Eucharists in which the community's boundaries withhold the bread and wine from the outsiders, those presiding at the Eucharists must issue a warm invitation to the outsiders to receive nonroutine, ritually rich blessings. They may also invite them to faith in Jesus Christ, culminating in baptism and discipleship.

Third, "bounded set" churches must be churches of many tables. If a church reserves its eucharistic table to baptized believers, it must offer many other meals in which it demonstrates that it knows that Jesus practiced radical hospitality. A church that does not compress its entire life into an hour on Sunday morning, that has a rich communal life, that greets the outsider with a multidimensional welcome at many tables in a life of fellowship and learning that is open to all—such a church can ask people to wait until they are baptized to participate in the Eucharist. Finally, the "bounded set" churches' boundaries must not lead communicants to be self-satisfied. Members must not think that only they—the baptized ones—have arrived, smug in their safety within the boundary. Instead the eucharistic meals must empower those who eat and drink at Christ's table to live the intriguing and insecure life of his disciples, moving with him beyond the boundaries toward the outsiders in whom the *missio Dei* may be at work.

An Emerging Approach in Post-Christendom: Eucharists Open to Outsiders
Until recently, "open communion" meant allowing members of other congregations or denominations to participate in the Communion services of one's own church. It signified that congregations recognized the baptism of other traditions and the common faith that they shared. Now it has come to mean the participation of unbaptized people. At the core of this approach is the memory of Jesus' radical hospitality. Especially in the Gospel of Luke, Jesus ate with people who did not fit within the boundaries of ritual and moral purity—and the result was transformation: Jesus' radical acceptance at table cleansed the outsider rather than polluting himself.[20]

The open table has many apparent advantages. It expresses hospitality, a central Christian virtue. It also expresses the joy of welcome. When the presider says, "Jesus invites everyone to his table," the church turns a smiling face toward the world and toward many people who have experienced deep wounds and profound exclusions. Further, the open table avoids embarrassment. The presider does not need to figure out how to invite some people but not others to take part in Communion; parents may be relieved when their unbaptized children are not excluded from the church's central rite; and many people, uncomfortable because their congregation is not growing, are grateful that they are not sending potential members away feeling unsatisfied and repulsed.

Indeed, how will the outsiders themselves interpret their lack of participation? In other areas of life they can produce a Visa card and experience instant gratification. Why must the church be the only area of society that views longing as a virtue? And we must reverently note that there is recurrent testimony of outsiders who have experienced God in the eucharistic meal that, for them, served as a "converting ordinance."[21] An emerging church leader states, "Nearly every week when we celebrate communion we have people accept Christ."[22] A Jewish student who was deeply drawn to the teaching and the Friday morning Eucharists of Henri Nouwen at Yale University testifies that "it was through Henri and partici-pating in his Eucharists that I came to believe that even as a Jew I belonged round the table"—and became a Ploughshares peace activist.[23] Sara Miles, a self-described "left-wing journalist with a habit of skepticism," came to worship in a California Episcopal church and reported that, to her astonishment, participating in "holy communion knocked me upside down and forced me to deal with the impossible reality of God."[24] When outsiders receive the Eucharist, clearly something missionally potent might happen.

How do we understand open eucharistic practice in post-Chris-tendom? The "set theory," as described by Stuart Murray, offers two understandings—the "open set" and the "centered set"—which invite the participation of the outsider in the Communion service. These understandings are very different from the "bounded set" of traditional eucharistic practice, which excludes the outsider.[25]

- *The open set*: According to this understanding, welcome is the community's defining characteristic. The open set has no bound-aries—all outsiders are encouraged to come to the table—and it is tolerant in accepting widely varying approaches to belief and lifestyle within the church. Baptism is not required. Eucharist might be the pathway to baptism.
- *The centered set*: This understanding is more rigorous than the open set but less constrictive than the bounded set. The centered set's defining characteristic is its adherence to core convictions that are "rooted in the story which has shaped the community—and ultimately in Jesus Christ."[26] The core convictions are countercultural and serve to sepa-rate the centered-set community from its pluralist milieu. The congregation's leaders devote themselves to helping the community keep moving toward a deep understanding and

radical appropriation of the core values. The congregation is hospitable to outsiders who explicitly wish to move toward the center—Jesus Christ—and welcomes them at its Communion services whether or not they have been baptized. Eucharist might be the pathway to baptism.

We find attractions in both of these understandings. They foster worship that in some dimensions elicit participation in God's mission. But we have questions:

- *Of the open set*: How does the radically open community express Jesus' demand as well as his gift, his meal of suffering as well as his feast of celebration? Is a church truly hospitable if it is not clear what its core convictions and ethical commitments are? Under the appearance of hospitality, is it prone to "a kind of laissez-faire, liberal Constantinianism, a notion that there is no boundary between the church and the world and so the table belongs to all"?[27] If its mission is one of inclusion at the table, which *overflows* into the feeding of hundreds of hungry people at the table of Christ and in Christ's name, this radically open church can also be a radical sign of God's kingdom.[28]
- *Of the centered set*: Who determines the community's core convictions? Who decides which people are walking toward Jesus and the core convictions, and are moving from outsider to insider and may participate in the community's Eucharists? What forms of discipline determine that, in an unbounded community, certain regular participants are moving away from the center and therefore are not appropriate participants in the Lord's table?
- *Of both the open set and centered set*: Why be baptized? How does a community, in opening the table to nonbaptized people impress on the nonbaptized person the importance of being baptized? As James Farwell has observed, "It is notoriously difficult to move people from the table to the commitment of the font."[29] How does the community pass on the faith from one generation to another? Can a community develop an inner group, rooted in covenant, that meets occasionally for prayer, confession, and reassessment of the core values and of the

community's faithfulness in living them?[30] What other, non-eucharistic meals does the community have that welcome the outsider? In the United Kingdom and North America today, there are cultures of consumer satisfaction and instant gratification; is the open table an appropriate indigenization of the gospel or a capitulation to an impatient cultural milieu?

We ourselves see the greatest strength in a sensitive application of the classic Christian approach. But we see value in all three understandings—bounded, open, and centered sets—for incorporating the outsider who comes to worship. All three hold out possibilities; all three elicit questions. We believe that the central questions come down to the church's ecclesiology and the depth of the church's worship of God. Is the Eucharist the act of a congregation that, as the body of Christ, offers worship as "the self-expression of the life of covenanted love given by the Spirit"?[31] Does it glorify the God whose mission is to reconcile all things in Christ? Does it shape believers whose lives are transformed into signs of God's shalom-ful mission? Does the worship, through the week as well as when the community gathers, form believers who are radically committed to love the stranger and welcome the "outsiders and unbelievers"?

Worship and Mission in a Body Made Whole

Worship and mission are both important. We have noted that in pre-Christendom the church's remarkable missional success grew out of its life of worship. We have also seen how, in the Christendom centuries, mission virtually vanished as the Christian population came to be identical to the civil population; in these centuries worship was the church's *raison d'être*. In the past three centuries in the West, mission has reappeared. At first, it recurred as the activity of enthusiastic but marginal Christians. Later, in a broader understanding, influential theologians have come to see mission as the primary theological category for understanding God. The *missio Dei*—God's passionate project to reconcile all things in Christ—alters everything. Worship, according to the classic statement, is to glorify God and sanctify humans. When our worship glorifies God, it does so by praising God for God's actions and attuning us to God's missional purposes. When God through our worship sanctifies us, God conforms us to God's missional character and empowers us to participate in the *missio Dei*.

It is because of the character and purpose of God that worship and mission are intertwined. Neither worship nor mission can take precedence over the other. Neither has the right to specialize itself and to declare that it can exist without symbiotic relationship with the other. The Christendom years show us that worship—as an activity that humans can control—tends to take precedence over mission. In Christendom, worship was the province of the religious professionals, the clergy. Within the past century, this has changed. According to Witvliet, "The growth of lay worship leaders has arguably been one of the most sweeping liturgical changes in the past century."[32] This has brought renewed life to many in the church, and it will reach its potential when the worship led by lay worship leaders equips the worshipping communities with a vision of the mission of God and empowers and emboldens them to take part in it. If the church is to have a future in post-Christendom, there must be renewed emphasis on mission, which is something that only God can control. There must be as many workshops and training weekends that alert people to God's mission and equip them to participate in it as there are on worship. Mission must join worship at the heart of the church's life, for in post-Christendom—after the supports of a sympathetic state and public have disappeared— "non-missional churches will not survive."[33]

But how satisfying, how sanctifying it is when Christians see worship and mission not dualistically, not in competition, but as the integrated action of a body that is made whole. We can view it as a gathering and sending—for we cannot spend all our time in the Christian assembly, and we cannot survive in our work if we do not gather to worship God. However, we find it more helpful to view the Christian life—with the worship and mission that are integral to it—as a matter of breathing.

Breathing In, Breathing Out

The Church's existence is a continual alternation between two phases. Like systole and exhalation in the process of breathing, assembly and mission succeed each other in the life of the Church. Discipleship would be stunted unless it included both the centripetal phase of worship and the centrifugal phase of mission.[34]

So wrote the late Cardinal Avery Dulles in his classic *Models of the Church*. He understood that, by God's design, there is a deep synergy between worship and mission. His observation negates assertions that worship is more important than mission (as it was in Christendom) or that mission is more important than worship (as it is in the view of some activists). Is inhaling more important than exhaling? Or exhaling than inhaling? There is instead a deep wholeness to which God calls us. God calls individual Christians, churches of all sorts, seminaries, bishops, pastors, and church bureaucrats to seek this wholeness vigilantly, critically, and above all hopefully. For through it all the mission of God is coursing. The reconciliation of people to God, of people to the estranged other, of people to the created order that we pillage—this vision is nurtured in acts of worship and embodied in lives of worshipful service.

It is God whose work brings cosmic reconciliation. It is Jesus Christ through whom God has definitively reconciled the world to God. It is the Holy Spirit who continues to nurture, nudge, and blaze forth to enable the impossible to happen. And we? We are God's children, God's servants, who ascribe worth to God by breathing in—worshipping the Lord with gladness—and by breathing out—collaborating with God as God continues the story and brings the peaceable kingdom.

Are Americans in Christendom?

Christendom Defined

"A culture seeking to subject all areas of human experience to the Lordship of Christ."[1] This involves

- a common belief (orthodox Christianity)
- a common belonging (membership of civil society and the Christian church coincides)
- a common behavior (living in ways commonly viewed as Christian, but not necessarily ways of living taught by Jesus Christ, which are viewed as extreme, suitable for religious professionals but not for ordinary citizens)
- enforcement by inducement or compulsion
- marked by control of the media and the "spectacles" (public events or entertainment)

It's Hard to Generalize

- America's religious origins are hybrid, involving a variety of communities: Christendom transplants (the Anglican establishment); those persecuted by Anglican Christendom who wanted to institute their own Christendoms (New England Puritans); Christians who feared and repudiated Christendom models (Quakers, Baptists, Mennonites, seekers); people (such as Benjamin Franklin and Thomas Jefferson) who espoused Enlightenment values; immigrants who arrived with many backgrounds, some of them deeply Christendom in character. The religious ethos of America has been influenced by the U.S. Constitution's First Amendment ("Congress shall make no law respecting an establishment of religion, or prohibiting the free exercise thereof"); American irreligion—and the need for "revivals"; and the phenomenon of "civil religion" (see below).

- Today there are varying patterns in different parts of the United States (and in Canada). For example, in the United States, the blue states are different from the red states; cities and university towns are different from farming towns; the "Bible Belt" is different from the Pacific Northwest. Some areas, both urban and rural, have concentrations of immigrants who adhere to various religions.

We Are in Christendom

- Church attendance on Sundays remains about 25 percent, which is high by Western standards;[2] some Americans go to church twice on Sunday and on Wednesday evening too.
- Many Americans assume that theirs is a Christian country and that on a questionnaire about religious observance it is "correct" to give a Christian answer.
- There are towns where it is widely (though often erroneously) assumed that everyone is a Christian, so mission is still "out there" in foreign lands.
- Many people assert that they believe in God, honor the Bible, and pray.
- Politicians in some areas gain support from their Christian profession; in this they are symptomatic of the Christendom trait that Christian adherence is a way to procure favor at court and succeed in business.
- Christian language and discourse are familiar in many circles.
- The current American president (Barack Obama) is a confessing Christian, uses religious language, occasionally attends worship services, and backs faith-based initiatives.
- Christianity is big business: The Christian music industry and Christian publications are flourishing. There are attempts to legislate Christian values, to promote Christian symbols, and to have prayer and religious observance in state-supported schools.
- The economic and sexual behavior of many Christians is not distinctively Christian.

- Intolerant attitudes to other religions and to Christians of heterodox views and practices are widespread.
- The powerful conundrum of "civil religion" persists. It is "a form of devotion, outlook, and commitment that deeply and widely binds the citizens of the nation together with ideas they possess and express about the sacred nature . . . of their country," and borrows heavily from Christian narratives and vocabulary, so that many Americans see no conflict between their civil religion and their Christian faith.[3] For many Americans, dying for their country means dying for the Christian faith, and serving the country is the same as serving God. Robert Bellah says that in the United States it is "difficult to see where church leaves off and world begins."[4] In our state, Indiana, on automobile license plates the phrase "In God we trust" is superimposed on an American flag.

We Are Not in Christendom

- In the United States Constitution there is a separation of church and state (Amendment 1).
- In the United States, great power is held by transnational corporations and "the market," which may have greater influence and elicit greater allegiance than either church or state.
- There is immense religious variety in America—for example, a Hmong Buddhist temple in the farming town of Mountain Lake, Minnesota, in which Mennonites used to be dominant.
- Church attendance is lower than polls indicate.[5] In some areas (for example, Oregon) few people go to church; in other areas that people assume to be "Christian," church attendance is lower than imagined. The national average is closer to 25 percent than the often cited 40 percent.
- Church attendance is less frequent than it used to be: many people attend "regularly"—not twice on Sunday but twice per month.
- In some communities, there is widespread Christian adherence as well as committed discipleship, but also a refusal to coerce or criticize the non-Christian nonconformists.
- There are believing Christians in American society who have given up on the church, yet are present, alienated, and nonobservant.

- There are communities of Christian immigrants from other countries who are infusing U.S. church life with new vigor and a different spirituality.
- There is widespread ignorance, even in churches, of the Bible and its story.
- The "blue laws," which prohibit certain activities on Sunday, no longer function; one can go to the movies on Sunday, and sports activities dominate weekends, including Sunday mornings.
- The secular institutions remain secular: public schools, network television, and radio stations.
- There is a vigorous culture of Christian institutions that parallel secular institutions: Christian schools and colleges, Christian television and radio stations. At its best, this is a mark of a confident but distinctive community offering alternatives to the rest of society; at its worst, it is Christendom preparing to reimpose itself.
- Economic power: people's attendance at the malls is more assiduous than their attendance in churches; there is an economic lordship that seems all-pervasive, and consumerism is a dominant value.
- Media power: people's consumption of entertainment—television, Internet, and music—defies Christian standards; most Christians give more time to the entertainment industry than they do to the church's activities and to prayer. In many Christian traditions, it is hard to persuade young people to give up entertainment and social activities for the sake of baptismal or confirmation classes.
- Individualism: people's ethical decisions—whether economic or sexual—are determined by individuals acting individualistically. Private judgments are more influential than the Bible or the teachings of the Christian tradition (for example, the failure of the Roman Catholic Church's attempts to get Catholics to practice natural methods of contraception). People know the church's teachings, and they ignore them.
- There are institutions—such as many universities—in which an ideology of "tolerance" leads to intolerance for faculty and students who try to function professionally as confessing Christians.

- There are American Christians, both Catholic and evangelical, who are working consciously to reestablish a Christendom culture that they say has largely disappeared.

The Struggle

- To worship God and follow Jesus freely, humbly, and articulately.
- To work and be neighbors as advocates of the mission and shalom of God, being both pilgrims within the dominant culture and yet comprehensible to it.
- To share the gospel of Jesus Christ humbly but candidly in situations in which some people associate Christianity with the coercing and crusading of Christendom.
- To act in question posing ways that validate the gospel of Jesus Christ—for example, to campaign for the protection of other religions or to practice restorative justice.
- To persuade other American Christians that, because Jesus' insights are true, authentic worship of God and Christian discipleship cannot be forced.
- To talk with other Christians about alternative approaches to ten: to emphasize the eight Beatitudes and the dual Great Commandment to love God and neighbor (8+2=10!), as much as or more than the Ten Commandments.
- To enable Christians in the United States to learn from Christians in Europe that the fruit of social or legal coercion is cynicism, resistance to Christianity, and the decline of the church.

Notes

Series Preface

1. Stuart Murray, *Post-Christendom: Church and Mission in a Strange New World* (Carlisle: Paternoster, 2004), 19.

Introduction

1. Robert N. Bellah, "God and King," in *God, Truth, and Witness: Engaging Stanley Hauerwas*, L. Gregory Jones, Reinhard Hütter and C. Rosalee Velloso Ewell (eds)(Grand Rapids, MI: Brazos Press, 2005), 125.

Chapter 1: Worship After Christendom

1. Wilbert R. Shenk, *Write the Vision: The Church Renewed* (Harrisburg, PA: Trinity Press International, 1995), 51–52.
2. For photos of the Ravenna mosaics see http://employees.oneonta.edu/farberas/arth/arth212/san_vitale.html.
3. *Codex Iustinianus* 1.11.10, cited in Alan Kreider, "Violence and Mission in the Fourth and Fifth Centuries," *International Bulletin of Missionary Research* 31:3 (2007): 130.
4. For photos of this church, see www.norfolkchurches.co.uk/tivetshallmargaret/tivetshallmargaret.htm.
5. J. Andrew Kirk, *What is Mission? Theological Explorations* (Minneapolis: Fortress Press, 2000), 187.
6. W. D. Maxwell, *An Outline of Christian Worship* (Oxford: Clarendon Press, 1936), 1.
7. Dan Kimball, *Emerging Worship: Creating Worship Gatherings for New Generations* (Grand Rapids: Zondervan, 2004), 112.
8. Sally Morgenthaler, *Worship Evangelism* (Grand Rapids: Zondervan, 1995), 23, 31.
9. Everett Ferguson, *The Churches of Christ: A Biblical Ecclesiology for Today* (Grand Rapids: Eerdmans, 1996), 208ff.; C. F. D. Moule, *Worship in the New Testament*, Grove Liturgical Study 12/13

(Nottingham: Grove Books, 1983), 74–76; I. Howard Marshall, "How Far Did the Early Christians Worship God?" *Churchman* 99 (1985): 216–29.

10. Rodney Clapp, *A Peculiar People: The Church as Culture in a Post-Christian Society* (Downer's Grove, IL: InterVarsity Press, 1996), 174.

11. Miguel A. Palomino and Samuel Escobar, "Worship and Culture in Latin America," in *Christian Worship Worldwide: Expanding Horizons, Deepening Practices*, ed. Charles E. Farhadian (Grand Rapids: Eerdmans, 2007), 126.

12. Thomas R. Yoder Neufeld, "Living the Word," *Christian Century*, August 26, 2008, 20.

13. Jonathan J. Bonk, *Missions and Money*, rev. ed., American Society of Missiology Series 15 (Maryknoll, NY: Orbis Books, 2006), 147.

14. Second Council of Nicaea (787), Nicene and Post-Nicene Fathers, 2nd ser., 14, p. 550; cf. Augustine *City of God* 10.1.

15. Philip Kenneson, "Gathering: Worship, Imagination and Formation," in *The Blackwell Companion to Christian Ethics*, eds. Stanley Hauerwas and Samuel Wells (Oxford: Blackwell Publishing, 2006), 54.

16. Nicholas Wolterstorff, "Justice as a Condition of Authentic Liturgy," *Theology Today*, 148.1 (1991): 14.

17. Millard Lind, *Biblical Foundations for Christian Worship* (Scottdale, PA: Herald Press, 1973), 25.

18. Wolterstorff, "Justice," 9, 16.

19. Ibid., 12. See also Christopher Marshall, *The Little Book of Restorative Justice* (Intercourse, PA: Good Books, 2005), 30: "In the absence of justice . . . religious performances merely nauseate God."

20. Cyprian *Ad Quirinum* 3.26.

21. Menno Simons, "Reply to False Accusations" (1552), in *Complete Writings*, ed. J. C. Wenger (Scottdale, PA: Herald Press, 1956), 559.

22. Doug Pagitt, cited in Eddie Gibbs and Ryan K. Bolger, *Emerging Churches: Creating Christian Community in Postmodern Cultures* (Grand Rapids: Baker Academic, 2005), 231.

23. John Witvliet, "Series Preface," in Charles E. Farhadian, *Christian Worship Worldwide: Expanding Horizons, Deepening Practices* (Grand Rapids: Eerdmans, 207), xiii.

24. Eugene H. Peterson, *Leap over a Wall: Earthy Spirituality for Everyday Christians* (San Francisco: HarperSanFrancisco, 1997), 152–53.

25. J. G. Davies, *Worship and Mission* (London: SCM, 1966), 71.

26. Craig Van Gelder, *The Ministry of the Missional Church: A Community Led by the Spirit* (Grand Rapids: Baker Books, 2007), 17–18.
27. Michael B. Aune, "Liturgy and Theology: Rethinking the Relationship—Part II," *Worship* 81:2 (2007): 167.
28. Gerhard Lohfink, *Does God Need the Church? Toward a Theology of the People of God* (Collegeville, MN: Liturgical Press, 1999), 217.
29. Bob Goudzwaard, Mark Vander Vennen, and David Van Heemst, *Hope in Troubled Times: A New Vision for Confronting Global Crises* (Grand Rapids: Eerdmans, 2007), 44.
30. Davies, *Worship and Mission*, 97–8.
31. Ibid., 106.
32. Jesus was quoting Isa 56:7; Jer 7:11.
33. Thomas Schattauer, ed., *Inside Out: Worship in an Age of Mission* (Minneapolis: Fortress Press, 1999), 3.
34. David Smith, *Mission After Christendom* (London: Darton, Longman & Todd, 2003), 3.
35. George G. Hunter III, "The Case for Culturally Relevant Congregations," in *Global Good News: Mission in a New Context*, ed. Howard Snyder (Nashville, TN: Abingdon Press, 2001), 98.
36. David W. Bebbington, "Evangelicals and Public Worship, 1965–2005," *Evangelical Quarterly* 79:1 (2007): 17.
37. Stephen R. Holmes, "Trinitarian Missiology: Towards a Theology of God as Missionary," *International Journal of Systematic Theology* 8:1 (2006): 89.

Chapter 2: Mission Under Christendom

1. David B. Barrett, Todd M. Johnson, and Peter F. Crossing, "Missiometrics 2007: Creating Your Own Analysis of Global Data," *International Bulletin of Missionary Research* 31:1 (2007): 31.
2. Lamin Sanneh, *Disciples of All Nations: Pillars of World Christianity* (New York: Oxford University Press, 2008), 131.
3. Dorothy S. McCammon, *We Tried to Stay* (Scottdale, PA: Herald Press, 1953).
4. Dorothy S. McCammon and Harriet L. Burkholder, eds., *Tragedy and Triumph: Courage and Faith Through Twenty-seven years in Chinese Prisons: The Story of Dr. Yu En-Mei* (San Francisco: Purple Bamboo Publishing, 1993).
5. Sanneh, *Disciples*, 270.
6. Miroslav Volf, "A Vision of Embrace: Theological Perspectives on Cultural Identity and Conflict," *Ecumenical Review* 47:2 (1995): 195.

7. Robert L. Ramseyer, ed., *Mission and the Peace Witness: The Gospel and Christian Discipleship* (Scottdale, PA: Herald Press, 1979), 117.

8. Pierre Charles, *Etudes Missiologiques*, Museum Lessianum, Section Missiologique 33 (Louvain: Desclée De Brouwer, 1956), 26.

9. Robin Lane Fox, *Pagans and Christians* (San Francisco: Harper & Row, 1986), 282, referring to Pantaenus and Gregory of Pontus.

10. H. H. Rosin, *"Missio Dei": An Examination of the Origin, Contents and Function of the Term in Protestant Missiological Discussion* (Leiden: Interuniversity Institute for Missiological and Ecumenical Research, Department of Missiology, 1972), 6.

11. Wolfgang Reinbold, *Propaganda und Mission im ältesten Christentum. Eine Untersuchung zu den Modalitäten der Ausbreitung der frühen Kirche*, Forschungen zur Religion und Literatur des Alten und Neuen Testaments 188 (Göttingen: Vandenhoeck & Ruprecht, 2000), 296. Our translation.

12. *Codex Theodosianus* 16.1.2; *Codex Iustinianus* 1.11.10.

13. Christoph Wolff, *Johann Sebastian Bach: The Learned Musician* (New York: Norton, 2000), 216.

14. Other Bach cantatas with similar themes are 42, 126, and 190.

15. Stuart Murray, *Beyond Tithing* (Carlisle: Paternoster, 2000), 133–41.

16. In the church of the East, in areas that had been parts of the Persian Empire and after the seventh century were under Islamic rule, mission continued into central Asia and China for many centuries. See Philip Jenkins, *The Lost History of Christianity* (New York: HarperCollins, 2008).

17. David J. Bosch, *Transforming Mission: Paradigm Shifts in Theology of Mission*, American Society of Missiology Series 16 (Maryknoll, NY: Orbis Books, 1991), 251.

18. Ibid., 228.

19. Wilbert R. Shenk, ed., *Anabaptism and Mission* (Scottdale, PA: Herald Press, 1984).

20. Andrew F. Walls, "The Missionary Movement: A Lay Fiefdom?" in *The Cross-Cultural Process in Christian History*, ed. Andrew F. Walls (Maryknoll, NY: Orbis Books, 2002), 231.

21. Bosch, *Transforming Mission*, 489.

22. Wilbert R. Shenk, *Write the Vision: The Church Renewed* (Harrisburg, PA: Trinity Press International, 1995), 50; Stuart Murray, *Post-Christendom: Church and Mission in a Strange New World* (Carlisle: Paternoster, 2004), 225.

23. Lesslie Newbigin, *Foolishness to the Greeks: The Gospel and Western Culture* (Geneva: World Council of Churches, 1986), 147.

24. Hartmut Lehmann, "Missionaries without Empire: German Protestant Missionary Efforts in the Interwar Period (1919–1939)," in *Missions, Nationalism, and the End of Empire*, ed. Brian Stanley (Grand Rapids: Eerdmans, 2003), 37.

25. Kevin Xiyi Yao, "At the Turn of the Century: A Study of the China Centenary Missionary Conference of 1907," *International Bulletin of Missionary Research* 32:2 (2008): 66.

26. W. B. Woodard, *The Allied Occupation of Japan, 1945–1952, and Japanese Religions* (Leiden: Brill, 1972), 281.

27. Karl Rahner, "Towards a Fundamental Theological Interpretation of Vatican II," *Journal of Theological Studies* 40 (1979): 717.

28. Owen Chadwick, *The Victorian Church*, 2 vols. (London: A. & C. Black, 1966–1970); Andrew F. Walls, "Structural Problems in Mission Studies," *International Bulletin of Missionary Research* 15:4 (1991): 146.

29. Walls, *Cross-Cultural Process*, 65.

30. Jehu Hanciles, "Transformations within Global Christianity and the Western Missionary Enterprise," *Mission Focus: Annual Review* 14 (2006): 7.

Chapter 3: Mission After Christendom: The *Missio Dei*

1. Maisie Ward, *France Pagan? The Mission of Abbé Godin* (London: Sheed & Ward, 1949).

2. Norman E. Thomas, ed., *Classic Texts in Mission and World Christianity*, American Society of Missiology Series 20 (Maryknoll, NY: Orbis Books, 1995), 105–6.

3. H. H. Rosin, *"Missio Dei": An Examination of the Origin, Contents and Function of the Term in Protestant Missiological Discussion* (Leiden: Interuniversity Institute for Missiological and Ecumenical Research, Department of Missiology, 1972), 13.

4. Georg F. Vicedom, *Missio Dei: Einführung in eine Theologie der Mission* (Munich: Chr. Kaiser Verlag, 1958); Georg F. Vicedom, *The Mission of God: An Introduction to a Theology of Mission*, trans. Gilbert A. Thiele and Dennis Hilgendorf (St. Louis: Concordia, 1965).

5. J. G. Davies, *Worship and Mission* (London: SCM, 1966), 33.

6. Stephen B. Bevans and Roger P. Schroeder, *Constants in Context: A Theology of Mission for Today*, American Society of Missiology Series 30 (Maryknoll, NY: Orbis Books, 2004), 290.

7. Wilbert R. Shenk, "The Mission Dynamic," in *In Bold Humility: David Bosch's Work Considered*, eds. Willem Saayman and Klippies Kritzinger (Maryknoll, NY: Orbis Books, 1996), 83–93.

8. "Reconciliation as the Mission of God: Faithful Christian Witness in a World of Destructive Conflicts and Divisions," Issue Group on Reconciliation under Lausanne Committee on World Evangelization, Pattya, Thailand, September–October 2004 (published 2005, available at www.reconciliationnetwork.com).

9. Christopher J. H. Wright, *The Mission of God: Unlocking the Bible's Grand Narrative* (Downers Grove, IL: InterVarsity Press, 2006).

10. Stephen R. Holmes, "Trinitarian Missiology: Towards a Theology of God as Missionary," *International Journal of Systematic Theology* 8:1 (2006): 82.

11. Ibid., 89.

12. Ibid., 82.

13. Wright, *Mission of God*, 24–25, who makes a useful distinction: the adjective *missionary* points to activities, whereas the adjective *missional* has to do with ethos, theology, and foundational orientation. We recognize that the word *missional* is a neologism, and gives problems to some people, in part because it seems like jargon.

14. Darrell L. Guder, ed., *Missional Church: A Vision for the Sending of the Church in North America* (Grand Rapids: Eerdmans, 1998); Lois Y. Barrett et al., eds., *Treasures in Clay Jars: Patterns in Missional Faithfulness* (Grand Rapids: Eerdmans, 2004).

15. Jean-Paul Audet, *The Gospel Project* (New York: Paulist Press, 1969).

16. Wright, *Mission of God*, 47.

17. Hans Walter Wolff, "Swords into Plowshares: Misuse of a Word of Prophecy?" in *The Meaning of Peace: Biblical Studies*, eds. Perry B. Yoder and Willard M. Swartley (Louisville, KY: Westminster John Knox, 1992), 116.

18. Carolyn J. Weekley, *The Kingdoms of Edward Hicks* (New York: Harry N. Abrams, 1999).

19. Willard M. Swartley, "The Evangel as Gospel of Peace," in *Evangelical, Ecumenical, and Anabaptist Missiologies in Conversation: Essays in Honor of Wilbert R. Shenk*, eds. James R. Krabill, Walter Sawatsky, and Charles E. Van Engen (Maryknoll, NY: Orbis Books, 2006), 69–77.

20. Eric Osborn, "Love of Enemies and Recapitulation," *Vigiliae Christianae* 54 (2000): 12–31.

21. Darrell L. Guder, *The Continuing Conversion of the Church* (Grand Rapids: Eerdmans, 2000), 74.
22. James D. G. Dunn, *Romans 1–8*, Word Biblical Commentary 38A (Dallas: Word, 1988), 481.
23. N. T. Wright, *The Letter to the Romans*, New Interpreters Bible 10 (Nashville, TN: Abingdon Press, 2002), 600–1.
24. Wright, *Mission of God*, 35.
25. David B. Barrett, Todd M. Johnson, and Peter F. Crossing, "Missiometrics 2007: Creating Your Own Analysis of Global Data," *International Bulletin of Missionary Research* 31:1 (2007): 31.
26. Jehu Hanciles, "Transformations within Global Christianity and the Western Missionary Enterprise," *Mission Focus: Annual Review* 14 (2006): 9.
27. Samuel Escobar, *The New Global Mission: The Gospel from Everywhere to Everyone* (Downers Grove, IL: InterVarsity Press, 2003).
28. Ibid., 25–26.
29. Davies, *Worship and Mission*, 86.
30. Cited by Glen Stassen, *Just Peacemaking: Ten Practices for Abolishing War*, rev. ed. (Cleveland: Pilgrim Press, 1998), 30.
31. Christopher J. H. Wright, "An Upside-Down World," *Christianity Today*, January 2007, 42.
32. Richard B. Hays, *The Moral Vision of the New Testament* (San Francisco: HarperSanFrancisco, 1996), 198–200.
33. N. T. Wright, *Paul in Fresh Perspective* (Minneapolis: Fortress Press, 2005), 114.
34. John Piper, *Let the Nations Be Glad! The Supremacy of God in Missions*, rev. ed. (Grand Rapids: Baker Academic, 1993), 17.
35. Nicholas Wolterstorff, *Until Justice and Peace Embrace* (Grand Rapids: Eerdmans, 1983), 72.
36. Jürgen Moltmann, *The Church in the Power of the Spirit: A Contribution to Messianic Ecclesiology* (New York: Harper & Row, 1977), 10.
37. Swartley, "Evangel," 69–77.
38. J. Andrew Kirk, "My Pilgrimage in Mission," *International Bulletin of Missionary Research* 28:2 (2004): 73.
39. Stephen Neill, *Creative Tension* (London: Edinburgh House Press, 1959), 81. William J. Abraham has usefully applied the same logic to evangelism: "If everything is evangelism, nothing is evangelism" (*The Logic of Evangelism* [Grand Rapids: Eerdmans, 1989], 44).
40. L. A. Hoedemaker, "The People of God and the Ends of the Earth," in *Missiology: An Ecumenical Introduction*, eds. F. J. Verstraelen

et al. (Grand Rapids: Eerdmans, 1995), 162–65. See also George Sumner, "What's Anglican About Mission?" *Anglican Theological Review* 89:3 (2007): 463: "The problem with this appealing term [*missio Dei*] has been that it remains devoid of content, and so is prone to be filled out with the favorite ideas of each user, in accordance with his or her ideological commitments."

41. Jim Reapsome, "Holistic Reach," *Christianity Today* 51:6 (June 2007): 73.

42. Eusebius *Oration in Praise of Constantine* (336), 2:3; 16:3–7; Lamin Sanneh, *Disciples of All Nations: Pillars of World Christianity* (New York: Oxford University Press, 2008), 282.

43. Compare three rather different criteria proposed by John V. Taylor (*The Go-Between God: The Holy Spirit and the Christian Mission* [London: SCM, 1972], 39): "Which factors of this situation are giving people the more intense awareness of some 'other' who claims their attention or of some greater 'whole'? Which factors are compelling people to make personal and responsible choices? Which factors are calling out from people self-oblation and sacrifice?"

44. George Monbiot, *Heat: How to Stop the Planet from Burning* (Cambridge, MA: South End Press, 2007).

45. Ibid., 148–54.

46. For the analysis and proposal in detail, see Alan Storkey, "A Motorway-based National Coach System," 2005, available from alan@storkey.com.

47. For samples of Alan Storkey's wide-ranging interests, see his *Transforming Economics: A Christian Way to Employment* (London: SPCK, 1986); *Marriage and Its Modern Crisis: Repairing Married Life* (London: Hodder & Stoughton, 1996); *Jesus and Politics: Confronting the Powers* (Grand Rapids: Baker Academic, 2005).

48. Rodney Clapp, *A Peculiar People: The Church as Culture in a Post-Christian Society* (Downer's Grove, IL: InterVarsity Press, 1996), 186.

Chapter 4: Post-Christendom Worship: The Recovery of Narrative

1. David F. Ford and Daniel W. Hardy, *Living in Praise: Worshipping and Knowing God* (Grand Rapids: Baker Academic, 2005), 23.

2. June Alliman Yoder, Marlene Kropf, and Rebecca Slough, *Preparing Sunday Dinner: A Collaborative Approach to Worship and Preaching* (Scottdale, PA: Herald Press, 2005), 158–62.

3. Robert N. Bellah et al., *Habits of the Heart: Individualism and Commitment in American Life* (New York: Harper & Row, 1985), 81.

4. Robert Pinsky, "Poetry and American Memory," *Atlantic Monthly*, October 1999. We owe this quote to Jonathan Bonk.

5. Richard T. Hughes, *Myths America Lives By* (Urbana, IL: University of Illinois Press, 2003).

6. We also learned from our Catholic friends that their schools and communities did not celebrate Guy Fawkes Day.

7. Mason Locke Weems, *The Life of George Washington; with Curious Anecdotes, Equally Honourable to Himself, and Exemplary to His Young Countrymen* (Philadelphia: J. B. Lippincott, n.d.), 15-16.

8. Walter Brueggemann, *Israel's Praise: Doxology against Idolatry and Ideology* (Philadelphia: Fortress Press, 1988), chap. 4.

9. J. G. Davies, *Worship and Mission* (London: SCM, 1966), 151.

10. Arthur C. Ainger, *Church Missionary Hymn Book*, 1899.

11. N. T. Wright, "How Can the Bible Be Authoritative?" *Vox Evangelica* 21 (1991): 7–32; N. T. Wright, *The New Testament and the People of God* (London: SPCK, 1992), 141–43.

12. Nigel G. Wright, *The Radical Evangelical: Seeking a Place to Stand* (London: SPCK, 1996): 54–56; Samuel Wells, *Improvisation: The Drama of Christian Ethics* (Grand Rapids: Brazos Press, 2004), 50–57; Christopher Rowland and Jonathan Roberts, *The Bible for Sinners: Interpretation in the Present Time* (London: SPCK, 2008), 6–8.

13. Craig G. Bartholomew and Michael W. Goheen, *The Drama of Scripture: Finding Our Place in the Biblical Story* (Grand Rapids: Baker Academic, 2004). In his *The New Testament and the People of God*, 141–43, Wright presents his scheme as follows: "1-Creation; 2-Fall; 3-Israel; 4-Jesus. The writing of the New Testament—including the writing of the gospels—would then form the first scene of the fifth act, and would simultaneously give hints (Romans 8, 1 Corinthians 15, parts of the Apocalypse) of how the play is supposed to end." Bartholomew and Goheen, p. 27, substantially agree with Wright's acts 1–4, but nuance act 5 differently and add act 6 as follows:

    Act 5   Spreading the News of the King: The Mission
            of the Church
        Scene 1   From Jerusalem to Rome
        Scene 2   And into All the World
    Act 6   The Return of the King: Redemption Completed

14. Wright, *New Testament*, 142.

15. Ephrem of Syrus, in Sebastian Brock, *The Luminous Eye: The Spiritual World Vision of St. Ephrem* (Kalamazoo: Cistercian Publications, 1985), 29; Jack W. Hayford, *Manifest Presence: Expecting a Visitation of God's Grace Through Worship* (Grand Rapids: Chosen Books, 2005), 52.

16. Steven J. Land, *Pentecostal Spirituality: A Passion for the Kingdom* (Sheffield: Sheffield Academic Press, 1993), 13, 136.

17. Walter Brueggemann, *Theology of the Old Testament: Testimony, Dispute, Advocacy* (Minneapolis: Fortress Press, 1997), 206.

18. This poem is one of the oldest writings in the Hebrew Scriptures. See Walter Brueggemann, *The Book of Exodus*, New Interpreter's Bible 1 (Nashville, TN: Abingdon Press, 1994), 799.

19. Richard Bauckham, *Jesus and the Eyewitnesses: The Gospels as Eyewitness Testimony* (Grand Rapids, MI: Eerdmans, 2006).

20. Walter Brueggemann, "Counterscript: Living with the Elusive God," *Christian Century*, November 29, 2005, 27.

21. John Paul Lederach, *The Moral Imagination: The Art and Soul of Building Peace* (New York: OUP, 2005), 146.

22. Jean Bethke Elshtain, "Theologian: Christian Contrarian," *Time*, September 17, 2001.

23. Jonathan J. Bonk, *Missions and Money*, rev. ed., American Society of Missiology Series 15 (Maryknoll, NY: Orbis Books, 2006), 94.

24. Christian Smith and Melinda Lundquist Denton, *Soul Searching: The Religious and Spiritual Lives of American Teenagers* (New York: Oxford University Press, 2005), 162–63; Philip Jenkins, *The New Faces of Christianity: Believing the Bible in the Global South* (New York: Oxford University Press, 2006), 114.

25. Rifat Sonsino, *Motive Clauses in Hebrew Law, Biblical Forms and Near Eastern Parallels* (Chico, CA: Scholars Press, 1980), 35–39, cited in Millard Lind, *The Sound of Sheer Silence and the Killing State: The Death Penalty and the Bible* (Telford, PA: Cascadia, 2004), 158; Christopher D. Marshall, *Beyond Retribution: A New Testament Vision for Justice, Crime, and Punishment* (Grand Rapids: Eerdmans, 2001), 260.

26. For example, Exod 22:21; Deut 24:17-22.

27. Matt 6:14-15; 18:32-33; Rom 15:7; 1 Pet 2:21.

28. Marshall, *Beyond Retribution*, 260.

29. Eugene H. Peterson, *Leap over a Wall: Earthy Spirituality for Everyday Christians* (San Francisco: HarperSanFrancisco, 1997), 44.

30. Pete Ward, *Selling Worship: How What We Sing Has Changed the Church* (Milton Keynes: Paternoster, 2005), 210.

31. *Worship Leader*, March/April 2006, 23. Brenton Brown, an American pastor in the Vineyard tradition, has found that "story songs help place us as individuals within the grander story of God's dealings with his people," but is aware of the danger of a dominating individualistic piety: "If you're going to use a narrative approach for congregational songs, you need to make sure that the story has a universal quality to it" ("Songcraft: Story Songs," *Worship Leader*, January/February 2008, 10).

32. Text by Christopher Ellis, in *Baptist Praise and Worship* (Oxford: Oxford University Press, 1991), 447.

33. Gail Ramshaw, "The Long and Short of Eucharistic Praying," *Call to Worship* 40:4 (2007): 33; for further reflections, see Anne Ferguson, "Making Eucharist in the Here and Now: The History and Present Practice of Locally-Authored and Extemporaneous Eucharistic Prayer," *Doxology* 24 (2007): 41.

34. James Wm. McClendon Jr., *Systematic Theology, II: Doctrine* (Nashville: Abingdon Press, 1994), 404.

35. Denis Edwards, "Eucharist and Ecology: Keeping Memorial of Creation," *Worship* 82:3 (2008): 212.

36. Emmanuel Charles McCarthy, "The Nonviolent Eucharistic Jesus: A Pastoral Approach," Center for Christian Nonviolence, accessible at http://www.lewrockwell.com/orig7/mccarthy1.html.

37. Davies, *Worship and Mission*, 151.

38. For encouraging examples of collects which express missional alertness, see the collects for the 13th and 15th Sundays after Trinity in *Common Worship* (London: Church House Publishing, 2000), 416–17. It would be useful to compile a new book—*Prayers for a Missional Church*—that provides prayers for the entire church year (Years A, B, and C), which gives thanks and praise to the God of the reconciling metanarrative and asks God graciously to empower God's people to participate in God's mission.

39. Arthur Paul Boers et al., eds., *Take Our Moments and Our Days: An Anabaptist Prayer Book—Ordinary Time* (Scottdale, PA: Herald Press, 2010), 272.

40. Life of Jesus Mafa, www.jesusmafa.com/anglais/accueil.htm, and Misereor, www.misereor.de/aktionen-kampagnen/hungertuch.html.

41. Eddie Gibbs and Ryan K. Bolger, *Emerging Churches: Creating Christian Community in Postmodern Cultures* (Grand Rapids: Baker Academic, 2005), 73–74, 177.

42. Bryan Stone, *Evangelism After Christendom: The Theology and Practice of Christian Witness* (Grand Rapids: Brazos Press, 2007), 109.

Chapter 5: Narrative Resources for Worship: Hoping the Past, Remembering the Future

1. Thereby they do an injustice to Robert E. Webber, whose "ancient-future" work was far more subtle than this; see, for example, his *Ancient-Future Evangelism* (Grand Rapids: Baker Books, 2003).
2. Philip Jenkins, *The Lost History of Christianity* (New York: HarperCollins, 2008).
3. C. Arnold Snyder, *Following in the Footsteps of Christ: The Anabaptist Tradition* (London: Darton, Longman & Todd, 2004), 48.
4. Joseph Kahn, "Where's Mao? Chinese Revise History Books," *New York Times*, September 1, 2006, A1, A6.
5. Frederick C. Bauerschmidt, "Baptism in the Diaspora," in *On Baptism: Mennonite-Catholic Theological Colloquium, 2001–2002,* ed. Gerald W. Schlabach (Kitchener, ON: Pandora Press, 2004), 21.
6. Helen Kolb Gates et al., *Bless the Lord O My Soul: A Biography of Bishop John Fretz Funk, 1835–1930* (Scottdale, PA: Herald Press, 1964).
7. John Bell, *The Singing Thing: A Case for Congregational Song* (Chicago: GIA Publications, 2000), 48.
8. For the entire text, see Littlemore Baptist Church's website, www. littlemorebaptist.org.uk/
9. Scott A. Ellington, "The Costly Loss of Testimony," *Journal of Pentecostal Theology* 16 (2000): 59.
10. Walter Brueggemann, *Theology of the Old Testament: Testimony, Dispute, Advocacy* (Minneapolis: Fortress Press, 1997), 117-44.
11. Ellington, "Costly Loss," 50–51. See John Bell, "The Lost Tradition of Lament," in *Composing Music for Worship,* eds. Stephen Darlington and Alan Kreider (Norwich: Canterbury Press, 2003), 104–16; Paul Bradbury, *Sowing in Tears: How to Lament in a Church of Praise,* Grove Worship Series 193 (Cambridge: Grove Books, 2007).
12. Gerhard Lohfink, *The Work of God Goes On* (Philadelphia: Fortress Press, 1987), 20.
13. Charles E. Farhadian, ed., *Christian Worship Worldwide: Expanding Horizons, Deepening Practices* (Grand Rapids: Eerdmans, 207), 61–62, 148–49.
14. Allen Bouley, OSB, *From Freedom to Formula: The Evolution of the Eucharistic Prayer from Oral Improvisation to Written Texts,* The Catholic University of America Studies in Christian Antiquity 21

(Washington, D.C.: Catholic University of America Press, 1981). Bouley gives a range of considerations that led to this change (155–58).

15. Mark R. Gornik, *To Live in Peace: Biblical Faith and the Changing Inner City* (Grand Rapids: Eerdmans, 2002), 165.

16. "UVF Ends Terror Campaign," *Independent*, May 3, 2007.

17. Cited by Jenkins, *New Faces*, 96.

18. This theme has recurred in recent writing. See David A. Hogue, *Remembering the Future, Imagining the Past: Story, Ritual, and the Human Brain* (Cleveland, OH: Pilgrim Press, 2003); Jacob W. Elias, *Remember the Future: The Pastoral Theology of Paul the Apostle* (Scottdale, PA: Herald Press, 2006); Andrew Walker and Luke Bretherton, eds., *Remembering Our Future: Explorations in Deep Church* (London: Paternoster, 2007).

19. Cited in David J. Bosch, *Transforming Mission: Paradigm Shifts in Theology of Mission*, American Society of Missiology Series 16 (Maryknoll, NY: Orbis Books, 1991), 498.

20. Lesslie Newbigin, *The Other Side of 1984: Questions for the Churches* (Geneva: World Council of Churches, 1983), 1.

21. Jonathan J. Bonk, *Missions and Money*, rev. ed., American Society of Missiology Series 15 (Maryknoll, NY: Orbis Books, 2006), 107.

22. Daniel Johnson, "Contrary Hopes: Evangelical Christianity and the Decline Narrative," in *The Future of Hope: Christian Tradition Amid Modernity and Postmodernity*, eds. Miroslav Volf and William Katerberg (Grand Rapids: Eerdmans, 2004), 41.

23. Rodney Clapp, *A Peculiar People: The Church as Culture in a Post-Christian Society* (Downer's Grove, IL: InterVarsity Press, 1996), 185.

24. Richard Bauckham, and Trevor Hart, *Hope Against Hope: Christian Eschatology at the Turn of the Millennium* (Grand Rapids: Eerdmans, 1999), 52.

25. Hans Walter Wolff, "Swords into Plowshares: Misuse of a Word of Prophecy?" in *The Meaning of Peace: Biblical Studies*, eds. Perry B. Yoder and Willard M. Swartley (Louisville, KY: Westminster John Knox, 1992), 110–26.

26. James W. Loewen, *Sundown Towns: A Hidden Dimension of American Racism* (New York: New Press, 2008).

27. Walter Brueggemann, *Isaiah 1–39* (Louisville, KY: Westminster John Knox, 1998), 42.

28. Jürgen Moltmann, *Theology of Hope: On the Ground and the Implications of a Christian Eschatology* (New York: Harper & Row, 1967), 328.

29. John Howard Yoder, "Peace without Eschatology," in *The Royal Priesthood: Essays Ecumenical and Ecclesiological*, ed. Michael G. Cartwright (Grand Rapids: Eerdmans, 1994), 152, 157.

Chapter 6: Early Christian Worship: Multivoiced Meals

1. Oscar Cullmann, *Early Christian Worship*, Studies in Biblical Theology 10 (London: SCM, 1953), 7, 12–15.
2. Dom Gregory Dix, *The Shape of the Liturgy*, 2nd ed. (London: Adam & Charles Black, 1945), 5, 36.
3. Paul F. Bradshaw, *The Search for the Origins of Christian Worship: Sources and Methods for the Study of Early Liturgy*, 2nd ed. (London and New York: SPCK and Oxford University Press, 2002), 34–36, 68–71, 53 (for the "pluriform nature of early Christianity").
4. Paul F. Bradshaw, "The Homogenization of Christian Liturgy— Ancient and Modern," *Studia Liturgica* 26 (1996): 1–15.
5. Maxwell E. Johnson, "The Apostolic Tradition," in *The Oxford History of Christian Worship*, eds. Geoffrey Wainwright and Karen B. Westerfield Tucker (New York: Oxford University Press, 2006), 32.
6. Paul F. Bradshaw, *Daily Prayer in the Early Church* (London: Alcuin Club/SPCK, 1981), 21–22, 44–45; John Koenig, *The Feast of the World's Redemption: Eucharistic Origins and Christian Mission* (Harrisburg, PA: Trinity Press International, 2000); Dennis E. Smith, *From Symposium to Eucharist: The Banquet in the Early Christian World* (Minneapolis: Fortress Press, 2003).
7. Lamin Sanneh, *Translating the Message: The Missionary Impact on Culture*, American Society of Missiology Series 13 (Maryknoll, NY: Orbis Books, 1989).
8. Andrew F. Walls, *The Missionary Movement in Christian History: Studies in the Transmission of Faith* (Maryknoll, NY: Orbis Books, 1996), 7–9. Across the centuries, missionally alert theologians have expressed these two principles in other ways. In the fourth century, Basil of Caesarea urged young Christians not to avoid pagan literature but to be like bees: "For these neither approach all flowers equally, nor in truth do they attempt to carry off entire those upon which they alight, but taking only so much of them as is suitable for their work, they suffer the rest to go untouched" (*Address to Young Men* 4). In the fourteenth century, Gregory Palamas used a different image: Christians should approach pagan thinking by discriminating between honey, which is sweet and nutritious, and hemlock, which is sweet and lethal (*The Triads* 28,

cited in William J. Abraham, *The Logic of Evangelism* [Grand Rapids: Eerdmans, 1989]), 170.

9. Stuart Murray, *Post-Christendom: Church and Mission in a Strange New World* (Carlisle: Paternoster, 2004), 66.

10. Bradshaw, *Search*, x.

11. Larry W. Hurtado, *One God, One Lord: Early Christian Devotion and Ancient Jewish Monotheism* (Philadelphia: Fortress Press, 1988), 11; Bradshaw, *Search*, 139; Smith, *From Symposium*, chap. 6.

12. Blake Leyerle, "Meal Customs in the Greco-Roman World," in *Passover and Easter: Origin and History to Modern Times*, eds. Paul F. Bradshaw and Lawrence A. Hoffman (Notre Dame, IN: University of Notre Dame Press, 1999), 31.

13. Smith, *From Symposium*, 281–82.

14. Part 1, the meal (Greek *deipnon* [Latin *cena*]), was served by slaves to diners reclining, two or three to a couch. After a ritual transition, which was a ceremonial blessing of the wine, part 2, the entertainment (Greek *symposion* [Latin *convivium*]) began, in which there was drinking, music, conversation, and at times philosophical discourse. In our text we will refer to the post-meal entertainment as a *symposium*.

15. Paul F. Bradshaw, *Eucharistic Origins* (New York: Oxford University Press, 2004), 43–44.

16. Smith, *From Symposium*, 216–17.

17. Ibid., 283.

18. Reta Halteman Finger, *Of Widows and Meals: Communal Meals in the Book of Acts* (Grand Rapids: Eerdmans, 2007), 52.

19. Examples from scholars of various Christian traditions include Jan Michael Joncas, "Tasting the Kingdom of God: The Meal Ministry of Jesus and Its Implications for Contemporary Worship and Life," *Worship* 74:4 (2000): 329–65; Robert Banks, *Paul's Idea of Community: The Early House Churches in Their Historical Setting* (Grand Rapids: Eerdmans, 1980); Koenig, *Feast*, 112–22; M. E. Johnson, "Apostolic Tradition," 46–49; Smith, *From Symposium*, chap. 7.

20. "Come together" (*synerchomai*) 11:17, 18, 33-34; 14:23, 26; "assembly/church" (*ekklesia*) 11:18, 22; 12:28; 14:4, 5, 12, 19, 23, 28; "body" (*sōma*) , 11:24, 27; 12:12-27.

21. Smith, *From Symposium*, 200.

22. Bradshaw, *Eucharistic Origins*, 71; cf. Smith, *From Symposium*, 200.

23. John Howard Yoder, *Body Politics: Five Practices of the Christian Community before the Watching World* (Nashville, TN: Discipleship Resources, 1992), 21.

24. Leyerle, "Meal Customs," 41.

25. Jerome Murphy-O'Connor, *St. Paul's Corinth: Texts and Archaeology*, 3rd ed. (Collegeville, MN: Liturgical Press, 2002), 184.

26. For four meanings that Paul may have intended in 1 Cor 11:29, see Dale B. Martin, *The Corinthian Body* (New Haven, CT: Yale University Press, 1995), 195.

27. Jerome Murphy-O'Connor, "Eucharist and Community in First Corinthians," *Worship* 51:1 (January 1977): 67–68, who espouses a "community interpretation of 11:29." See also Richard B. Hays, *First Corinthians*, Interpretation, A Bible Commentary for Teaching and Preaching (Louisville, KY: John Knox Press, 1997), 200.

28. Andrew McGowan points out that the Jesus of the Gospels "did not preside over a distinctive meal tradition." He attended banquets, which others hosted, at which he ate and drank with others, including marginal people. This was "a model of sharing openly in the meals of others" ("The Meals of Jesus and the Meals of the Church: Eucharistic Origins and Admission to Communion," in *Studia Liturgica Diversa: Essays in Honor of Paul F. Bradshaw*, eds. Maxwell E. Johnson and L. Edward Phillips (Portland, OR: Pastoral Press, 2004), 110–11.

29. Yoder, *Body Politics*, 23.

30. Christopher J. Ellis argues convincingly that the English Baptist tradition, in which Communion is celebrated monthly rather than weekly, accords to the Lord's Supper a significance that is "*central rather than normative*": *Gathering: A Theology and Spirituality of Worship in Free Church Tradition* (London: SCM, 2004), 183.

31. Quoted in Richard Gaillardetz, *Transforming Our Days* (New York: Crossroad, 2000), 123–24.

32. Smith, *From Symposium*, 212.

33. Koenig, *Feast*, 121.

34. Smith, *From Symposium*, 207.

35. Hays, *First Corinthians*, 238–39.

36. It is variously translated into English as "build up," "edify," or "strengthen." The translators of the REB, NJB, and NRSV have preferred "build up"; the NIV translators render it both with "edify," familiar from the KJV, and with the paraphrase "strengthen."

37. Hermas *Vision* 3.9.2-7.

38. Gordon D. Fee, *God's Empowering Presence: The Holy Spirit in the Letters of Paul* (Peabody, MA: Hendrickson, 1994), 889.

39. Gerhard Lohfink, *Jesus and Community* (Philadelphia: Fortress Press, 1982), 122–32. The lives of individual Christian disciples and the corporate body of Christ were essential elements of Jesus' missional strategy—salt (scattered individuals) and light (gathered community). See Alan Kreider, *Social Holiness: A Way of Living for God's Nation* (Eugene, OR: Wipf & Stock, 2008), 242–43, 288–89.

40. Robert Banks provides a credible reconstruction of an early Christian house church meeting in his *Going to Church in the First Century*, 2nd ed. (Paramatta, NSW: Hexagon Press, 1985).

41. James Farwell finds in this passage a "clear logic of participation," rooted in the necessity of discerning the unity of the body of Christ, according to which only certain participants would take part in the meal ritual (1 Cor 11:27ff.): "Baptism, Eucharist, and the Hospitality of Jesus: On the Practice of 'Open Communion,'" *Anglican Theological Review* 86:2 (2004): 222–23; see also Koenig, *Feast*, 254.

42. Ben Witherington III, *Conflict and Community in Corinth: A Socio-Rhetorical Commentary on 1 and 2 Corinthians* (Grand Rapids: Eerdmans, 1995), 284.

43. David G. Horrell, "Domestic Space and Christian Meetings at Corinth," *New Testament Studies* 50:3 (2004): 349–69; Robert Jewett, "Tenement Churches and Pauline Love Feasts," *Quarterly Review* 14 (Spring 1994): 43–58.

44. John Christopher Thomas, *Footwashing in John 13 and the Johannine Community*, JSNT Supplement Series 61 (Sheffield: Sheffield Academic Press, 1991), 184–85.

45. Justin wrote (1 *Apology* 66): "This food we call Eucharist, of which no one is allowed to partake except one who believes that the things we teach are true and has received the washing for forgiveness of sins and for rebirth, and who lives as Christ handed down to us." Many Christian traditions have taken seriously Justin's concern for right belief and baptism, but have ignored his insistence that the participants in the meal behave as Christ taught.

46. See the parallel passage in Eph 5:18-20, which significantly begins with the admonition, "Do not get drunk with wine," which refers to its location in a meal event, after dinner and after the ritual blessing of the cup of wine, which articulated the transition to the *symposium*.

47. See parallels of reportage and testimony in a liturgical text (Ps 40:10) and in a parable of Jesus (Luke 15:9).

48. Willard M. Swartley, *Covenant of Peace: The Missing Peace in New Testament Theology and Ethics* (Grand Rapids: Eerdmans, 2006), 208–11; Ulrich Mauser, *The Gospel of Peace: A Scriptural Message for Today's World* (Louisville, KY: Westminster/John Knox Press, 1992), 23–34.

49. William T. Cavanaugh, *Torture and Eucharist: Theology, Politics, and the Body of Christ* (Oxford: Blackwell Publishing, 1998), 229; Peter Dula, "Easter in Baghdad: Theology in the Shadow of War," *Commonweal*, March 26, 2006, 19.

50. Justin 1 *Apology* 14 alludes to many of these concerns in second-century Rome.

Chapter 7: After Christendom: Multivoiced Worship Returns

1. For a discussion of changing approaches in domestic worship leading to the third-century emergence of the sermon, see Alistair Stewart-Sykes, *From Prophecy to Preaching: A Search for the Origins of the Christian Homily*, Supplements to *Vigiliae Christianae* 59 (Leiden: Brill, 2001).

2. According to *Didache* 9.5, unbaptized people were apparently still in the assembly, but were not to participate in the Eucharist (Paul Bradshaw, "The Reception of Communion in Early Christianity," *Studia Liturgica* 37 [2007]: 67). For the more general exclusion of unbaptized people from the Christian meetings, see Alan Kreider, *Worship and Evangelism in Pre-Christendom*, Alcuin/GROW Joint Liturgical Studies 32 (Cambridge: Grove Books, 1995), 8–9.

3. Minucius Felix *Octavius* 9.6.

4. Tertullian *Apology* 39.16–19. That the North African Christians called their meal *Agape* did not mean that they differentiated it from another meal that they called *Eucharist*. In this period there is no evidence for two different kinds of meals: Andrew McGowan, "Rethinking Agape and Eucharist in Early North African Christianity," *Studia Liturgica* 34 (2004): 166, 168–72.

5. The *agape* continued in many places. See, for example, the evidence of the Council of Laodicea (canons 27–28) from mid-fourth-century Asia Minor: Charles Joseph Hefele, *Histoire Des Conciles D'après Les Documents Originaux*, I.2, ed. J. Leclerq (Paris: Letouzey et Ané, 1907), 1015.

6. Pliny *Epistle* 10.96.7.

7. Murphy-O'Connor, on the basis of a "sumptuous" villa excavated in Corinth, has estimated that a "base figure" for the "whole church" in Corinth in Paul's time was "between forty and fifty persons" (*St. Paul's Corinth: Texts and Archaeology*, 3rd ed. [Collegeville, MN: Liturgical Press, 2002], 178, 182). David Horrell, pointing to recent archaeology of less sumptuous dwellings in Corinth in which Christians might have met upstairs, has argued that the number of people in the meetings of the Corinthian congregation may have been somewhat smaller than that ("Domestic Space," 349–69).

8. Alistair Stewart-Sykes, "The Domestic Origins of the Liturgy of the Word," *Studia Patristica* 40 (2006): 115–20.

9. Dennis E. Smith, *From Symposium to Eucharist: The Banquet in the Early Christian World* (Minneapolis: Fortress Press, 2003), 21.

10. Gordon W. Lathrop, *Holy Things: A Liturgical Theology* (Minneapolis: Fortress Press, 1993).

11. John Koenig, *Soul Banquets: How Meals Become Mission in the Local Congregation* (Harrisburg, PA: Morehouse Publishing, 2007), 26.

12. Origen *Contra Celsum* 7.8.

13. James Cooper, ed., *Testamentum Domini* (Edinburgh, T. & T. Clark, 1902), 1.22-23. For the date and provenance of this document, see Grant Sperry-White, ed., *The Testamentum Domini: A Text for Students* (Bramcote, Nottingham: Grove Books, 1991), 6.

14. Andrew McGowan, "Food, Ritual and Power," in *A People's History of Christianity, II: Late Ancient Christianity*, ed. Virginia Burrus (Minneapolis: Fortress Press, 2005), 147.

15. McGowan, "Rethinking Agape," 169–71.

16. Maureen A. Tilley, ed., *Donatist Martyr Stories: The Church in Conflict in Roman North Africa*, Translated Texts for Historians 24 (Liverpool: Liverpool University Press, 1996), 36–37.

17. Alexander Schmemann, *Introduction to Liturgical Theology*, 2nd ed. (Leighton Buzzard: Faith Press, 1975), 93.

18. Allen Bouley, OSB, *From Freedom to Formula: The Evolution of the Eucharistic Prayer from Oral Improvisation to Written Texts*, The Catholic University of America Studies in Christian Antiquity 21 (Washington, D.C.: Catholic University of America Press, 1981), 245–52.

19. *Apostolic Constitutions* 2.57.

20. Paul F. Bradshaw, "The Homogenization of Christian Liturgy—Ancient and Modern," *Studia Liturgica* 26 (1996): 1–15.

21. *Apostolic Constitutions* 8.12. For further theological developments, see William R. Crockett, *Eucharist: Symbol of Transformation* (New York: Pueblo Publishing, 1989), 107.

22. Bradshaw, "The Effects of the Coming of Christendom on Early Christian Worship," in *The Origin of Christendom in the West*, ed. Alan Kreider (Edinburgh: T. & T. Clark, 2001), 278.

23. John Chrysostom, "Homily 36 on 1 Corinthians," in Judith L. Kovacs, *I Corinthians: Interpreted by Early Christian Commentators*, The Church's Bible (Grand Rapids: Eerdmans, 2005), 238.

24. For contrasting understandings of 1 Cor 14:34-35 on the part of two evangelical commentators, see Gordon D. Fee, *The First Epistle to the Corinthians* (Grand Rapids: Eerdmans, 1987), 699–709; and Ben Witherington III, *Conflict and Community in Corinth: A Socio-Rhetorical Commentary on 1 and 2 Corinthians* (Grand Rapids: Eerdmans, 1995), 287–88. Fee argues that Paul's argument in chapter 14 makes better sense without these verses, that they contradict his teaching in 11:2-16 that women may pray and prophesy in the assembly, and have appeared in ancient manuscripts at various places; in his view they are a "very early marginal gloss," an interpolation. Therefore, this passage is not a binding prohibition of women's participation in worship. Witherington admits the textual problems, but does not see these as decisive. He argues that during the weighing of prophecies, some women, probably married, disrupted the worship by asking inappropriate questions. Paul urges them to remain silent and to ask questions at home; in this way Paul corrects an abuse, but does retract the right of women to speak in worship, which he had asserted in chapter 11. Cf. A. C. Wire, *The Corinthian Women Prophets* (Minneapolis: Fortress Press, 1990), 152–58, 229–32.

25. Martin Luther, "The Misuse of the Mass," in *Luther's Works* 36, ed. A. R. Wentz (Philadelphia: Muhlenberg Press, 1959), 149–50.

26. Martin Luther, "On the Councils and the Church (1539)," in *Luther's Works* 41, ed. Eric W. Gritsch (Philadelphia: Fortress Press, 1966), 154–55.

27. The text of this anonymously authored document, which survives in a codex of 1590, is being prepared for publication by C. Arnold Snyder. In 1560 Heinrich Bullinger incorporated an abbreviated version of this text, emanating from the 1540s, without quotes from Luther, in his anti-Anabaptist writing *Der Widertoeuffern ursprung* (Zürich: Christoph Froschauer, 1560). For the text

as rendered by Bullinger, see Shem Peachey and Paul Peachey, "Answer of Some Who are Called (Ana)Baptists Why They Do Not Attend the Churches: A Swiss Brethren Tract," *Mennonite Quarterly Review* 45 (1971): 5–32.

28. Marpeck, "Concerning the Lowliness of Christ (1547)," in William Klassen and Walter Klaassen, eds., *The Writings of Pilgram Marpeck* (Scottdale, PA: Herald Press, 1978), 442.

29. Christopher J. Ellis, *Gathering: A Theology and Spirituality of Worship in Free Church Tradition* (London: SCM, 2004), 46–47; Christopher Hill, *The World Turned Upside Down: Radical Ideas During the English Revolution* (New York: Viking, 1972), 95, 104–5.

30. Horton Davies, *Worship and Theology in England*, vol. 2 (Grand Rapids: Eerdmans, 1996), 513–14.

31. Michael L. Budde, "Collecting Praise," in *The Blackwell Companion to Christian Ethics*, eds. Stanley Hauerwas and Samuel Wells (Oxford: Blackwell Publishing, 2006), 128.

32. James Wm. McClendon Jr., *Systematic Theology, II: Doctrine* (Nashville: Abingdon Press, 1994), 187.

33. Nicholas Wolterstorff, *Until Justice and Peace Embrace* (Grand Rapids: Eerdmans, 1983), 161.

34. Eleanor Kreider, *Communion Shapes Character* (Scottdale, PA: Herald Press, 1997), 189–95; also as *Given for You: A Fresh Look at Communion* (Leicester: IVP, 1998), 167–72.

35. Doug Pagitt, *Church Re-Imagined: The Spiritual Formation of People in Communities of Faith* (Grand Rapids: Zondervan, 2005), 97; Eddie Gibbs and Ryan K. Bolger, *Emerging Churches: Creating Christian Community in Postmodern Cultures* (Grand Rapids: Baker Academic, 2005), 228, 232.

36. Henry H. Knight III and Steven J. Land, "On Being a Witness: Worship and Holiness in the Wesleyan and Pentecostal Traditions," in *Liturgy and the Moral Self: Essays in Honor of Don E. Saliers*, eds. E. Byron Anderson and Bruce T. Morrill, SJ (Collegeville, MN: Liturgical Press, 1998), 87.

37. Dana L. Robert and M. L. Daneel, "Worship among Apostles and Zionists in Southern Africa," in *Christian Worship Worldwide: Expanding Horizons, Deepening Practices*, ed. Charles E. Farhadian (Grand Rapids: Eerdmans, 207), 61–62.

38. Brian Haymes, "Towards a Sacramental Understanding of Preaching," in *Baptist Sacramentalism*, eds. Anthony R. Cross and Philip E. Thompson (Carlisle: Paternoster, 2003), 266.

39. Even the hymns which, according to 1 Cor 14:26, might be proposed by any member, are now controlled by clergy in collaboration with church musicians.

40. Charles Pinches, "Proclaiming: Naming and Describing," in Hauerwas and Wells, *Christian Ethics*, 180.

41. Stewart-Sykes, *From Prophecy*, 279–80.

42. Justin 1 *Apology* 67; Alan Kreider, *Worship and Evangelism*, 36–39.

43. Charles E. Farhadian, "Worship as Mission: The Personal and Social
Ends of Papuan Worship in the Glory Hut," in Farhadian, *Christian Worship Worldwide*, 190–91; see also 60–61, 154.

44. David C. Norrington, *To Preach or Not to Preach? The Church's Urgent
Question* (Carlisle: Paternoster, 1996); Jeremy Thomson, *Preaching
as Dialogue*, Grove Pastoral Series 68 (Cambridge: Grove Books,
1996); Leo Hartshorn, *Interpretation and Preaching as Communal
and Dialogical Practice: An Anabaptist Perspective* (Lewiston, NY:
Edwin Mellen Press, 2006); http://interactivepreaching.net.

45. Our Mennonite congregation in Indiana, which has a long tradition of
all-age Sunday school, has for many years had a "sermon-response"
intergenerational class in which participants discuss what they
heard in the morning sermon, and apply its message to their lives.

46. Gerard W. Hughes, SJ, *In Search of a Way: Two Journeys of Discovery*
(Rome: E. J. Dwyer, 1978).

47. Stuart Murray and Anne Wilkinson-Hayes, *Hope from the Margins:
New Ways of Being Church*, Grove Evangelism Series 49 (Cambridge: Grove Books, 2000).

48. "Urban Expression Newsletter," United Kingdom, June 2008.

49. John V. Taylor, *The Go-Between God: The Holy Spirit and the Christian Mission* (London: SCM, 1972), 148.

50. Mike Breen and Bob Hopkins, *Clusters: Creative Mid-sized Missional
Communities* (3DM Publications, 2007).

51. Lois Y. Barrett et al., eds., *Treasures in Clay Jars: Patterns in Missional
Faithfulness* (Grand Rapids: Eerdmans, 2004), 26–27.

52. Walter Brueggemann, *Theology of the Old Testament: Testimony,
Dispute, Advocacy* (Minneapolis: Fortress Press, 1997), 271.

53. J. G. Davies, "The Missionary Dimension of Worship," *Studia Liturgica*
6 (1969): 84.

54. David Peterson, *A Biblical Theology of Worship* (Grand Rapids: Eerdmans,
1993), 214–15.

55. Augustine *Sermon* 272, in Augustine *Sermons* III/7, ed. John E.
Rotelle (New Rochelle, NY: New City Press, 1993); *Sacrosanctum*

Concilium, 1.7, in *Vatican II: The Conciliar and Post-Conciliar Documents*, ed. Austin Flannery (Wilmington, DE: Scholarly Resources, 1975), 4–5; Judith M. Kubicki, *The Presence of Christ in the Gathered Assembly* (New York: Continuum, 2006).

56. Jan Michael Joncas, "Tasting the Kingdom of God: The Meal Ministry of Jesus and Its Implications for Contemporary Worship and Life," *Worship* 74:4 (2000): 329–65.

57. Gerhard Lohfink, *Does God Need the Church? Toward a Theology of the People of God* (Collegeville, MN: Liturgical Press, 1999), 228.

58. Gordon D. Fee, God's *Empowering Presence: The Holy Spirit in the Letters of Paul* (Peabody, MA: Hendrickson, 1994), 889.

59. Lohfink, *Does God*, 228; Fee, *God's Empowering Presence*, 891.

60. Darrell L. Guder, *The Continuing Conversion of the Church* (Grand Rapids: Eerdmans, 2000), 77, citing Arne Rasmussen, *The Church as Polis* (Notre Dame: University of Notre Dame Press, 1995), 195, who comments on Stanley Hauerwas's view of "sin as control": "Christians must . . . be a people that risk trusting others and not fear the new, the different, and the surprising."

61. The literature on testimony is large and growing: Paul Ricoeur, "The Hermeneutics of Testimony," in Lewis Mudge, ed., *Essays on Biblical Interpretation* (Philadelphia: Fortress Press, 1980), 119–54; Thomas Hoyt Jr., "Testimony," in *Practicing Our Faith*, ed. Dorothy C. Bass (San Francisco: Jossey-Bass, 1997), 91–104; Mark J. Cartledge, *Testimony, Its Importance, Place and Potential*, Grove Renewal Series 9 (Cambridge: Grove Books, 2002); Thomas G. Long, *Testimony: Talking Ourselves into Being Christian* (San Francisco: Jossey-Bass, 2004); Alan Jacobs, *Looking Before and After: Testimony and the Christian Life* (Grand Rapids: Eerdmans, 2008).

62. Fee, *God's Empowering Presence*, 888, 891.

63. McClendon, *Systematic Theology, II*, 188.

64. Wolterstorff, "Justice," 17.

65. Cf. Cartledge, *Testimony*, 22–24.

66. Lillian Daniel, *Tell It Like It Is: Reclaiming the Practice of Testimony* (Herndon, VA: Alban Institute, 2006), 10–11.

67. Ibid., 151–58.

68. Jean-Daniel Plüss, *Therapeutic and Prophetic Narratives in Worship* (Frankfurt-am-Main: Peter Lang, 1988), 187.

69. For an eloquent statement of difficulties in current North American Mennonite practice of "sharing time," see Arthur Paul Boers, "Thank You for Debra Mussels, Asian Ladybugs and Sharing?" *The Mennonite*, February 21, 2006, 8–11.

70. Vera Duncanson, Brian Johnson, and Stefanie Weisgram, OSB, eds. *Stories from Christian Neighbors: A Heart for Ecumenism* (Collegeville, MN: Liturgical Press, 2003), xi.

71. Boers, "Thank You," 11.

72. *Book of Discipline of the Yearly Meeting of the Religious Society of Friends* (London: Britain Yearly Meeting of the Religious Society of Friends, 1999), sec. 12.12, 12.17. We owe these references to Christine Trevett.

73. Andrew F. Walls, "The Ephesians Moment in Worldwide Worship: A Meditation on Revelation 21 and Ephesians 2," in Farhadian, *Christian Worship Worldwide*, 37. Liturgical scholar James F. White, taking a broad view of Christian practice at the end of the last century, asked pointedly, "Who knows how many sacraments there are?" ("How Do We Know It Is Us?" in Anderson and Morrill, *Liturgy and the Moral Self*, 62).

74. Robert and Daneel, "Worship among Apostles," 60–63.

75. Martin D. Stringer, *A Sociological History of Christian Worship* (Cambridge: Cambridge University Press, 2005), 238.

76. Thomas Stransky, "From Vatican II to *Redemptoris Missio*: A Development in the Theology of Mission," 142, cited in Kirk, *What Is Mission?* 90.

Chapter 8: Worship Forms Mission I: Glorifying God, Sanctifying Humans

1. George G. Hunter III, "The Case for Culturally Relevant Congregations," in *Global Good News: Mission in a New Context*, ed. Howard Snyder (Nashville, TN: Abingdon Press, 2001), 99.

2. Ibid., 102, 105.

3. Rodney Stark, *The Rise of Christianity: A Sociologist Reconsiders History* (Princeton, NJ: Princeton University Press, 1996), 6.

4. Dom Gregory Dix, *The Shape of the Liturgy*, 2nd ed. (London: Adam & Charles Black, 1945), 16, 35; Alan Kreider, *Worship and Evangelism in Pre-Christendom*, Alcuin/GROW Joint Liturgical Studies 32 (Cambridge: Grove Books, 1995), 8–9.

5. Minucius Felix *Octavius* 38.6.

6. Origen *Contra Celsum* 3.55; *Canons of Hippolytus* 19.

7. Justin 1 *Apology* 67.

8. Tertullian *To His Wife* 2.6.

9. Alan Kreider, "'They Alone Know the Right Way to Live': The Early Church and Evangelism," in *Ancient Faith for the Church's Future*,

eds. Mark Husbands and Jeffrey P. Greenman (Downers Grove, IL: InterVarsity Press, 2008), 169–86.

10. John L. Allen Jr., *The Rise of Benedict XVI* (New York: Doubleday, 2005), 10, quoting *The Ratzinger Report* (1985).

11. Alan Kreider, *The Change of Conversion and the Origin of Christendom* (Harrisburg, PA: Trinity Press International, 1999), chap. 5.

12. Eusebius *Life of Constantine* 4.54.

13. Wilbert R. Shenk, *Write the Vision: The Church Renewed* (Harrisburg, PA: Trinity Press International, 1995), 35.

14. Ibid., 61. See also Dickson D. Bruce Jr., *And They All Sang Hallelujah: Plain-Folk, Camp-Meeting Religion, 1800–1845* (Knoxville, TN: University of Tennessee Press, 1980), 61–79.

15. See, for example, Ronald J. Sider, *The Scandal of the Evangelical Conscience: Why Are Christians Living Just Like the Rest of the World?* (Grand Rapids: Baker, 2005).

16. Brad J. Kallenberg, *Live to Tell: Evangelism in a Postmodern World* (Grand Rapids: Brazos Press, 2002), 50.

17. Don E. Saliers, "Liturgy and Ethics: Some New Beginnings," in *Liturgy and the Moral Self: Essays in Honor of Don E. Saliers*, eds. E. Byron Anderson and Bruce T. Morrill, SJ (Collegeville, MN: Liturgical Press, 1998), 28.

18. Stanley Hauerwas and Samuel Wells, "The Gift of the Church and the Gifts God Gives It," in *The Blackwell Companion to Christian Ethics*, eds. Stanley Hauerwas and Samuel Wells (Oxford: Blackwell Publishing, 2006), 25.

19. Gerhard Lohfink, *Does God Need the Church? Toward a Theology of the People of God* (Collegeville, MN: Liturgical Press, 1999), 302.

20. Graham Tomlin, *The Provocative Church* (London: SPCK, 2002).

21. John Francis Kavenaugh, SJ, *Following Christ in a Consumer Society: The Spirituality of Cultural Resistance* (Maryknoll, NY: Orbis, 1981).

22. Michael L. Budde, "Collecting Praise," in Hauerwas and Wells, *Christian Ethics*, 124.

23. Rodney Clapp, "On the Making of Kings and Christians," in *The Conviction of Things Not Seen: Worship and Ministry in the 21st Century*, ed. Todd E. Johnson (Grand Rapids: Brazos Books, 2002), 122.

24. Mark R. Gornik, *To Live in Peace: Biblical Faith and the Changing Inner City* (Grand Rapids: Eerdmans, 2002), 110, 55.

25. Andrew F. Walls, *The Missionary Movement in Christian History: Studies in the Transmission of Faith* (Maryknoll, NY: Orbis Books, 1996), 3–6; James F. White, "How Do We Know It Is Us?" in

Anderson and Morrill, *Liturgy and the Moral Self*, 58–9; Charles E. Farhadian, ed., *Christian Worship Worldwide: Expanding Horizons, Deepening Practices* (Grand Rapids: Eerdmans, 2007).
26. Nathan B. Hege, *Beyond Our Prayers: Anabaptist Church Growth in Ethiopia, 1948–1998* (Scottdale, PA: Herald Press, 1998), chap. 14.
27. Saliers, "Liturgy and Ethics," 33.

Chapter 9: Worship Forms Mission II: Actions of Worship
1. Studies that survey the actions of Christian worship from the vantage of mission include J. G. Davies, *Worship and Mission* (London: SCM, 1966), 113–41, and, for the early church, Alan Kreider, *Worship and Evangelism in Pre-Christendom*, Alcuin/GROW Joint Liturgical Studies 32 (Cambridge: Grove Books, 1995), 28–39. Lillian Daniel, "Empire's Sleepy Embrace: The View from the Pew," in *Anxious About Empire: Theological Essays on the New Global Realities*, ed. Wes Avram (Grand Rapids: Brazos Press, 2004), 173–86, surveys the actions of worship from the perspective of peace. R. Jerome Boone's perspective on the actions of worship is the freedom and spontaneity of the Spirit: "Community and Worship: The Key Components of Pentecostal Christian Formation," *Journal of Pentecostal Theology* 8 (1996): 138ff. Stanley Hauerwas and Samuel Wells's *The Blackwell Companion to Christian Ethics* (Oxford: Blackwell Publishing, 2006) is a leisurely, detailed, and rewarding examination of Christian worship from the perspective of ethics—and, in our view, of mission as well.
2. Philip Kenneson, "Gathering: Worship, Imagination and Formation," in Hauerwas and Wells, *Christian Ethics*, 65.
3. Ibid., 58–60.
4. Larry Miller, "The Church as Messianic Society: Creation and Instrument of Transfigured Mission," in *The Transfiguration of Mission*, ed. Wilbert R. Shenk (Scottdale, PA: Herald Press, 1993), 137.
5. Charles E. Farhadian, *Christian Worship Worldwide: Expanding Horizons, Deepening Practices* (Grand Rapids: Eerdmans, 207), 286–87.
6. J. H. Yoder, *Body Politics: Five Practices of the Christian Community before the Watching World* (Nashville, TN: Discipleship Resources, 1992), 38–39.
7. Farhadian, *Christian Worship Worldwide*, 288–89.
8. Graham Cray, *Youth Congregations and the Emerging Church*, Grove Evangelism Series 57 (Cambridge: Grove Books, 2002), 15.

9. Stuart Murray, *Church After Christendom* (Milton Keynes: Paternoster, 2004), 83.

10. Shana Peachey Boshart, "Christian Formation and Catechesis in Mennonite Churches: A Dialogue," paper for "Mission and Peace," INT 521, Associated Mennonite Biblical Seminary, Spring 2007.

11. S. J. D. Green, *Religion in the Age of Decline: Organisation and Experience in Industrial Yorkshire, 1870–1920* (Cambridge: Cambridge University Press, 1996), 389–90.

12. Judith M. Lieu, *Christian Identity in the Greco-Roman World* (Oxford: Oxford University Press, 2004), 259–64.

13. Kevin J. Vanhoozer, "Praising in Song: Beauty and the Arts," in Hauerwas and Wells, *Christian Ethics*, 110.

14. David F. Ford and Daniel W. Hardy, *Living in Praise: Worshipping and Knowing God* (Grand Rapids: Baker Academic, 2005), 15.

15. Walter Brueggemann, *Israel's Praise: Doxology against Idolatry and Ideology* (Philadelphia: Fortress Press, 1988), chap. 4.

16. Steven J. Land, *Pentecostal Spirituality: A Passion for the Kingdom* (Sheffield: Sheffield Academic Press, 1993), 139, 142.

17. Janet Elaine Rasmussen, "Praise, Our Mother Tongue," in *Our Worship and Our Work* (Elkhart, IN: Associated Mennonite Biblical Seminary, 2008), 53–58.

18. Luke Bretherton, *Hospitality as Holiness: Christian Witness Amid Moral Diversity* (Aldershot, UK: Ashgate, 2006), 129.

19. Bob Goudzwaard, Mark Vander Vennen, and David Van Heemst. *Hope in Troubled Times: A New Vision for Confronting Global Crises* (Grand Rapids: Eerdmans, 2007), 81, 44.

20. "Reflections on the Fiftieth Anniversary of World War II and the Tasks of Japanese Christians" (April 10, 1995), in *The Japanese Emperor System: The Inescapable Missiological Issue*, ed. Robert Lee (Tokyo: Tokyo Mission Research Institute, 1995), 141. A salient parallel would be American Christians confessing their repentant grief at the 1945 fire-bombing of Tokyo and the nuclear devastation of Hiroshima and Nagasaki.

21. N. T. Wright, *What St. Paul Really Said* (Grand Rapids: Eerdmans, 1997), 56.

22. John L. Allen Jr., *The Rise of Benedict XVI* (New York: Doubleday, 2005), 156.

23. Dallas Willard, *Renovation of the Heart: Putting on the Character of Christ* (Colorado Springs, CO: NavPress, 2002), 244.

24. James Wm. McClendon Jr., *Systematic Theology, II: Doctrine* (Nashville: Abingdon Press, 1994), 381.

25. Stanley Hauerwas, "Character, Narrative, and Growth in the Christian Life," in *The Hauerwas Reader*, eds. John Berkman and Michael Cartwright (Durham, NC: Duke University Press, 2001), 252.

26. Andrew Kreider, "But Seriously," at www.andrewkreider.com.

27. McClendon, *Systematic Theology, II*, 382, defines these as "instances of the distinctive guidance God gives to individual lives for designated Kingdom tasks."

28. Robert Schreiter, CPPS, *Reconciliation, Mission and Ministry in a Changing Social Order* (Maryknoll, NY: Orbis Books, 1992), 60.

29. William A. Barry and William J. Connolly, *The Practice of Spiritual Direction* (New York: Seabury Press, 1982), 8.

30. Yoder, *Body Politics*, 32.

31. Cited in Davies, *Worship and Mission*, 91.

32. Walter Wink, *Engaging the Powers: Discernment and Resistance in a World of Domination* (Minneapolis: Fortress Press, 1992), 23.

33. Michael L. Budde, "Collecting Praise," in Hauerwas and Wells, *Christian Ethics*, 128.

34. *Epistle to Diognetus* 5.

35. Alan Kreider, "Baptism and Catechesis as Spiritual Formation," in Andrew Walker and Luke Bretherton, eds., *Remembering Our Future: Explorations in Deep Church* (London: Paternoster, 2007), 175.

36. William T. Cavanaugh, *Torture and Eucharist: Theology, Politics, and the Body of Christ* (Oxford: Blackwell Publishing, 1998), 229.

37. Davies, *Worship and Mission*, 94.

38. Balthasar Hubmaier, "Form for the Lord's Supper" (1527), in *Balthasar Hubmaier: Theologian of Anabaptism*, eds. H. Wayne Pipkin and John H. Yoder (Scottdale, PA: Herald Press, 1989), 404.

39. Davies, *Worship and Mission*, 98.

40. Borgmann's ideas are summarized in Richard Gaillardetz, *Transforming Our Days* (New York: Crossroad, 2000).

41. Marty Troyer, "As Christ was in the World, so shall we be: The Formative Effect of Communion," CHM 522, Associated Mennonite Biblical Seminary, 19 April 2008.

42. Ambrose *De Mysteriis* 6.31-33; Thomas M. Finn, "It Happened One Saturday Night: Ritual and Conversion in Augustine's North Africa," *Journal of the American Academy of Religion* 58/4 (1990), 593n. In the early sixth century, Gallic bishop Caesarius of Arles applied the baptismal footwashing to hospitality: "Let them

receive strangers and, in accord with what was done for themselves in baptism, wash the feet of their guests" (*Sermon* 204).

43. Paul D. Duke, "John 13:1-17, 31b-35," *Interpretation*, 49:4 (1995): 399.

44. See above, chap. 3.

45. Samuel Wells, "Sent Out," *Christian Century*, June 28, 2005, 9.

46. Mark Thiessen Nation, "Washing Feet: Preparation for Service," in Hauerwas and Wells, *Christian Ethics*, 449.

47. Two models we have encountered in which footwashing has been a special gift:

- An ecumenical rite. Bridgefolk—North American Catholics who are committed to community and peacemaking and Mennonites who are sacramentally-minded gather for an annual meeting—have discovered that footwashing can be a powerful ritual. It enables Christians who are deeply committed to each other to commune together even if they cannot come to the table together.

- In churches that practice the "open table" in their public services and "bounded" Communion in a separate service that is restricted to baptized Christians. Footwashing can become a significant part of the intimate, "close" Communion services, possibly held in the evening, in which members express their deepest commitment to each other in private, in ways that might be off-putting to casual visitors at a Sunday morning service.

48. Cyprian *Ad Quirinum* 3.26.

49. Daniel M. Bell, "Deliberating: Justice and Liberation," in Hauerwas and Wells, *Christian Ethics*, 192.

50. Eleanor Kreider, "Let the Faithful Greet Each Other: The Kiss of Peace," *Conrad Grebel Review* 5 (1987): 29–49; William Klassen, "The Sacred Kiss in the New Testament: An Example of Social Boundary Lines," *New Testament Studies* 39 (1993): 122–35.

51. *Didache* 14.1-2.

52. Cyprian *The Lord's Prayer* 23.

53. Alan Kreider, "Peacemaking in Worship in the Syrian Church Orders," *Studia Liturgica* 34:2 (2004): 177–90.

54. *Didascalia Apostolorum* 2.53–54.

55. *Acts of Perpetua* 21; *Martyrdom of Shamuna, Guria and Habib* (Ante-Nicene Fathers 8: 701).

56. John Bossy, *Peace in the Post-Reformation*, The Birkbeck Lectures, 1995 (Cambridge: Cambridge University Press, 1998), 2 and passim.
57. Colin Buchanan, *The Kiss of Peace*, Grove Worship Series 80 (Bramcote, Nottingham: Grove Books, 1982), 15.
58. Tertullian *On Prayer* 29.
59. Tertullian *Apology* 39.
60. Tertullian *On Prayer* 29.
61. Alan Kreider, Eleanor Kreider, and Paulus S. Widjaja, *A Culture of Peace: God's Vision for the Church* (Intercourse, PA: Good Books, 2005).
62. R. Scott Appleby, *The Ambivalence of the Sacred: Religion, Violence, and Reconciliation* (Lanham, MD: Rowman & Littlefield, 2000), 7.
63. Janet Wootton, "The Future of the Hymn," in *Composing Music for Worship*, ed. Stephen Darlington and Alan Kreider (Norwich: Canterbury Press, 2003), 119–27.
64. Nicholas Wolterstorff, "Thinking About Church Music," in *Music in Christian Worship*, ed. Charlotte Kroeker (Collegeville, MN: Liturgical Press, 2005), 11–13.
65. Ibid., 13.
66. Ibid., 14–15.
67. Adam Tice, "Who Do You Sing That I Am?" Senior Integration Paper, Associated Mennonite Biblical Seminary, March 2007.
68. George S. Hendry, *Theology of Nature* (Philadelphia: Westminster Press, 1980), 24. We owe this reference to Ben Ollenburger.
69. Ross Langmead, "Music in Worship," Whitley College, Melbourne, Australia, School of Ministry, 28 June 2005, http://jmm.aaa.net.au/articles/15430.htm.
70. Thomas H. Troeger, "The Hidden Stream that Feeds: Hymns as a Resource for the Preacher's Imagination," *The Hymn* 43:3 (1992): 12, cited by Marlene Kropf and Kenneth Nafziger, *Singing: A Mennonite Voice* (Scottdale, PA: Herald Press, 2001), 118.
71. C. Michael Hawn, *Gather into One: Praying and Singing Globally* (Grand Rapids: Eerdmans, 2003), xvi–xvii.
72. Robin Lane Fox, *Pagans and Christians* (San Francisco: Harper & Row, 1986), 330.
73. Justin 1 *Apology* 67, translated by Everett Ferguson, *Early Christians Speak* (Austin, TX: Sweet Publishing Company, 1971), 94.
74. Yves Congar, OP, *Lay People in the Church* (1959), 175, cited by Davies, *Worship and Mission*, 81.
75. Ulrich Luz, *Matthew 1–7: A Commentary* (Minneapolis: Augsburg, 1989), 212–13.

76. Yoder, *Body Politics*, 67–68.

77. Arthur Paul Boers, "Pastors, Prophets, and Patriotism: Leading Pastorally during These Times," in Avram, *Anxious About Empire*, 161–62.

78. John Koenig, *Soul Banquets: How Meals Become Mission in the Local Congregation* (Harrisburg, PA: Morehouse Publishing, 2007), 26.

79. *Acts of the Abitinian Martyrs* 12, in Maureen A. Tilley, ed., *Donatist Martyr Stories: The Church in Conflict in Roman North Africa*, Translated Texts for Historians 24 (Liverpool: Liverpool University Press, 1996), 36–37.

80. Gaillardetz, *Transforming Our Days*, 113; Ion Bria, *Go Forth in Peace: Orthodox Perspectives on Mission* (Geneva: World Council of Churches, 1980), 66–71, cited in David J. Bosch, *Transforming Mission: Paradigm Shifts in Theology of Mission* (Maryknoll, NY: Orbis Books, 1991), 210.

81. Mark R. Gornik, *To Live in Peace: Biblical Faith and the Changing Inner City* (Grand Rapids: Eerdmans, 2002), 165.

Chapter 10: Worship Forms Mission III: Worshipping Christians in the World

1. Jill Lawless, "Atheists Spread Word in London: It's 'No'," *Chicago Tribune*, October 23, 2008, 10.

2. John Howard Yoder, *The Priestly Kingdom* (Notre Dame, IN: University of Notre Dame Press, 1984), 56.

3. For example, Theophilus *Ad Autolycum* 3.14; Athenagoras *Legatio* 11.2; Justin 1 *Apology* 14.

4. Neal Blough, *Christ in Our Midst: Incarnation, Church and Discipleship in the Theology of Pilgram Marpeck*, Anabaptist and Mennonite Studies 8 (Kitchener, ON: Pandora Press, 2007), 245–47.

5. Don E. Saliers, "Liturgy and Ethics: Some New Beginnings," in *Liturgy and the Moral Self: Essays in Honor of Don E. Saliers*, eds. E. Byron Anderson and Bruce T. Morrill, SJ (Collegeville, MN: Liturgical Press, 1998), 16–17.

6. Frank Furedi, *Culture of Fear Revisited: Risk-taking and the Morality of Low Expectation*, 4th ed. (London: Continuum, 2006), xi.

7. Scott Bader-Saye, *Following Jesus in a Culture of Fear* (Grand Rapids: Brazos Press, 2007), 28.

8. Steven J. Land, *Pentecostal Spirituality: A Passion for the Kingdom* (Sheffield: Sheffield Academic Press, 1993), 123, 139.

9. Ibid., 136.

10. Philip Kenneson, "Gathering: Worship, Imagination and Forma-tion," in Stanley Hauerwas and Samuel Wells, eds., *The Blackwell Companion to Christian Ethics*, (Oxford: Blackwell Publishing, 2006), 63–64.
11. Robert Jenson, "How the World Lost Its Story," *First Things* 36 (October 1993): 23.
12. Steven J. Schweitzer, "Utopia and Utopian Literary Theory: Some Preliminary Observations," in *Utopia and Dystopia in Prophetic Literature*, ed. Ehud Ben Zvi (Göttingen: Vandenhoeck & Ruprecht, 2006), 22–23.
13. Bob Goudzwaard, Mark Vander Vennen, and David Van Heemst. *Hope in Troubled Times: A New Vision for Confronting Global Crises* (Grand Rapids: Eerdmans, 2007), 177.
14. John Howard Yoder, "Armaments and Eschatology," *Studies in Christian Ethics*, 1:1 (1988): 58; cited by Stanley Hauerwas, *With the Grain of the Universe* (Grand Rapids: Brazos Press, 2001), 6.
15. Tertullian *Apology* 50.14
16. Alan Kreider, "'They Alone Know the Right Way to Live': The Early Church and Evangelism," in *Ancient Faith for the Church's Future*, eds. Mark Husbands and Jeffrey P. Greenman (Downers Grove, IL: InterVarsity Press, 2008), 172–76.
17. Cyprian *On Mortality* 28–31.
18. Bryan Stone, *Evangelism After Christendom: The Theology and Practice of Christian Witness* (Grand Rapids: Brazos Press, 2007), 39.
19. William T. Cavanaugh, "Discerning: Politics and Reconciliation," in Hauerwas and Wells, *Christian Ethics*, 207.
20. Donald B. Kraybill, Steven M. Nolt, and David L. Weaver-Zercher, *Amish Grace: How Forgiveness Transcended Tragedy* (San Francisco: Jossey-Bass, 2007), 90–95.
21. Margaret R. Pfeil, "Liturgy and Ethics: The Liturgical Asceticism of Energy Conservation," *Journal of the Society of Christian Ethics* 27:2 (2007): 127–49; Voluntary Gas Tax, http://voluntarygastax.org.
22. Kim Tan, *The Jubilee Gospel: The Jubilee, Spirit and the Church* (Milton Keynes: Authentic Media, 2008), 131.
23. Buy Nothing Christmas, http://www.buynothingchristmas.org.
24. David W. Boshart, *Becoming Missional: Denominations and New Church Development in Complex Social Contexts* (Eugene, OR: Wipf & Stock, 2011), 125.
25. Jennifer L. Boen, "A Lifesaving Gift," *Fort Wayne News Sentinel*, June 19, 2007.

26. Lois Y. Barrett et al., eds., *Treasures in Clay Jars: Patterns in Missional Faithfulness* (Grand Rapids: Eerdmans, 2004), 49–50.
27. Alan J. Roxburgh and Fred Romanuk, *The Missional Leader* (San Francisco: Jossey-Bass, 2006), 16.
28. Stone, *Evangelism*, 56.
29. David J. Bosch, *Transforming Mission: Paradigm Shifts in Theology of Mission* (Maryknoll, NY: Orbis Books, 1991), 11.
30. Eddie Gibbs and Ryan K. Bolger, *Emerging Churches: Creating Christian Community in Postmodern Cultures* (Grand Rapids: Baker Academic, 2005), 120.
31. John D. Witvliet, "Afterword: Inculturation, Worship, and Dispositions for Ministry," in Charles E. Farhadian, ed., *Christian Worship Worldwide: Expanding Horizons, Deepening Practices* (Grand Rapids: Eerdmans, 207), 282.
32. Stuart Murray, *Church After Christendom* (Milton Keynes: Paternoster, 2004), 157.
33. Wendell Berry, *The Way of Ignorance* (Berkeley, CA: Shoemaker & Hoard, 2005), 45; Benedict, *Rule* 58.
34. Jeremy Hall, OSB, *Silence, Solitude, Simplicity* (Collegeville, MN: Liturgical Press, 2007), 10.

Chapter 11: Missional Worship in a Worldwide Church

1. William T. Cavanaugh, "The City: Beyond Secular Parodies," in *Radical Orthodoxy*, eds. John Milbank, Catherine Pickstock, and Graham Ward (London: Routledge, 1999), 189.
2. *Epistle to Diognetus* 5; Aristeides *Apology* 16.5.
3. Pakisa K. Tshimika and Tim Lind, *Sharing Gifts in the Global Family of Faith: One Church's Experiment* (Intercourse, PA: Good Books, 2003), 32.
4. Ibid., 17.
5. Andrew F. Walls, "The Ephesians Moment in Worldwide Worship: A Meditation on Revelation 21 and Ephesians 2," in Charles E. Farhadian, *Christian Worship Worldwide: Expanding Horizons, Deepening Practices* (Grand Rapids: Eerdmans, 207), 27.
6. *Martyrdom of Polycarp* 5 (Herbert Musurillo, *The Acts of the Christian Martyrs* [Oxford: Clarendon Press, 1972], 7).
7. Eusebius, *Ecclesiastical History* 5.1.3 (Musurillo, *Acts*, 63).
8. Karl Leo Noethlichs, "Die 'Christianisierung' des Krieges vom spätantiken bis zum frühmittelalterlichen und mittelbyzantinischen Reich," *Jahrbuch für Antike und Christentum* 44 (2001): 22. Our translation.

9. LeRoy Walters, "Historical Applications of the Just War Theory," in *Love and Society*, eds. J. T. Johnson and D. H. Smith (Missoula, MT: Scholars Press, 1974), 135.

10. John Howard Yoder, *The Priestly Kingdom* (Notre Dame, IN: University of Notre Dame Press, 1984), 156.

11. Cavanaugh, "City," 188–89.

12. Hilaire Belloc, *Europe and the Faith* (New York: Paulist Press, 1921), Introduction.

13. Timothy C. Tennent, *Theology in the Context of World Christianity* (Grand Rapids: Zondervan, 2007), 8.

14. For example, Paul Gifford, "A View of Ghana's New Christianity," in *The Changing Face of Christianity: Africa, the West, and the World*, eds., Lamin Sanneh and Joel A. Carpenter (New York: Oxford University Press, 2005), 82–96; Emmanuel M. Katongole, "Hauerwasian Hooks and the Christian Social Imagination: Critical Reflections from an African Perspective," in *God, Truth, and Witness: Engaging Stanley Hauerwas*, eds. L. Gregory Jones, Reinhard Hütter, and C. Rosalee Velloso Ewell (Grand Rapids: Brazos Press, 2005), 148–51.

15. Andrew F. Walls, ed., *The Cross-Cultural Process in Christian History* (Maryknoll, NY: Orbis Books, 2002), 70.

16. Tshimika and Lind, *Sharing Gifts*, 5.

17. Jonathan J. Bonk, *Missions and Money*, rev. ed., American Society of Missiology Series 15 (Maryknoll, NY: Orbis Books, 2006).

18. Everett Thomas, "Global Church Faces Wealth Gap," *Mennonite Weekly Review*, March 27, 2006, 1–2.

19. Miranda K. Hassett, *Anglican Communion in Crisis: How Episcopal Dissidents and Their African Allies are Reshaping Anglicanism* (Princeton, NJ: Princeton University Press, 2007), 202.

20. J. Andrew Kirk, *What is Mission? Theological Explorations* (Minneapolis: Fortress Press, 2000), 203.

21. C. Kirk Hadaway and Penny Long Marler, "How Many Americans Attend Church Each Week? An Alternative Approach to Measurement," *Journal for the Scientific Study of Religion* 44:1 (2005): 307–22.

22. Walls, *Cross-Cultural Process*, 69.

23. Phil Groves, *Global Partnerships for Local Mission*, Grove Pastoral Series 106 (Cambridge: Grove Books, 2006), 7.

24. Emmanuel Katongole, "Greeting: Beyond Racial Reconciliation," in Hauerwas and Wells, *Christian Ethics*, 80; cf. Hassett, *Anglican Communion*, 184–85.

25. Lesslie Newbigin, *Foolishness to the Greeks: The Gospel and Western Culture* (Geneva: World Council of Churches, 1986), 9; Walls, *Cross-Cultural Process*, 69.

26. Darrell L. Guder, *The Continuing Conversion of the Church* (Grand Rapids: Eerdmans, 2000), 80.

27. Tshimika and Lind, *Sharing Gifts*, 21.

28. Ibid., 38.

29. Philip Jenkins, *God's Continent: Christianity, Islam, and Europe's Religious Crisis* (New York: Oxford University Press, 2007), 92.

30. I (Eleanor Kreider) was a member of this delegation.

31. Christine Pohl, "Hospitality: Ancient Resources and Contemporary Challenges," in *Ancient Faith for the Church's Future*, eds. Mark Husbands and Jeffrey P. Greenman (Downers Grove, IL: InterVarsity Press, 2008), 151.

32. Jonathan J. Bonk, "Thinking Small: Global Missions and American Churches," *Missiology* 28:2 (2000): 154–55.

33. Tshimika and Lind, *Sharing Gifts*, 70.

34. Scott Bader-Saye, *Following Jesus in a Culture of Fear* (Grand Rapids: Brazos Press, 2007), 57–58.

35. Alison Phelps, email to Alan and Eleanor Kreider, January 19, 2009.

36. Rod Stafford, email to Alan and Eleanor Kreider, March 5, 2009.

37. Interview with Neil Amstutz, Tina Stoltzfus Schlabach, and Rod Hollinger-Janzen, October 14, 2008.

38. In conversation, February 2006.

39. Stanley Hauerwas, "Enduring, or, How Rowan Greer Taught Me to Read," in *Reading in Christian Communities: Essays on Interpretation in the Early Church*, eds. Charles A. Bobertz and David Brakke (Notre Dame, IN: University of Notre Dame Press, 2002), 212.

40. Kirk, *What is Mission?* 93

41. Tshimika and Lind, *Sharing Gifts*, 98.

42. Katongole, "Greeting," 80.

43. Paul F. Bradshaw, "The Homogenization of Christian Liturgy— Ancient and Modern," *Studia Liturgica* 26 (1996): 14–15.

44. C. Michael Hawn, "Praying Globally: Pitfalls and Possibilities of Cross-cultural Liturgical Appropriation," in Farhadian, *Christian Worship Worldwide*, 211.

45. Ibid., 207. For further questions Hawn urges congregations to ask when appropriating global Christian materials and practices, see Hawn, "Praying," 219; Hawn, *Gather into One: Praying and Singing Globally* (Grand Rapids: Eerdmans, 2003), 14–16.

46. Elias Schad, "True Account of an Anabaptist Meeting at Night in a Forest and a Debate Held There with Them," *Mennonite Quarterly Review* 58 (1984): 292.

47. Hawn, *Gather into One*, 16.

48. It has been included in a recent Mennonite hymnal, *Sing the Story* (Scottdale, PA: Faith & Life Resources, 2007), 40.

49. *Bonhoeffer*, DVD directed by Martin Doblmeier, 2003; Eberhard Bethge, Dietrich Bonhoeffer (New York: Harper & Row, 1970), 109.

50. John Bell, *Sent by the Lord: Songs of the World Church* (Glasgow: Wild Goose Publications, 1991).

51. Ibid., 7.

52. Ross Langmead, "Music in Worship," Whitley College, Melbourne, Australia, School of Ministry, 28 June 2005, http://jmm.aaa. net.au/articles/15430.htm.

53. Hawn, *Gather into One*, 272–73.

54. Ibid., 14–16. Hawn's Criteria for "liturgical plurality": (1) it is not ethno-tourism; (2) it embraces a variety of practice with attentiveness to tradition; (3) it does not imply a synthesis of styles into a universal form; (4) it is a countercultural expression of faith; (5) it does not deny the validity of an individual culture, but celebrates God's presence as transcultural for all of us; (6) it raises to our consciousness the voices of the voiceless and the awareness of those who have been invisible to us; and (7) it expresses hope for what is yet to be, a taste of the world to come.

55. Mary Oyer, "A Conversation with Mary Oyer," in *Music in Christian Worship*, ed. Charlotte Kroeker (Collegeville, MN: Liturgical Press, 2005), 182.

56. John D. Witvliet, *Worship Seeking Understanding: Windows into Christian Practice* (Grand Rapids: Baker Academic, 2003), 256.

57. Ibid., 277.

58. Tshimika and Lind, *Sharing Gifts*, 100–1.

59. For examples, sponsored by the German Catholic aid organization Misereor, see www.albertusmagnus-archiv.de/text/hunger_1.htm.

60. Patricia C. Pongracz, Volker Küster, and John W. Cook, *The Christian Story: Five Asian Artists Today* (London: D. Giles/New York: Museum of Biblical Art, 2007).

61. *A New Zealand Prayer Book; He Karakia Mihinare o Aotearoa* (Auckland: William Collins, 1989).

62. Walls, *Cross-Cultural*, 41.

63. Jenkins, *God's Continent*, chap. 4; Stuart Murray, *Church After Christendom* (Milton Keynes: Paternoster, 2004), 118–22.

64. Kirk, *What is Mission?* 194.

65. John S. Mbiti, "Theological Impotence and the Universality of the Church," in *Mission Trends 3: Third World Theologies*, eds. Gerald H. Anderson and Thomas F. Stransky, CSP (New York: Paulist Press, 1976), 17.

66. Jonathan J. Bonk, "Ecclesiastical Cartography and the Invisible Continent," *International Bulletin of Missionary Research* 28:4 (2004): 153–58. See the product of an international three-year research study on ways Christians in different cultures read the story of Jesus' interaction with the Samaritan woman (John 4:1-42): Hans De Wit, Louis Jonker, Marleen Kool, and Daniel Schipani, eds., *Through the Eyes of Another: Intercultural Reading of the Bible* (Elkhart, IN: Institute of Mennonite Studies; Amsterdam: Vrije Universiteit, 2004).

67. Lamin Sanneh, *Whose Religion is Christianity? The Gospel Beyond the West* (Grand Rapids: Eerdmans, 2003), 35.

Chapter 12: Outsiders Come to Worship I: What the Outsiders Experience

1. In the Christendom era, the only "outsiders" that some European people knew were Jews, whom the laws exempted from church attendance. Of course, church leaders knew that many people attended church services irregularly; there were occasional parish missions that attempted to revive the faith and sacramental practice of the unobservant.

2. George Lings and Stuart Murray, *Church Planting: Past, Present and Future*, Grove Evangelism Series 61 (Cambridge: Grove Books, 2003), 24: "In specific mission contexts do we need a moratorium on the word 'church' when we mean Christian communities or groups of Jesus' disciples?"

3. John Drane, *After McDonaldization: Mission, Ministry, and Christian Discipleship in an Age of Uncertainty* (Grand Rapids: Baker Academic, 2008), 89–90; Robert L. Wilken, *The Christians as the Romans Saw Them* (New Haven, CT: Yale University Press, 1984), 82.

4. John V. Taylor, *The Go-Between God: The Holy Spirit and the Christian Mission* (London: SCM, 1972), 134.

5. Linford Stutzman, *With Jesus in the World: Mission in Modern Affluent Societies* (Scottdale, PA: Herald Press, 1992), chap. 3.

6. John Finney, *Finding Faith Today: How Does It Happen?* (Swindon: British and Foreign Bible Society, 1992), 43.

7. Alan J. Roxburgh, *The Missionary Congregation, Leadership and Liminality* (Harrisburg, PA: Trinity Press International, 1997), chap. 2.

8. Drane, *After McDonaldization*, 91.

9. Richard Rohr, OFM, *Simplicity: The Art of Living* (New York: Crossroad, 1991), 59.

10. David Myers, *The American Paradox* (2000), cited by Rodney Clapp, "On the Making of Kings and Christians," in *The Conviction of Things Not Seen: Worship and Ministry in the 21st Century*, ed. Todd E. Johnson (Grand Rapids: Brazos Books, 2002), 114–15.

11. Robert E. Webber, *Ancient-Future Evangelism* (Grand Rapids: Baker Books, 2003), 67.

12. Rowan Williams, *Mission and Christology*, J. C. Jones Memorial Lecture (Church Missionary Society, Welsh Members' Council, 1994), 18.

13. Andrew F. Walls, ed., *The Cross-Cultural Process in Christian History* (Maryknoll, NY: Orbis Books, 2002), 8.

14. Cited in Robert Lee, *The Clash of Civilizations: An Intrusive Gospel in Japanese Civilization* (Harrisburg, PA: Trinity Press International, 1999), 4.

15. Rodney Clapp, *Johnny Cash and the Great American Contradiction* (Louisville, KY: Westminster John Knox, 2008).

16. George G. Hunter III, "The Case for Culturally Relevant Congregations," in *Global Good News: Mission in a New Context*, ed. Howard Snyder (Nashville, TN: Abingdon Press, 2001), 97, 99, 107. Cf. Sally Morgenthaler, who calls for "cross-cultural worship music" that will be accessible to regular worshippers and to the "unchurched/unbeliever": *Worship Evangelism* (Grand Rapids: Zondervan, 1995), 213.

17. Anscar J. Chupungco, *Liturgical Inculturation: Sacramentals, Religiosity, and Catechesis* (Collegeville, MN: Liturgical Press, 1992); for an accessible statement of his position, see his article "Inculturation" in *The New SCM Dictionary of Liturgy and Worship*, ed. Paul Bradshaw (London: SCM Press, 2002), 244–51.

18. Thomas A. Kane, "Celebrating Pentecost in Leauva'a: Worship, Symbols, and Dance in Samoa," in Charles E. Farhadian, *Christian Worship Worldwide: Expanding Horizons, Deepening Practices* (Grand Rapids: Eerdmans, 207), 162.

19. Cited by Patricia Harkins-Pierre, "Religion Bridge: Translating Secular into Sacred Music: A Study of World Christianity Focusing

on the U.S. Virgin Islands," in *The Changing Face of Christianity: Africa, the West, and the World*, eds., Lamin Sanneh and Joel A. Carpenter (New York: Oxford University Press, 2005), 40.

20. Darrell L. Guder, *The Continuing Conversion of the Church* (Grand Rapids: Eerdmans, 2000), 200.

21. J. G. Davies, *Worship and Mission* (London: SCM, 1966), 147.

22. Rodney Clapp, *A Peculiar People: The Church as Culture in a Post-Christian Society* (Downer's Grove, IL: InterVarsity Press, 1996), 75.

23. "The Nairobi Statement" (1994), in Farhadian, *Christian Worship Worldwide*, 285–90.

24. Stuart Murray and Anne Wilkinson-Hayes, *Hope from the Margins: New Ways of Being Church*, Grove Evangelism Series 49 (Cambridge: Grove Books, 2000); Jeanne Hinton, *Church at the Edge: Exploring New Ways of Being Church* (Stowmarket, UK: Kevin Mayhew, 2006); Joseph G. Healey and Jeanne Hinton, eds., *Small Christian Communities Today: Capturing the New Moment* (Maryknoll, NY: Orbis Books, 2006).

25. Robert Banks and Julia Banks, *The Church Comes Home* (Peabody, MA: Hendrickson, 1998).

26. Phyllis Tickle, *The Great Emergence: How Christianity is Changing and Why* (Grand Rapids: Baker Books, 2008); George Barna, *Revolution* (Carol Stream, IL: Tyndale House, 2005).

27. C. Michael Hawn, "Praying Globally: Pitfalls and Possibilities of Cross-cultural Liturgical Appropriation," in Farhadian, *Christian Worship Worldwide*, 227.

28. Dorothy C. Bass, ed., *Practicing Our Faith*, (San Francisco: Jossey-Bass, 1997); cf. Peter Brierley, *Pulling Out of the Nosedive* (London: Christian Research, 2006), 163, who sees middle-sized churches as "a slowly reducing portion of the whole," because they are "caught in the middle" between large and small churches.

29. Daniel T. Benedict and Craig K. Miller, *Contemporary Worship for the 21st Century: Worship or Evangelism?* (Nashville, TN: Discipleship Resources, 1994); Martin Robinson, *A World Apart: Creating a Church for the Unchurched* (Tunbridge Wells: Monarch, 1992). See www.willowcreek.org.

30. F. Dean Lucking, "Liturgical Evangelism: the Finnish Experiment," in *Christian Century*, June 13, 2006, 10–11; Tuomasmessu, www.tuomasmessu.fi/?sid=25.

31. Gerhard Lohfink, *Does God Need the Church? Toward a Theology of the People of God* (Collegeville, MN: Liturgical Press, 1999), 27.

32. Christopher J. H. Wright, *The Mission of God: Unlocking the Bible's Grand Narrative* (Downers Grove, IL: InterVarsity Press, 2006), 473.

33. Emmanuel M. Katongole, "Hauerwasian Hooks and the Christian Social Imagination: Critical Reflections from an African Perspective," in *God, Truth, and Witness: Engaging Stanley Hauerwas*, eds., L. Gregory Jones, Reinhard Hütter, and C. Rosalee Velloso Ewell (Grand Rapids: Brazos Press, 2005), 137.

34. Nicholas Lash, *Theology on the Way to Emmaus* (London: SCM Press, 1986), 201.

35. Scott A. Ellington, "The Reciprocal Reshaping of History and Experience in the Psalms: Interactions with Pentecostal Testimony," *Journal of Pentecostal Theology* 16:1 (2007): 27.

36. Clapp, "On the Making," 122.

37. Rowan Williams, *Eucharistic Sacrifice: The Roots of a Metaphor* (Bramcote, Nottingham: Grove Books, 1982), 29, cited in Koenig, *Feast*, 243.

38. Joseph G. Healey and Jeanne Hinton, eds., *Small Christian Communities Today: Capturing the New Moment* (Maryknoll, NY: Orbis Books, 2006), 92.

39. Stuart Murray, *Church Planting: Laying Foundations* (Carlisle: Paternoster, 1998), 175; also (Scottdale, PA: Herald Press, 2001), 159.

40. Stuart Murray, *Church After Christendom* (Milton Keynes: Paternoster, 2004), 126.

41. Rodney Clapp, "Anabaptism and the Obstacles that Make for Vocation," in *Engaging Anabaptism: Conversations with a Radical Tradition*, ed. John Roth (Scottdale, PA: Herald Press, 2001), 143.

42. Eleanor Kreider, *Communion Shapes Character* (Scottdale, PA: Herald Press, 1997), 189–95; also as *Given for You: A Fresh Look at Communion* (Leicester, UK: IVP, 1998), 167–72.

43. Gerard Hughes, SJ, *The God of Surprises* (London: Darton, Longman & Todd, 1985), 34–36.

44. Jonathan J. Bonk, "Thinking Small: Global Missions and American Churches," *Missiology* 28:2 (2000): 154.

45. Peter Brown, *The Rise of Western Christendom*, 2nd ed. (Oxford: Blackwell, 2003), 466.

46. James J. Stamoolis, *Eastern Orthodox Mission Theology Today*, American Society of Missiology Series 10 (Maryknoll, NY: Orbis Books, 1986), 95–96.

47. Richard B. Hays, *The Moral Vision of the New Testament* (San Francisco: HarperSanFrancisco, 1996), 39.

Chapter 13: Outsiders Come to Worship II: Hospitality and Wholeness

1. Ambrose *Epistle* 40.8.
2. Karl Rahner, SJ, *The Shape of the Church to Come* (New York: Seabury Press, 1974), 23–4, 57.
3. On the importance of hospitality in Christians' daily lives, see Michele Hershberger, *A Christian View of Hospitality: Expecting Surprises* (Scottdale, PA: Herald Press, 1999).
4. Christine D. Pohl, *Making Room: Recovering Hospitality as a Christian Tradition* (Grand Rapids: Eerdmans, 1999), 157.
5. Patrick R. Keifert, *Welcoming the Stranger: A Public Theology of Worship and Evangelism* (Minneapolis: Augsburg Fortress, 1992), 113.
6. Alison Gilchrist, *Creating a Culture of Welcome in the Local Church*, Grove Evangelism Series 66 (Cambridge: Grove Books, 2004), 17.
7. John D. Witvliet, "The Cumulative Power of Transformation in Public Worship: Cultivating Gratitude and Expectancy for the Holy Spirit's Work," in *Worship that Changes Lives: Multidisciplinary and Congregational Perspectives on Spiritual Transformation*, ed. Alexis D. Abernethy (Grand Rapids: Baker Academic, 2008), 57.
8. Keifert, *Welcoming the Stranger*, 110–13.
9. Walter Brueggemann, *Biblical Perspectives on Evangelism: Living in a Three-Storied Universe* (Nashville, TN: Abingdon, 1993), 89, 94.
10. Heribert Mühlen, cited in Wolfgang Vondey, "New Evangelization and Liturgical Celebration in the Roman Catholic Church," *Studia Liturgica* 36 (2006): 241, 246–48.
11. Mark R. Gornik, *To Live in Peace: Biblical Faith and the Changing Inner City* (Grand Rapids: Eerdmans, 2002), 90.
12. For examples of catechesis in the Roman Catholic and Baptist traditions in the United Kingdom, see Stuart Wilson, "'At Your Word, Lord': Renewal Program in the Diocese of Westminster," in *Small Christian Communities Today: Capturing the New Moment*, eds., Joseph G. Healey and Jeanne Hinton (Maryknoll, NY: Orbis Books, 2006), 90–98; Ian Stackhouse, "Deep Church 4: Believing and Belonging," *Baptist Times*, May 22, 2008, 12.
13. Alan Kreider, "Baptism and Catechesis as Spiritual Formation," in Walker and Bretherton, *Remembering Our Future*, 170–206.
14. Lee C. Camp, *Mere Discipleship: Radical Christianity in a Rebellious World* (Grand Rapids: Brazos Press, 2003), 114.
15. We must acknowledge the Churches of Christ and the Plymouth Brethren traditions, in which Communion has from the beginning been observed weekly, with all members communicating.

16. L. Michael White, "Regulating Fellowship in the Communal Meal: Early Jewish and Christian Evidence," in *Meals in a Social Context: Aspects of the Communal Meal in the Hellenistic and Roman World*, eds. Inge Nielsen and Hanne Sigismund Nielsen (Aarhus: Aarhus University Press, 2001), 180.

17. *Didache* 5.9; Paul Bradshaw, "The Reception of Communion in Early Christianity," *Studia Liturgica* 37 (2007): 167.

18. Justin 1 *Apology* 66.

19. John D. Rempel, *The Lord's Supper in Anabaptism*, Studies in Anabaptist and Mennonite History 33 (Scottdale, PA: Herald Press, 1993), 33–37.

20. Luke Bretherton, *Hospitality as Holiness: Christian Witness Amid Moral Diversity* (Aldershot, UK: Ashgate, 2006), 129–31.

21. John Wesley, *Journal*, June 27, 1740, in W. Reginald Ward, ed., *Works of John Wesley* (Nashville, TN: Abingdon Press, 1990), 158.

22. Sally Morgenthaler, "Out of the Box: Authentic Worship in a Postmodern Culture," *Worship Leader*, May/June 1998, 27.

23. Michael J. Ford, *Wounded Prophet: A Portrait of Henri J. M. Nouwen* (New York: Doubleday, 1999), 57.

24. Sara Miles, *Take This Bread: A Radical Conversion* (New York: Ballantine Books, 2007), xiv, xvi.

25. Stuart Murray, *Church After Christendom* (Milton Keynes: Paternoster, 2004), 26–38, which develops the work of Paul Hiebert, *Anthropological Reflections on Missiological Issues* (Grand Rapids: Baker, 1994), 107–36. Murray adds the "open set" to Hiebert's three-set schema. Murray and Hiebert both note an additional set, the "fuzzy set," which has boundaries that are ill-defined and a center that the members—who disagree with each other—cannot agree on or specify clearly (Murray, 27).

26. Murray, *Church After Christendom*, 29.

27. James Farwell, "Baptism, Eucharist, and the Hospitality of Jesus: On the Practice of 'Open Communion,'" *Anglican Theological Review* 86:2 (2004): 232.

28. Miles, *Take This Bread*, 116, 222.

29. Farwell, "Baptism," 236.

30. Murray, *Church After Christendom*, 37–38.

31. Rempel, *Lord's Supper*, 34.

32. Witvliet, *Worship*, 271.

33. Murray, *Church After Christendom*, 146.

34. Avery Dulles, SJ, *Models of the Church: A Critical Assessment of the Church in All its Aspects*, 2nd ed. (New York: Doubleday, 1987), 220.

Appendix

1. Alan Kreider, *The Change of Conversion and the Origin of Christendom* (Harrisburg, PA: Trinity Press International, 1999), 91–98.
2. C. Kirk Hadaway and Penny Long Marler, "How Many Americans Attend Church Each Week? An Alternative Approach to Measurement," *Journal for the Scientific Study of Religion* 44:1 (2005): 307–22.
3. Harry S. Stout, *Upon the Altar of the Nation: A Moral History of the American Civil War* (New York: Viking, 2006), xviii.
4. Robert N. Bellah, "God and King," in *God, Truth, and Witness: Engaging Stanley Hauerwas*, eds., L. Gregory Jones, Reinhard Hütter, and C. Rosalee Velloso Ewell (Grand Rapids: Brazos Press, 2005), 125.
5. Hadaway and Marler, "How Many," 307–22.

Bibliography

Anderson, E. Byron, and Bruce T. Morrill, SJ, eds. *Liturgy and the Moral Self: Humanity at Full Stretch Before God.* Collegeville, MN: Liturgical Press, 1998.

Bader-Saye, Scott. *Following Jesus in a Culture of Fear.* Grand Rapids: Brazos Press, 2007.

Barrett, Lois Y., et al. *Treasures in Clay Jars: Patterns in Missional Faithfulness.* Grand Rapids: Eerdmans, 2004.

Bonk, Jonathan J. *Missions and Money.* Rev. ed., American Society of Missiology Series 15. Maryknoll, NY: Orbis Books, 2006.

———. "Thinking Small: Global Missions and American Churches." *Missiology* 28.2 (2000): 149–61.

Bosch, David J. *Transforming Mission: Paradigm Shifts in Theology of Mission.* American Society of Missiology Series 16. Maryknoll, NY: Orbis Books, 1991.

Bouley, Allen, OSB. *From Freedom to Formula: The Evolution of the Eucharistic Prayer from Oral Improvisation to Written Texts.* The Catholic University of America Studies in Christian Antiquity 21. Washington, DC: Catholic University of America Press, 1981.

Bradshaw, Paul F. *Eucharistic Origins.* New York: Oxford University Press, 2004.

———. "The Homogenization of Christian Liturgy—Ancient and Modern." *Studia Liturgica* 26 (1996): 1–15.

Brueggemann, Walter. *Biblical Perspectives on Evangelism: Living in a Three-Storied Universe.* Nashville, NT: Abingdon Press, 1993.

———. *Israel's Praise: Doxology against Idolatry and Ideology.* Philadelphia, PA: Fortress Press, 1988.

———. *Theology of the Old Testament: Testimony, Dispute, Advocacy.* Minneapolis: Fortress Press 1997.

Budde, Michael L. "Collecting Praise: Global Culture Industries." In Hauerwas and Wells, *Blackwell Companion,* 123–37.

Cavanaugh, William T. "Discerning: Politics and Reconciliation." In Hauerwas and Wells, *Blackwell Companion*, 53–67.

———. "The City: Beyond Secular Parodies." In *Radical Orthodoxy*. Edited by John Milbank, Catherine Pickstock and Graham Ward. London: Routledge, 1999, 182–200.

Clapp, Rodney. *A Peculiar People: The Church as Culture in a Post-Christian Society*. Downers Grove, IL: InterVarsity Press, 1996.

———. "On the Making of Kings and Christians." In *The Conviction of Things Not Seen: Worship and Ministry in the 21st Century*. Edited by Todd E. Johnson. Grand Rapids: Brazos Books, 2002, 109–22.

Daniel, Lillian. *Tell It Like It Is: Reclaiming the Practice of Testimony*. Herndon, VA: Alban Institute, 2006.

Davies, J. G. *Worship and Mission*. London: SCM Press, 1966.

Ellington, Scott A. "The Costly Loss of Testimony." *Journal of Pentecostal Theology* 16 (2000): 48–59.

Farhadian, Charles E., ed. *Christian Worship Worldwide: Expanding Horizons, Deepening Practices*. Grand Rapids: Eerdmans, 2007.

Farwell, James. "Baptism, Eucharist, and the Hospitality of Jesus: On the Practice of 'Open Communion.'" *Anglican Theological Review* 86.2 (2004): 215–38.

Gibbs, Eddie, and Ryan K. Bolger. *Emerging Churches: Creating Christian Community in Postmodern Cultures*. Grand Rapids: Baker Academic, 2005.

Gornik, Mark R. *To Live in Peace: Biblical Faith and the Changing Inner City*. Grand Rapids: Eerdmans, 2002.

Goudzwaard, Bob, Mark Vander Vennen, and David Van Heemst. *Hope in Troubled Times: A New Vision for Confronting Global Crises*. Grand Rapids: Eerdmans, 2007.

Guder, Darrell L. *The Continuing Conversion of the Church*. Grand Rapids: Eerdmans, 2000.

Hauerwas, Stanley. "Character, Narrative, and Growth in the Christian Life." In *The Hauerwas Reader*. Edited by John Berkman and Michael Cartwright. Durham, NC: Duke University Press, 2001, 221–54.

Hauerwas, Stanley and Samuel Wells, eds. *The Blackwell Companion to Christian Ethics*. Oxford: Blackwell Publishing, 2006.

Hawn, C. Michael. *Gather into One: Praying and Singing Globally*. Grand Rapids: Eerdmans, 2003.

—————. "Praying Globally: Pitfalls and Possibilities of Cross-cultural Liturgical Appropriation." In Farhadian, *Christian Worship Worldwide*, 205–29.

Hunter, George G., III. "The Case for Culturally Relevant Congregations." In *Global Good News: Mission in a New Context*. Edited by Howard Snyder. Nashville, TN: Abingdon Press, 2001, 96–110.

Jenkins, Philip. *The New Faces of Christianity: Believing the Bible in the Global South*. New York: Oxford University Press, 2006.

Joncas, Jan Michael. "Tasting the Kingdom of God: The Meal Ministry of Jesus and its Implications for Contemporary Worship and Life." *Worship* 74.4 (2000): 329–65.

Kallenberg, Brad J. *Live to Tell: Evangelism in a Postmodern World*. Grand Rapids: Brazos Press, 2002.

Kenneson, Philip. "Gathering: Worship, Imagination, and Formation." In Hauerwas and Wells, *Blackwell Companion*, 53–67.

Kirk, J. Andrew. *What is Mission? Theological Explorations*. Minneapolis: Fortress Press, 2000.

Knight, Henry H., III, and Steven J. Land. "On Being a Witness: Worship and Holiness in the Wesleyan and Pentecostal Traditions." In Anderson and Morrill, *Liturgy and the Moral Self*, 79–93.

Koenig, John. *The Feast of the World's Redemption: Eucharistic Origins and Christian Mission*. Harrisburg, PA: Trinity Press International, 2000.

Kreider, Alan. *The Change of Conversion and the Origin of Christendom*. Harrisburg, PA: Trinity Press International, 1999; Eugene, OR: Wipf & Stock, 2007.

—————. *Worship and Evangelism in Pre-Christendom*, Alcuin/GROW Joint Liturgical Studies 32. Cambridge: Grove Books Ltd, 1995.

Kreider, Eleanor. *Communion Shapes Character*. Scottdale, PA: Herald Press, 1997; also as *Given for You: A Fresh Look at Communion*. Leicester: IVP, 1998.

Land, Steven J. *Pentecostal Spirituality: A Passion for the Kingdom*. Sheffield: Sheffield Academic Press, 1993.

Lohfink, Gerhard. *Does God Need the Church? Toward a Theology of the People of God*. Collegeville, MN: Liturgical Press, 1999.

Marshall, Christopher D. *Beyond Retribution: A New Testament Vision for Justice, Crime, and Punishment*. Grand Rapids: Eerdmans, 2001.

McClendon, James Wm., Jr. *Systematic Theology II, Doctrine*. Nashville, TN: Abingdon Press, 1994.

McGowan, Andrew. "Rethinking Agape and Eucharist in Early North African Christianity." *Studia Liturgica* 34 (2004): 133–46.

Morgenthaler, Sally. *Worship Evangelism*. Grand Rapids: Zondervan, 1995.

Murray, Stuart. *Church After Christendom*. Milton Keynes: Paternoster, 2004.

————. *Post-Christendom: Church and Mission in a Strange New World*. Carlisle: Paternoster, 2004.

Murray, Stuart, and Anne Wilkinson-Hayes. *Hope from the Margins: New Ways of Being Church*. Grove Evangelism Series 49. Cambridge: Grove Books, 2000.

Pohl, Christine D. *Making Room: Recovering Hospitality as a Christian Tradition*. Grand Rapids: Eerdmans, 1999.

Saliers, Don E. "Liturgy and Ethics: Some New Beginnings." In Anderson and Morrill, *Liturgy and the Moral Self*, 15–35.

Sanneh, Lamin. *Disciples of All Nations: Pillars of World Christianity*. New York: Oxford University Press, 2008.

Sanneh, Lamin, and Joel A. Carpenter, eds. *The Changing Face of Christianity: Africa, the West, and the World*. New York: Oxford University Press, 2005.

Shenk, Wilbert R. *Write the Vision: The Church Renewed*. Harrisburg, PA: Trinity Press International, 1995.

Smith, Dennis E. *From Symposium to Eucharist: The Banquet in the Early Christian World*. Minneapolis: Fortress Press, 2003.

Stewart-Sykes, Alistair. *From Prophecy to Preaching: A Search for the Origins of the Christian Homily*, Supplements to *Vigiliae Christianae* 59. Boston: Brill, 2001.

Stone, Bryan. *Evangelism After Christendom: The Theology and Practice of Christian Witness*. Grand Rapids: Brazos Press, 2007.

Tshimika, Pakisa K., and Tim Lind. *Sharing Gifts in the Global Family of Faith: One Church's Experiment*. Intercourse, PA: Good Books, 2003.

Walls, Andrew F. *The Cross-Cultural Process in Christian History*. Maryknoll, NY: Orbis Books, 2002.

————. *The Missionary Movement in Christian History: Studies in the Transmission of Faith*. Maryknoll, NY: Orbis Books, 1996.

Webber, Robert E. *Ancient-Future Evangelism: Making Your Church a Faith-Forming Community*. Grand Rapids: Baker Books, 2003.

White, James F. "How Do We Know It Is Us?" In Anderson and Morrill, *Liturgy and the Moral Self*, 55–65.

Witvliet, John D. *Worship Seeking Understanding: Windows into Christian Practice*. Grand Rapids: Baker Academic, 2003.

Wolterstorff, Nicholas. "Justice as a Condition of Authentic Liturgy." *Theology Today* 48.1 (1991): 6–21.

Wright, Christopher J. H. *The Mission of God: Unlocking the Bible's Grand Narrative*. Downers Grove, IL: InterVarsity Press, 2006.

Wright, N. T. *The New Testament and the People of God*. London: SPCK, 1992.

Yoder, John Howard. *Body Politics: Five Practices of the Christian Community Before the Watching World*. Nashville, TN: Discipleship Resources, 1992.

Index

A

Abraham, William J., 271
Affections, 181-83, 214
African Initiated Churches, 121
Agape, 100-1, 114-15, 120, 282
Algonquins, 47, 87-88
Alpha Courses, 135
Amish, 184
Anabaptists, 117-18, 181, 209-10
  Swiss Brethren, 117, 284-85
Apostolic Constitutions, 116
Appleby, R. Scott, 170

B

Bach, J. S., 39, 172
Bader-Saye, Scott, 182, 202
Banquet for all nations, 47
Banquet, Greco-Roman, 94-96
Baptism, 38-39, 51-52, 139, 160-62,
  235, 248, 249-54
"Baptismal ordination", 175
Baptists, 118, 280
Barth, Karl, 43-44
Bartholemew, Craig, 63
Basil of Caesarea, 278
Bauckham, Richard, 87
Bell, Daniel, 167
Bell, John, 81, 211
Belloc, Hilaire, 194
Benedict of Nursia, 188
Benedict XVI, 139
Berry, Wendell, 187-88

Bible reading, 70
Boers, Arthur Paul, 287
Bonhoeffer, Dietrich, 211
Bonk, Jonathan, 28, 68, 86
Borgmann, Albert, 163
Bosch, David, 40, 187
Bradshaw, Paul, 91-92, 208, 282
Bretherton, Luke, 154
Brethren, Plymouth, 118
Bria, Ion, 178
Bridgefolk, 293
Brierley, Peter, 303
Brown, Brenton, 275
Brueggemann, Walter, 82, 88, 152,
  247
Budde, Michael, 162
Bullinger, Heinrich, 284-85

C

Caesarius of Arles, 292-93
Camp, Lee, 248
Catechesis, 139, 161-62, 248, 305
Cavanaugh, William, 184, 190, 194
Chadwick, Owen, 42
Charismata, 102-5, 114
Charles, Pierre, 38
Children's time, 70
China, 35-37
Christ Community Church, Des
  Moines, 125-26
Christendom, 220-21, 301
  Definitions, 15-16, 19, 38

Decline of, 43-44, 119
Late Christendom, 140
Post Christendom, 15, 139, 183-4
Chrysostom, John, 116-17
Chupungco, Anscar, 228
Church anniversaries, 80-81
Clapp, Rodney, 142-43
Clergy, 39-40
Collection, Paul's, 192
Congar, Yves, OP, 175
Confess "Jesus is Lord", 154-57
Constantine I, 38, 54, 115-16
Conversion, 41
Corinthian worship, 94-109
Cray, Graham, 150
Creation reconciled, 46-47, 64
Cullmann, Oscar, 91
Cyprian, Bishop of Carthage, 30, 167-69

D
Daniel, Lillian, 131
Davies, J. G., 21, 32, 44, 52, 62, 72, 126, 163, 229
Dawkins, Richard, 179-80
Denton, Melinda Lundquist, 68
Didache, 106, 168, 250, 282
Didascalia Apostolorum, 168-69
Dix, Dom Gregory, 91
Donatists, 178
Drama, 73
Drama, Five-act, 63-64
Dulles, Avery, SJ, 257

E
Ecology, 57, 72, 184-85
Ecumenical Councils
Fourth Lateran Council (1215), 25, 39
Seventh Ecumenical Council (787), 28
Edwards, Denis, 72

Ellis, Christopher J., 280
Emerging churches, 124, 249, 252
Enlightenment, 194
Eschaton, 183
Escobar, Samuel, 51
Ethos, 237-38
Eucharist, 25, 112, 115, 120, 162-64, 235, 282
Also see Lord's Supper
Extemporaneous Eucharistic prayer, 275
Participation in, 248-55
Eusebius of Caesarea, 54
Evangelism, 41, 53-54, 138-39, 140, 220, 246-47, 271
Exodus, 62, 66, 68-69

F
Farhadian, Charles, 21, 143
Farwell, James, 254, 281
Fawkes, Guy, 60
Fee, Gordon, 129, 284
Focal practices, 163-64
Footwashing, 67, 164-67, 235, 292-93
Ford, David, 152
Fourth-century shift, 38, 74, 92, 115-16, 139, 193, 220
Friendship, 223-24
Funk, John, 80
Furedi, Frank, 181

G
Gathering, 147-52
Catholicity, 148-50
George, M. V., 240
Gibbs, Eddie, 71
Global Christianity, 194-95
Global gift sharing, 191-93, 196-98, 201-7, 216-18
Goheen, Michael, 63
Gornik, Mark, 143, 247

Goudzwaard, Bob, 156
Great Commission
  Johannine, 48-49, 50-51
  Matthean, 40, 50-51
Gregory Palamas, 278-79
Guder, Darrell, 49, 197-98, 228-29
H
Hall, Jeremy, OSB, 188
Hanciles, Jehu, 42
Hardy, Dan, 152
Harris, Elder, 178
Hart, Trevor, 87
Hartenstein, Karl, 44
Hauerwas, Stanley, 68, 158
Hawn, C. Michael, 174, 208, 210, 212, 231, 300
Hendry, George, 173
Hermas, 103, 113
Hicks, Edward, 46-47, 87-88
Hiebert, Paul, 306
Hildebrand-Schlegel, Harold, 207
Holiness, experience of, 176-77
Holmes, Stephen, 24, 44
Hope, 86-88, 90, 118-19
Horrell, David, 283
Hospitality, 154-55, 200, 244-48, 292-93
Hovda, Bob, 100-1
Hubmaier, Balthasar, 163
Hughes. Gerard, SJ, 123, 239
Hunter, George G, III, 137, 228-29
I
Ignatius, of Loyola, 40
Inculturation, 41, 134-36, 142, 190, 224, 227-30, 278
  By Paul in Corinth, 93-96
  Indigenizing and pilgrim, 94-95, 227-30
J
Japan, 156, 196, 227

Jesus, 30, 32, 47, 48-49, 50-51, 53, 54, 55-56, 69, 93, 99, 154-57, 163, 164-67, 168, 190, 223, 224, 235, 239, 240, 244, 248, 249, 250-51, 252, 253-54, 280
John Bunyan Baptist Church, Cowley, 213
Joncas, Jan Michael, 128-29
Justin Martyr, 71, 106-7, 113-14, 122, 249, 281
Justinian I, 23, 38
K
Katongole, Emmanuel, 197
Keepers of the memory, 81
Kenneson, Philip, 28, 147, 182
Kirk, Andrew, 54, 207, 216
Koenig, John, 101, 178
Koinonia, 99
Koontz, Ted, 52
L
Land, Steven, 65, 182
Lane Fox, Robin, 175
Langmead, Ross, 211
Liminality, 187-88, 225-27
Lind, Tim, 191, 198, 207
Littlemore Baptist Church, 81
Liturgical Movement, 120, 248-49
Liturgical plurality, 300
Liturgical year, 74
Liturgy, *see* Worship
  Also see Eucharist
Lohfink, Gerhard, 32, 83, 129
Lord's Prayer, 73, 184
Lord's Supper, 67, 71-72, 93, 97-101, 120-21, 177, 280
Luther, Martin, 117-18
M
MacArthur, Douglas, 41
McCammon, Don and Dorothy, 35-37, 56

McCarthy, Emmanuel Charles, 72
McClendon, James Wm., Jr., 71, 120, 130, 157, 159
McGowan, Andrew, 115, 280
Magesa, Laurenti, 200
Marpeck, Pilgram, 118
Marshall, Christopher, 69, 266
Maxwell, W. D., 25-26
Mbiti, John, 216-17
Megachurch, 231
Menno Simons, 30-31
Mennonite, 163-64, 196
Messiaen, Olivier, 178
Miles, Sara, 253
Mission, 38-42, 53, 214-15
Mission, classical
    Characteristics, 36-38
    Christendom origins, 38-40
    In late Christendom, 40-42
Missio Dei, 34, 43-58, 59, 79, 100, 131, 138, 143, 144, 148, 153, 154-55, 161, 174, 189, 248, 255, 272
    Characteristics, 49-53
    Criteria for discernment, 55-56
    Implications, 53-55
    Means of God's sending, 48-49
Missional, 45, 187, 270
Missionaries, 35-38, 39-42
Missionary, 45
Moltmann, Jürgen, 53, 89
Monbiot, George, 56-57
Morgenthaler, Sally, 26, 302
Motive clause, 68-70, 173
Multivoiced worship, 121-22, 175-76
Murphy-O'Connor, Jerome, OP, 283
Murray, Stuart, 94, 150, 237, 253, 306
Music, 170-74, 210-12, 236

N
Nagasaki, 194, 291
Nairobi Statement on Worship and Culture, 148-50
Narrative–*see* story, worship
Nation, Mark Thiessen, 167
Neill, Stephen, 54
Nero, 111
Newbigin, Lesslie, 41, 86
Nouwen, Henri, 253

O
Offering, 214
Oikodome, 102-4
Origen, 114
Orthodox, 65, 240
Outsiders in worship, 104-5, 106-7, 219-41
Oyer, Mary, 212

P
Pagitt, Doug, 121
Passover, 62
Paul, 26-27, 29, 47-48, 51, 69, 92-109, 111, 120-23, 127-30, 191-92, 219, 224-25, 231, 246, 249-50, 284
Peace, 38, 167-70
Peace greeting, 168
"Peaceable Kingdom", 46-47, 87-88
Peacemaking, 170, 186, 235-36
Pentecostal, 65, 121, 127-28, 177, 182, 240
Peterson, David, 127
Peterson, Eugene, 31
Phelps, Alison, 202-3
Pinches, Charles, 122
Pinsky, Robert, 60
Pohl, Christine, 200, 245
Polycarp, 193
Praise, 152-54, 233
Prayer, 71-72, 73, 159-60, 167-70, 209-10, 235-36, 275

Principalities and powers, 56, 142-43
Prophetic utterances, 102-4, 129
Psalms, 66, 77-78
Q
Quakers, 46-47, 87-88, 118, 133
R
Rahner, Karl, SJ, 41, 243-44
Ramshaw, Gail, 71
Ravenna, church of San Vitale, 23-24
Reformation, Protestant, 194
Rembrandt Van Rijn, 74, 213
Resident aliens, 162, 193
Revival meetings, 140, 220
Richter, Julius, 41
Rituals, 246
Robert the Bruce, 60
Rohr, Richard, OFM, 226
S
Sacrament, 100, 134, 288
St Thomas Crookes, Sheffield, 125
Saints, 80
Saliers, Don, 181
Sanneh, Lamin, 36, 217, 228
Schreiter, Robert, CPPS, 159
Sets: bounded, centered, open, 251-55, 306
Sepangi, Kefa, 85
Sermon, 70, 121-23, 246-48, 286
Shalom, 34, 45, 47, 53-54, 59, 87, 98, 119, 128, 134, 143, 147, 180-81, 186
Sharing Time, 132-33, 287
Shenk, Wilbert, 44
Simons, Menno, 30-31
Singh, Bakht, 239-40
Smith, Christian, 68
Snyder, C. Arnold, 284
Songs, hymns, 71, 210-12, 275

Spence, Gusty, 84
Spiritual gifts, 97
Stafford, Rod, 204
Stewart-Sykes, Alistair, 122
"Stoics", 152
Storkey, Alan, 57-58
Story
  Bible's story-odd, 67-70, 153
  Biblical metanarrative, 63-64, 74-75, 153, 234
  Community ballad, 81
  Christendom stifling of story, 61-63
  "Gap" years, 78-80
  Orient by "tradition", 99
  Origin stories, 69-70
  Power of story, 60-61
  Telling the story in worship, 67-75, 273
Stransky, Thomas, CSP, 135
Stringer, Martin, 134
Suhard, Emmanuel, 43
Sumner, George, 272
Symposium, 95-96, 101, 111, 114, 122, 126, 127, 129, 134, 135, 279
T
Table churches, 123-24, 249-50
Table worship
  Paul's ideal for, 106-9
  Disappearance of, 112-15
Taizé, 174, 232, 240
Taofinu'u, Pio, 228
Taylor, John V., 125, 223, 272
Tertullian, 112, 115, 125, 169-70, 184
Testament of Our Lord, 114
Testimony, 75, 81-85, 121-22, 130-33, 159-60, 176, 234, 246
Theodosius I, 38
Thomas Mass, 232

Tivetshall St. Margaret, Norfolk, 24
Transfiguration Parish, New York, 126
Troeger, Thomas, 174
Troeltsch, Ernst, 86
Tshimika, Pakisa, 191, 196, 198, 207

U
Uchimura, Kanzo, 227

V
Vicedom, Georg, 44
Visuals, 73-74, 213

W
Walls, Andrew, 42, 93-94, 195, 197, 215
Ward, Pete, 71
Warneck, Gustav, 40-41
Washington, George, 60-61
Waterford Mennonite Church, 205-6
Weems, Mason Locke, 60
Wells, Samuel, 166
White, James F., 288
Willard, Dallas, 157
Williams, Rowan, 227
Winter, Gibson, 161
Witherington, Ben, III, 284
Wittenberg, University of, 39
Witvliet, John, 187, 212, 246, 256
Wolff, Hans Walter, 46
Wolterstorff, Nicholas, 29-30, 53, 120, 130, 171
Women in worship, silencing, 117, 284
Worship and mission, 119, 221-24, 255-57
In three time dimensions, 64-65
In 1 Corinthians 10-14, 92-93
Worship, authenticity, 30

Worship, definitions, 25-29
All of life, 29-31
English worth-ship, 28
Glorification/sanctification, 141-43
New Testament words, 26-28
Worship "builds up", 138
Worship, evaluation, 34, 59, 65
Worship, free and orderly, 107-8
Worship, fruits of
Character of worshippers, 158
Worship, "homogenization", 92
Worship, multivoiced, 121, 123, 175-76, 236
Worship, narrative that shapes, 67-70, 172
Worship, reflects God's character, 31-34
God's action in, 32
Worship
Outsiders, 104-5, 111, 138
Role in post-Christendom, 140-41
Transforming power, 175-78, 181-88
Unjust, 29-30, 97-98, 100
Wright, Christopher, 44, 45, 50, 233, 270
Wright, N. T., 63, 156, 273

Y
Yoder, John Howard, 89-90, 97, 180, 194

The Authors

Alan and Eleanor Kreider's entire lives have been immersed in mission and worship. Both grew up among missionaries, in Japan and India respectively. Their academic studies took them in divergent directions—Alan to English Reformation history (Harvard Ph.D.) and Eleanor to piano performance (Michigan M.Mus.). But after completing their studies, they joined forces as Mennonite missionary teachers in England, where they lived for thirty years and found their interests overlapping.

In England they discovered the early church, which they studied seriously. Eleanor did advanced liturgical study at King's College, London, and both were active in the peace and radical discipleship movements. Initially they were based in London, where they directed the London Mennonite Centre, founded its Cross-Currents teaching program, and were pastors in the London Mennonite Fellowship. As speakers they traveled extensively, teaching in churches and conferences of many denominations. In their final years in England, they worked at Regent's Park College, Oxford University, where Eleanor taught worship and Alan directed the college's Centre for Christianity and Culture. Their wide ecumenical openness was coupled with their discovery that in post-Christendom the Anabaptist tradition provided resources for Christians of many traditions; they helped to found the UK-wide Anabaptist Network made up of Christians from many denominations.

Since 2000 Eleanor and Alan have lived in Elkhart, Indiana, which has been their base for teaching assignments throughout

North America and in many countries. Alan has been professor of church history and mission at Associated Mennonite Biblical Seminary. Both have continued to write books and articles. Representative titles are (Eleanor) *Communion Shapes Character* (Herald Press, 1997), (Alan) *Worship and Evangelism in Pre-Christendom* (Grove Books, 1995), and together with Paulus Widjaja, *A Culture of Peace: God's Vision for the Church* (Good Books, 2005). They are members of Prairie Street Mennonite Church, and are parents of Andrew, who with his wife Katie has three children.

pp 49-53   CHRISTENDOM   MISSIONAL / MISSIO-DEI

SENDER   Church   God
TERRITORY   "Go"   "As you go"
AGENTS   Select few   All in Christ
GOAL   Save souls   New creation
                Build church   Peaceable kingdom
                                        Renewal of cosmos

pp 184-186
Something "more interesting" inspired by hope.

pp 220-221

Worship w/o outsiders
Worship w/o outsiders — for security
Worship to attract outsiders
Worship amid outsiders.